DATA PROCESSING THE EASY WAY

Lawrence S. Leff

Assistant Principal and
Chairman, Department of Mathematics
Franklin D. Roosevelt High School
Brooklyn, New York

Barron's Educational Series, Inc.
Woodbury, New York / London / Toronto / Sydney

© Copyright 1984 by Barron's Educational Series, Inc.

All inquiries should be addressed to:
Barron's Educational Series, Inc.
113 Crossways Park Drive
Woodbury, New York 11797

Library of Congress Catalog No. 84-394

International Standard Book No. 0-8120-2627-6

Library of Congress Cataloging in Publication Data
Leff, Lawrence S.
  Data processing the easy way.

  1. Electronic data processing.   2. Electronic
digital computers.   I. Title.
QA76.L425   1984   001.64   84-394
ISBN 0-8120-2627-6

PRINTED IN THE UNITED STATES OF AMERICA

4 5 6 7   100   9 8 7 6 5 4 3 2 1

ACKNOWLEDGMENTS

I wish to express my thanks to my friend and colleague, Ms. Gabrielle Edwards, who encouraged me to take on this project. Mr. Stephen Miller came to my rescue by helping to secure several photos that appear in this book. Steve also read several sections of the manuscript and made a number of insightful remarks which led to the manuscript's improvement.

CONTENTS

CHAPTER

3 COMPUTER MEMORY AND TECHNOLOGY 65

CHAPTER

4 INPUT/OUTPUT 89

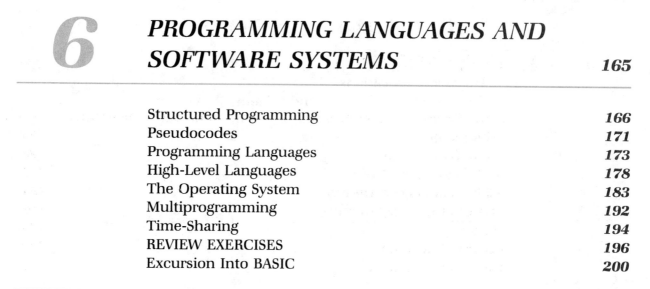

CHAPTER

PRINCIPLES OF FILE ORGANIZATION AND DATA MANAGEMENT

205

CHAPTER

DATA COMMUNICATIONS

231

CHAPTER

9 BINARY NUMBERS AND DATA REPRESENTATION 259

PREFACE

Every type of organization in our society, regardless of how small or large, must find effective ways of dealing with the piles and piles of information and statistics which it accumulates and uses in conducting its daily affairs. The study of data processing centers on how facts and figures can be organized and managed for efficient storage, processing, and retrieval and on what electronic equipment can be used to simplify these tasks. This book covers the major issues related to modern data processing using the computer as a focal point. In the course of our development of the subject of data processing, some of the questions that will be addressed are:

- What is a computer and how does it work?

- Why are computers used and what are their limitations?

- How are data and instructions prepared so that they can be fed into a computer?

- What types of auxiliary equipment are needed to make a computer system more versatile and permit it to operate more efficiently?

- What are the current trends in computer hardware, in the development of software systems, and in data communications?

The easy-to-follow style of presentation, the organization of topics, and the abundance of explanatory figures and illustrative examples should make this book attractive to individuals engaged in self-study. The nature and extent of the topics covered and the numerous objective review exercises (with solutions) should make this book a valuable resource to students enrolled in a formal course in data processing or computer literacy or in a programming course having a computer science component.

Recognizing the widespread use of desk-top computers in business, scientific research, and the home, two types of computer environments are described: large (mainframe) computer systems and microcomputer-based data processing systems. Rather than being treated as a separate unit of study, discussions relating to microcomputers (and the BASIC programming language) are woven into the text and serve to enhance the material that relates to computer mainframe systems.

In order to help reinforce and illustrate computer concepts, actual programming examples and activities are included. A unique feature of the book is the spiralled development of the essential elements of the BASIC programming language—the most common language of small computers. Each chapter ends with an Excursion Into BASIC which builds on the BASIC instructions developed in the previous chapters. Furthermore, in most instances the BASIC material that is discussed relates either directly or indirectly to the data processing concepts that were developed in the body of the chapter.

A feature of the presentation that may not be obvious from a survey of the table of contents relates to the author's concern over how much detail is necessary. Rather than overwhelming a reader by giving comprehensive coverage of a topic in a particular chapter, many topics are introduced and then returned to in succeeding chapters where their special features are further elaborated upon. This tends to give a reader more of an opportunity to digest the material and to appreciate its significance. For example, disk storage is informally discussed in Chapter 1 in the context of a microcomputer system. Chapter 2 includes a more detailed discussion of the fundamental characteristics of magnetic disk and tape storage in a mainframe computer environment. Chapter 4 focuses on the particulars of these devices (as well as other input/output devices), offering the reader some statistical facts related to disk storage (storage capacity, access times, etc.). Chapter 7 goes into considerable detail in describing the different file organizations that are possible with disk storage. An added benefit of this approach is that it takes into account that not all readers require the same depth of coverage; the topical organization allows a reader to omit selectively certain later sections which expand on a topic introduced earlier in the text.

Lawrence S. Leff

October, 1983

THE NATURE OF DATA

PROCESSING WITH AP

PLICATIONS TO BASIC

E NATURE OF DATA PRO

APPLICATIONS TO BAS

CHAPTER

1

THE NATURE OF DATA PROCESSING
WITH APPLICATIONS TO BASIC

DATA PROCESSING WIT

APPLICATIONS TO BASI

INTRODUCTION

You are standing in line at a checkout counter at your local supermarket. It's your turn. You place each of your groceries on the conveyor belt which sends them to the cashier. As the cashier reads each item for its stamped or printed price, he presses the appropriate cash register keys in order to *input* the prices. The cash register temporarily *stores* each price. The prices are *processed* when the cash register calculates any associated sales tax and then adds the figures to find the total grocery bill. The result of this processing is also temporarily stored in the cash register.

When the cashier presses an appropriate key, the cash register produces as *output* an itemized listing of the prices of each grocery item purchased and the grand totals, which are printed on a paper cash register receipt.

The activity just described represents a data processing system. Every data processing system is characterized by four major functions: *input, processing, storage,* and *output.* (See Figure 1-1.) The study of data processing centers on each of these four functions and how they interrelate.

In the pages and chapters ahead, we shall consider some questions that arise naturally in the study of data processing: How are data organized and prepared to ensure accurate and efficient handling? What types of processing are normally performed with data? What types of electronic equipment can be used to facilitate the processing of data? What is a computer, why is it used, and how does it work? How can we "talk" to a computer? How can data and instructions be stored for later use and then retrieved?

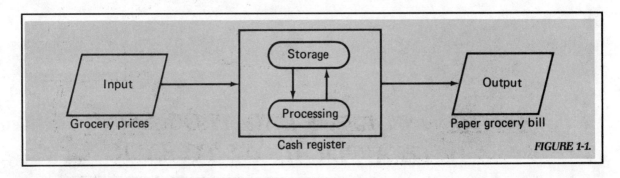

FIGURE 1-1.

DATA, DATA PROCESSING, AND RELATED TERMS

The term *data* is usually understood to mean any set of facts and numbers, regardless of whether they are related or seem to make sense. Some people distinguish between the terms *data* and *information* by insisting that data represents raw, or unprocessed, facts and numbers while information is a meaningful set of facts and numbers. Since both data and information may serve as input into a data processing system, we shall find it convenient to use these terms interchangeably. Examples of data include: a population census; stock market price quotations; an inventory listing; a schedule of airline departures and arrivals; the number of hours an employee works during a given week; a graph of economic growth; a weather map. In most data processing environments, data are not communicated verbally—they must be recorded. The form or document that is used to record data for entry into a data processing system is called a *source document*. The financial page of a daily newspaper may serve as the source document for communicating stock market price quotations. An employee's time card may serve as a source document for entering the number of hours the employee works into a data processing system.

In its most general sense, data processing may be defined as the manipulation of data in order to achieve some desired result or goal. It is important to keep in mind that data processing neither implies nor requires that there be a computer or any other type of physical equipment present. For example, suppose a person is given data in the form of a list of people's names. It is desired that the list of names be arranged in alphabetical order. The manipulation of the data is the work or processing necessary to organize the names into an alphabetical sequence. The output of the system must represent the achievement of that goal. A printed list of the names arranged in alphabetical order would represent the output of the system. This list may have some immediate use or be stored for future reference. (See Figure 1-2.)

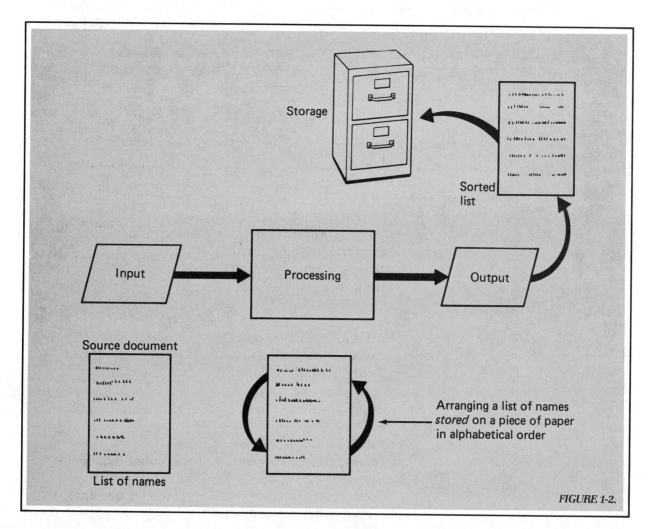

Storage

Sorted list

Input

Processing

Output

Source document

List of names

Arranging a list of names *stored* on a piece of paper in alphabetical order

FIGURE 1-2.

We now summarize the four basic operations of a data processing system:

■ *Input.* Original data are gathered and recorded on a source document. Data appearing on the source document are entered into the data processing system. Precisely how the data are read from the source document and get processed will depend upon the nature of the system. Methods of data entry will vary depending upon the sophistication of the system and whether a computer or some other special type of equipment will be used to facilitate the processing.

■ *Processing.* During this phase of the data processing cycle the data are manipulated in an effort to transform the input into the desired final result.

■ *Storage.* This term refers to both the *temporary* storage of data, instructions, and processing results as well as the more *permanent* storage of output necessary for subsequent data processing. For example, when a student takes a mathematics exam, intermediate results in performing a lengthy computation may be stored on scrap paper. The final answer may be stored on the answer paper that will be submitted to and graded by the teacher. The scrap paper represents the temporary storage of intermediate results in processing, while the answer paper corresponds to the permanent storage of final output results.

■ *Output.* This is the end product of the processing. Output that is printed onto a form or document is called *hard copy*. A savings account passbook is an example of hard copy. Output which appears on the video screen of a personal microcomputer is *not* hard copy. Hard copy that will subsequently be used as input is called a *turnaround document*. Bill statements are frequently used as turnaround documents. When paying bills, particularly utility or credit account bills, a punch card or a tear-off stub is included with the bill and must be returned with the payment. This card or stub then serves as input data when the payment is processed.

Exercises

1. A pocket calculator is used to multiply 10 by 23. Entering the numbers and the multiplication symbol × corresponds to the _____ phase; pressing the key that will perform the multiplication and yield the answer (usually the = key) represents the _____ phase; the number 230 represents the _____ phase.

2. A homeowner returns part of the electric bill statement with his or her payment. The bill is an example of a _____ document.

In each of the following examples, state whether the activity represents the input, processing, output, or storage phase of a corresponding data processing system.

3. Last month's canceled bank checks are placed in a file folder.

4. An airline reservation is made.

5. The interest on a customer's savings account balance is determined.

6. After having calculated an employee's weekly earnings, a bookkeeper writes a payroll check.

THE PROCESSING PHASE

During the processing phase of data processing, data may be manipulated in a variety of ways. For example, any one or any combination of the following types of operations may be required:

- *Sorting.* Arranging a set of words in an alphabetical sequence or listing a set of numbers in either ascending order (e.g., 10, 17, 33, 50, 78, 94) or descending order (e.g., 86, 77, 61, 49, 22, 9).

- *Classifying.* Using some given guideline to separate data items into one or more categories. Employment applications, for example, may be separated into three distinct groups based upon education: college graduates, high school graduates, and people lacking any higher education.

- *Comparing.* Determining whether two items are the same, or whether one number is less than, greater than, or equal to another number. For example, in a certain school any student who has a cumulative average that is greater than 90% is placed on the school's honor roll. In order to determine which students will be placed on the honor roll, each student's average must be compared to 90.

- *Calculating.* Performing mathematical computations with numerical data. In processing a payroll, it would be necessary to multiply the number of hours worked by the hourly wage in order to calculate the gross pay for an individual worker. Various payroll taxes must also be computed and then subtracted from the gross pay in order to calculate the net pay.

- *Summarizing.* Organizing summary information into a convenient, printed format. This usually involves one or more of the previously discussed processing operations. A checking account statement issued to a customer by the bank is the result of a summarizing operation. In addition to information that identifies the account, a summary of the account's activities over a given time period is shown. The following information is normally included: opening and closing account balances; the sum of the credits (deposits to the account) and the sum of the debits (checks drawn against the account); a listing of the individual account transactions, sorted in either check number sequence or chronological order according to the dates the transactions were processed. The document on which the output of a summarizing operation appears, and which is intended for distribution, is called a *report document*. A document that lists those checking accounts that are overdrawn during a given month is an example of a report document. At an annual stockholder meeting, a report document which describes a company's economic health (assets, liabilities, etc.) is always available for distribution to the stockholders.

Exercises

In each of the following examples, identify the processing activity as sorting, classifying, comparing, calculating, or summarizing.

7. Determining the interest on the unpaid balance of a credit card account.

8. Producing a credit account customer's monthly statement.

9. Given the sales figures for a group of salespersons, determining which salespersons have sold merchandise whose value exceeds $500.

10. Separating a group of people into the following categories: married, divorced, and single without ever having been married.

11. Arranging books on a shelf alphabetically according to the authors' names.

Multiple Choice

12. Which of the following operations may be included in the summarizing operation?
   a. Sorting **b.** Classifying **c.** Calculating
   d. Comparing **e.** All of these

13. Which is *not* an example of a report document?
   a. The yearly W-2 wage and tax statement
   b. A student's academic transcript
   c. A sales receipt
   d. A telephone bill
   e. A weekly listing of television programs

A DATA PROCESSING CYCLE ILLUSTRATED

A credit account customer, Peter Q. Public, has a credit account, number 5109, at Cheap Charlie's Discount Department Store. At Cheap Charlie's, computers are frowned upon. All credit account purchases and related bookkeeping procedures are handled without the aid of a computer.

On October 23, 1983, Mr. Public uses his credit card to purchase a pair of men's slacks for $34.95, including sales tax. Frank, the sales clerk, uses a preprinted credit account sales receipt form to write up the purchase. In order to simplify matters, the form requires that specific information be entered in specified blocks of reserved columns, called *fields*. Frank completes the sales receipt form by entering the appropriate *characters* into each field. A character is a letter (A–Z), a digit (0-9), or a special symbol (?, %, +, punctuation mark, blank space). (See Figure 1-3.)

A field may be classified by the types of characters it may include. A field that may hold only digits is called a *numeric* field. The account-number field (columns 41–44) is a numeric field. A field that may include letters (and blanks) with no digits or special characters is called an *alphabetic* field. Columns 1–10, the field that contains the customer's first name, is an alphabetic field. A field that may include combinations of digits, letters, and special characters is called an *alphanumeric* field. The street-address field (columns 22–40) is an alphanumeric field.

The maximum number of characters a field may contain is called the *width* of the field. The width of the account-number field is 4. The width of the amount-of-sale field is 6. In the first-name field (columns 1–10), the first name, Peter, does not occupy all the spaces in the field. When the width of an alphabetic field ex-

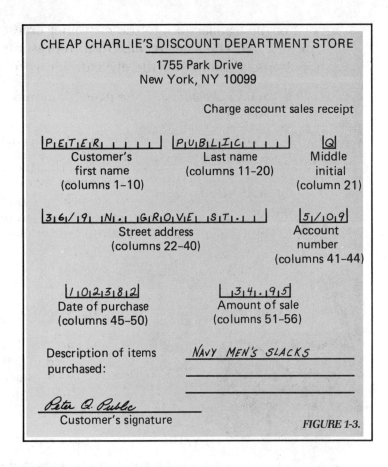

FIGURE 1-3.

ceeds the number of letters in the word that will be entered into the field, the first letter must be placed in the leftmost column position of the field. This is called *left-justification*. Notice that in the amount-of-sale field (columns 51–56) the first column is left blank. When entering digits into a numeric field, the last digit of the number must occupy the rightmost column position. This is called *right-justification*. (See Figure 1-4.)

All the fields on the sales receipt form describe a single purchase made by the same individual, that is, all the fields involve either the purchase itself or the individual making the purchase. Since all the fields are related, we may refer to the fields collectively as a *record*. A record is any set of related fields.

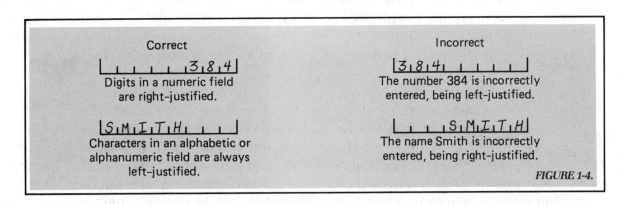

FIGURE 1-4.

Frank completes the sales receipt form, reads it over to verify the accuracy of the information entered, and then gives it to Mr. Public to sign. Mr. Public leaves with his purchase while Frank takes the sales receipt form, which represents a record of the transaction, to the customer credit accounts office on the fifth floor for processing. The sales receipt form represents a *transaction* (or *detail*) record. While Frank is waiting for the elevator, let us review some important definitions.

- *Source document.* The paper or form on which gathered data are recorded for subsequent processing.

- *Character.* A letter, digit, punctuation mark, or special character. A blank space is considered a character.

- *Field.* A related set of characters that usually represents a unit of information, such as a name field, an age field, or an address field. On a document, a field refers to a consecutive group of column positions which is reserved for a particular type of data item. Numeric data are right-justified when entered into a numeric field. Alphanumeric data are left-justified when entered into an alphanumeric field.

- *Record.* A set of related fields. A record that describes a single activity is a transaction (or detail) record.

An opinion poll survey is to be taken by telephone. The set of people who will be called is determined by opening a telephone directory to any page, tearing out the page, and giving it to a telephone operator. The telephone operator then calls each person on the list, asks a question, and records the responses.

The telephone page represents a *source document* to the operator.

Each group of columns that contain the persons' names, or addresses, or telephone numbers is a *field.* The letters, digits, or special characters that are entered in each field are called *characters.*

The name, address, and telephone fields for the *same* individual form a *record.* If the source document (telephone page listing) lists 100 people, then the page contains 100 records.

The elevator reaches the fifth floor, and Frank delivers the sales receipt form to Clara, the credit clerk in the credit department. Frank then returns to his counter in the men's furnishings department. Clara is very organized. Information regarding each credit account customer is maintained on separate index cards filed in a cabinet. Each index card includes information such as the customer's name, account number, address, and place of employment. Also included is a listing of the dates and amounts of all purchases and payments. This type of record contains information of a permanent, biographical, or historical nature. Such a record is called a *master* record.

The collection of customer credit account master records must be pulled from a file cabinet (see Figure 1-5) and Mr. Public's account master record located in order that it may be *updated,* or made more current, by recording the latest purchase. The transaction record (sales receipt) is then used to make an appropriate entry onto the corresponding master record. The entire collection of account master records is then returned to its storage location. A set of related records is called a *file;* a group of related master records is called a *master* file. A set of related transaction records is called a *transaction* file. The set of the day's credit account sales receipts would form a transaction file. The transaction record is also stored in the event of a customer inquiry.

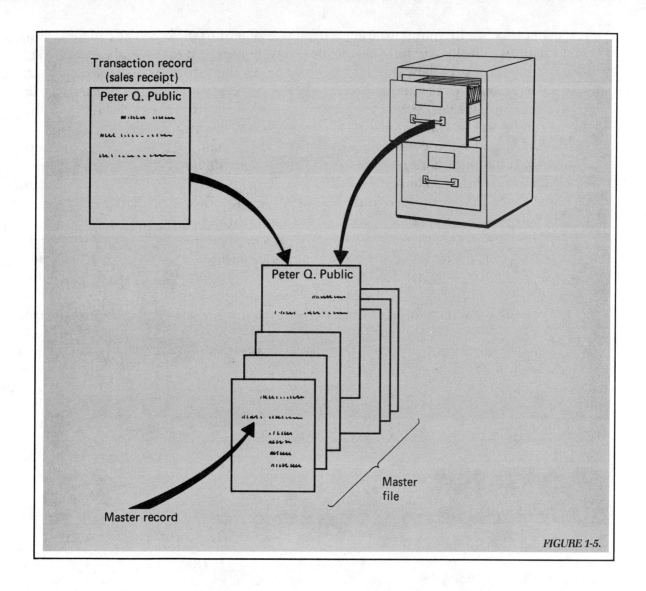

Transaction record
(sales receipt)

Peter Q. Public

Peter Q. Public

Master
file

Master record

FIGURE 1-5.

Exercises

14. Which is the fundamental unit of information in a data processing system?
 a. field **b.** record **c.** file **d.** source document

15. Which of the following data concepts encompasses the other three?
 a. field **b.** file **c.** character **d.** record

16. Typical information that may be included in a customer master record is:
 a. Social Security number **d.** outstanding balance
 b. birth date **e.** all of these
 c. annual income

17. An individual savings account withdrawal slip is an example of a:
 a. transaction record **c.** transaction file
 b. master record **d.** master file

18. The group of all savings account deposit slips accumulated at a bank during a particular business day is an example of a
 a. transaction record **c.** transaction file
 b. master record **d.** master file

Let us briefly return to the credit office where Clara has just finished storing the customer credit account master file. Frank enters the office with another sales receipt in his hand. Clara calmly suggests that in the future Frank hold or *batch* all the sales receipts until the end of the day so that she can process the transaction file (the set of all sales receipt records) at one time. Clara informs Frank that this procedure is more efficient and is called *batch processing*.

Any processing cycle in which the goal is to have the master file reflect the latest available information is referred to as *master file updating*. The customer records in the master file must be *updated* in order to reflect the most recent purchases. The addition of new credit accounts and the deletion of old credit accounts also must be accomplished through a master file updating procedure. When a customer notifies the credit office of a change in address, the customer credit account master file must be updated so that the corresponding customer credit account master record reflects the new address.

At the end of the month, Clara thumbs through the account master file and writes a bill to each customer who has an outstanding account balance. The return of the customer's payment initiates another data processing cycle. The set of all monthly payments made by credit account customers (recorded on the appropriate source documents) forms a transaction file. A master file update procedure is required in order to have each payment posted on the appropriate customer credit account master record.

SUMMARY

The data processing activities just described illustrate a sequential series of steps that is typical of a business data processing cycle. A business data processing cycle in which master records are updated usually includes the following ten activities:

1. Gathering data.

2. Recording data onto source documents so that each source document includes one or more individual transaction records.

3. Verifying that the data have been entered correctly.

4. Processing the transaction records either individually or in batches. When it is not essential that an individual transaction be processed immediately, batch processing tends to increase system efficiency.

5. Locating the appropriate master file.

6. Matching the transaction file against the master file by locating within the master file the master records that correspond to the transaction records being processed. This activity is called *merging* files.

7. Updating each master record that has a corresponding transaction record so that it now reflects the information on the transaction record.

8. Writing any required report documents.

9. Storing the updated master and transaction files.

10. Periodically writing additional report documents based on the updated master file.

In our department store example each of these activities was accounted for:

Steps in a Data Processing Cycle	Corresponding Department Store Activities
1 to 3	Completing the sales receipt and then scanning it for accuracy.
4	Taking the sales receipts accumulated during the day to the credit office.
5 to 6	Locating the file cabinet that houses the credit account master records and pulling those master records for which there are sales receipts.
7 and 9	Entering the transactions on the appropriate customer master records. Returning the master records to the master file cabinet. Storing the transaction file in case of a customer inquiry.
8 and 10	At the end of the month (customer billing period), producing a credit account statement for each customer who has an outstanding balance.

MICROCOMPUTERS AND DATA PROCESSING

Clara, the credit clerk, is overwhelmed by the volume of credit transactions and the preparation of the monthly billing statements. In order to assist Clara, Charlie, the proprietor, purchases an impressive looking microcomputer system. Clara eyes the computer with a bewildered expression. She frantically explains to Charlie that she doesn't know the first thing about computers. "Never fear," says Charlie. Charlie then picks up the phone and dials User-Friendly Computer Consultants, Inc. They advise Charlie and Clara that they will promptly send a representative to explain the nature of a microcomputer system. (See Figure 1-6.)

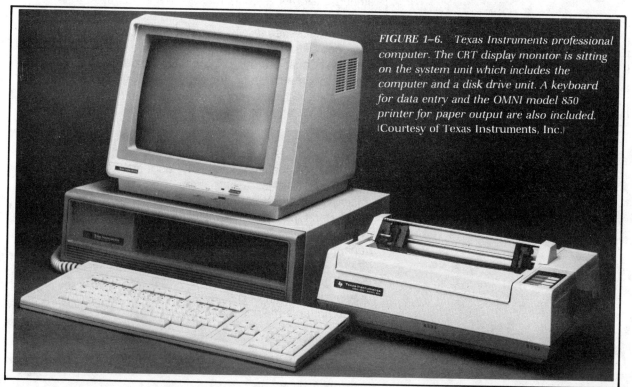

FIGURE 1–6. Texas Instruments professional computer. The CRT display monitor is sitting on the system unit which includes the computer and a disk drive unit. A keyboard for data entry and the OMNI model 850 printer for paper output are also included. (Courtesy of Texas Instruments, Inc.)

The representative, Peter, arrives and explains that the microcomputer, like the human brain, may be considered to be a data processing center. As in all data processing systems, there are four functions characteristic of all microcomputers, regardless of the manufacturer. Let us review these functions and identify the corresponding computer components:

Data Processing Function	Corresponding Computer Component
Input	*Keyboard.* Clara need not make any handwritten entries. Data and instructions are entered by pressing the appropriate typewriter-like keys.
Processing	*Electronic parts.* Clara has more free time; she no longer has to perform calculations, pull files, sort records within a file, or prepare customer bills. When commanded to execute a stored set of instructions, the computer performs these tasks electronically.
Storage	*Primary storage.* Instructions, calculations in progress, and final results of a current processing operation may be stored temporarily through electronic means inside the computer "box," in what is referred to as *main memory*. When the power is turned off, however, these stored items are lost.
	Secondary storage. Data, instructions, and processing results which need to be saved for future processing may be routed to an auxiliary, or secondary, storage device, such as a cassette tape or a disk drive unit. A cassette tape drive uses ordinary magnetic cassette tapes. A disk drive will typically store information on a flexible magnetic platter-like surface called a *floppy disk* or *diskette*. The diskette comes packaged in a protective envelope and is typically about the same size as a 45 rpm record, but rectangular in shape. Instead of storing customer account master files in tall metal cabinets, Clara will maintain them on lightweight and compact diskettes. (See Figure 1-7.) Although some microcomputers have either cassette tape or disk drive units built into the same cabinet that houses the microcomputer itself, these storage devices are still considered *peripheral* devices, that is, external to the microcomputer itself.
Output	*Video or TV monitor.* Current data and processing results are displayed to the "outside world" on a TV-like screen, sometimes referred to as a cathode-ray tube (CRT). Hard copy output may be produced by routing the output to an external electronically connected typewriter-like printer. A printer is another example of a peripheral device. Output may also be transmitted to a secondary storage device (cassette tape or disk drive units) for more permanent storage. (See Figure 1-8.) When needed, information stored previously on tape or disk may be copied back into the computer's main memory unit.

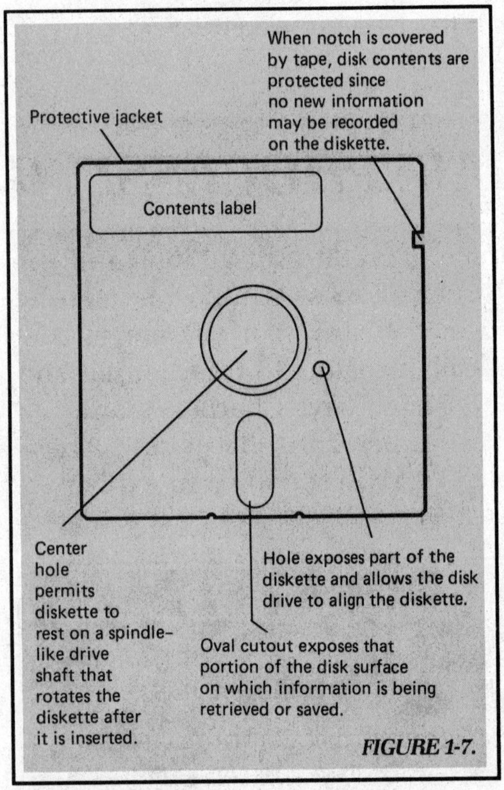

Figure 1-7 labels:

When notch is covered by tape, disk contents are protected since no new information may be recorded on the diskette.

Protective jacket

Contents label

Center hole permits diskette to rest on a spindle-like drive shaft that rotates the diskette after it is inserted.

Hole exposes part of the diskette and allows the disk drive to align the diskette.

Oval cutout exposes that portion of the disk surface on which information is being retrieved or saved.

FIGURE 1-7.

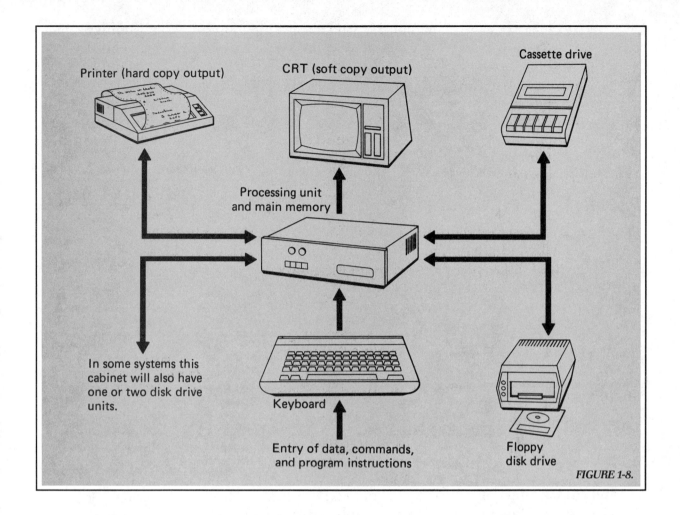

Printer (hard copy output)

CRT (soft copy output)

Cassette drive

Processing unit
and main memory

In some systems this
cabinet will also have
one or two disk drive
units.

Keyboard

Entry of data, commands,
and program instructions

Floppy
disk drive

FIGURE 1-8.

MORE ON SECONDARY STORAGE

When the power is turned off, all information that the user entered into the computer's internal memory is lost. Magnetic tape and diskettes provide a means for saving information for future use. Saving or copying information from the computer's main memory onto a cassette tape is very similar to recording a song from a radio that is connected to an audio cassette system.

A phonograph turntable is roughly analogous to a disk drive with the long-playing vinyl record album corresponding to the magnetic disk. A phonograph turntable and a disk drive both require that the corresponding platter-like disk be placed on a rotating spindle, which is rooted to a drive shaft. Using a disk drive, this is accomplished merely by inserting the diskette into a window-like slot. As the disk rotates, a mechanism attached to an arm reads information that has been previously encoded on the magnetic disk surface. A phonograph arm uses a stylus/cartridge assembly, while a disk drive arm is equipped with a read/write head. The phonograph sends information in the form of music to loudspeakers, while a disk drive transmits information into computer memory. Actually, main memory (computer people don't say "*the* main memory") only receives a *copy* of the information that is stored on the diskette. The read/write head of a disk drive permits data to be read from the disk (and then loaded into main memory) or information to be written to (saved on) the disk.

A cassette storage system is less expensive than a floppy disk storage system. However, the computer can locate and transfer information between the disk drive and main memory much faster than with a cassette storage system. A floppy disk drive can typically store about 140,000 characters on a diskette. (Larger or smaller storage capacities are not uncommon.) This translates into the equivalent of about 40 single-spaced typewritten pages. Some disk drives have a pair of read/write heads, one on each side of the disk's surface. When a double-sided disk is used, information may be stored on either side, thus effectively doubling the storage capacity of a single disk.

Magnetic disks are available in floppy (flexible) and hard (metal-based) formats. Floppy disks come in three sizes: $3\frac{1}{2}$, $5\frac{1}{4}$, and 8 inches square. The $5\frac{1}{4}$-inch size is the most common. Hard disks generally offer greater storage capacity than floppy disks and are not interchangeable with floppy disks, requiring special disk drives. Hard disks will be discussed in Chapter 2.

COMMUNICATING WITH THE COMPUTER

Clara is anxious to know how we "talk" to a computer. Peter explains that an agreed-upon language is used, which is part English-like and part mathematical. Let's start at the beginning.

A person speaking French into a telephone receiver to a person who speaks and understands only Russian cannot communicate with that individual. Communication requires that there be a *common* language. In order to be able to get a computer to perform a desired processing task, we must first communicate our wishes to the machine using a common language. Our thoughts and desires must be expressed in the form of an explicit step-by-step list of instructions, called a *program*. How would a chef communicate the procedure for preparing a cheese cake to a person who has never baked before? The recipe that might follow is similar in concept to a computer program. The instructions in a computer program, however, must be written in a language common to the user *and* the machine. It is extremely difficult for a person to learn the computer's "native" language, called *machine language*. It is even more difficult for the computer to be taught a person's native language, say, English. We must therefore seek a compromise. Whereas English has rules like "i before e except after c . . . except words like weird . . . ," unambiguous computer languages with no grammatical exceptions have been developed which are part symbolic and part English. Some computer languages resemble English more than others. *COBOL*, for example, is a business-oriented language that is English-like in appearance. *FORTRAN*, on the other hand, is algebra-like in structure and is used in engineering and scientific computing environments.

Computer programs, regardless of the language in which they are written, represent the *software* component of a computer system. The "nuts and bolts" computer equipment, which runs the software and stores, inputs, and outputs data, is referred to as the *hardware* component of a computer system. Software provides the instructions necessary to direct the operation of the hardware toward the achievement of some goal.

BASIC (Beginner's All-purpose Symbolic Instructional Code) is the language most often used when communicating with a personal microcomputer. Most microcomputers have been "taught" BASIC by including in the machine a special language interpreter that translates BASIC language statements into its own native machine language. It is then the responsibility of the human user who wishes to make up a set of instructions for the computer to follow to learn to "speak" BASIC. Unfortunately BASIC, like some other foreign languages (for example, Chinese), has many dialects. While some language dialects depend upon the geographic region from which the person comes, dialects of BASIC depend on the brand name of the microcomputer. We say therefore that BASIC is a *machine-dependent* language. The grammatical structure of the BASIC language will vary slightly depending upon whether the machine is manufactured by IBM, Radio Shack, Apple, Epson, or Commodore, to name a few.

By this time Clara is having heart palpitations, fearing that Charlie will ask her to write the complicated programs that will process sales transactions. In order to allay her fears, Peter informs Clara and Charlie that special applications software packages are available which will meet their needs, although some may require customizing, which can be accomplished by a programming specialist like himself.

Although the dominant theme of this book remains data processing, exposure to the basic elements of an actual programming language will help illustrate both the power and the limitations of a computer. Furthermore, many data processing concepts become easier to understand when reference can be made to a particular programming language, such as BASIC. Why BASIC? The simplicity of the BASIC programming language, its accessibility via the personal microcomputer, and its widespread use in small business computer systems make it the logical choice. The remainder of this chapter will be devoted to offering an introduction to BASIC. The appendices located at the end of each chapter will seek to build systematically on this knowledge.

VARIABLE VERSUS CONSTANT DATA VALUES

In a computer program there are generally two types of data values: variable and constant. In a program designed to process a company payroll, for example, the FICA (Social Security) tax *rate*, is known to the programmer when preparing the program, since it is fixed by the federal government and the same for every employee. The FICA tax rate is an example of a *constant data value*. The number of hours worked and the hourly wage rate, for example, vary from employee to employee and are not necessarily known to the programmer when the program instructions are written. The quantities must therefore be represented by a symbol, called a *variable name*. A program may have one or a great number of variables, depending on the nature and complexity of the processing required. A variable may be used to represent the value of a data item that is not currently known, but which will be supplied by the user of the program when the program is ready to be executed. Variables are also introduced by the programmer to refer to, and to keep track of, data items whose values may change during the execution of the program. In processing an individual's checking account transactions, a variable would be needed to represent the person's current balance. However, the value of this variable would change during the execution of the program, depending on the type of transaction processed (deposit or debit) and its amount.

Although the programmer normally selects the symbolic variable names that will be used in a program, the *syntax* (grammatical structure) of the particular programming language being used must be followed. There are specific guidelines that must be strictly adhered to in each programming language when names for variables are selected. A BASIC variable may consist of the following:

- A single letter (A, B, C, ... , Z)

- Two consecutive letters

- A letter immediately followed by a single digit (0, 1, 2, ... , 9)

J1, WB, and N are examples of legal BASIC variable names; 3A is *not* a valid BASIC variable name since the first character is a digit.

> Note: The rules for naming BASIC variables may vary slightly from machine to machine. The user's manual which accompanies the computer should be consulted in order to establish the correct set of guidelines to be followed.

AN INSIDE LOOK AT COMPUTER MEMORY

The ability to remember is intimately related to a person's ability to process information. For example, a person cannot be successful at multiplying two numbers unless he or she remembers the instructions for finding the product of two numbers as well as recalling which particular two data values are to be multiplied. Memory plays an equally important role in electronic data processing.

Walking into the lobby of a large apartment building, one notices an area reserved for several rows of consecutive mailboxes, one for each apartment. Essentially we have just described what the computer memory looks like. Instead of a letter carrier placing letters in the boxes, data values (numbers and alphanumeric characters) are stored in a computer's mailboxes, which are sometimes referred to as *memory cells* or *storage locations*.

How does a letter carrier know in which particular mailbox to place a letter that is addressed to a tenant? Simple. The mailboxes are labeled with the apartment number, the person's name, or both. Similarly, each computer memory cell is labeled so that it can be distinguished from other memory cells. The label or "apartment number" of a memory cell is referred to as the *address* of the memory cell. The data value (that is, the "mail") that is stored in a memory cell is referred to as the *contents* of that memory cell or storage location.

When a new tenant moves into an apartment building, a label bearing the tenant's name is usually affixed to the appropriate mailbox. Similarly, when a programmer introduces a variable into the program, a memory cell will be labeled automatically with the variable name. For example, suppose that in a certain program the variable B represents a person's savings account balance. Assume that the current balance is 487 dollars. In mathematical terms, we say that B equals 487 (B = 487). In a programming context, however, the variable name B represents the address of a memory location, while 487 represents its stored contents. (See Figure 1-9.)

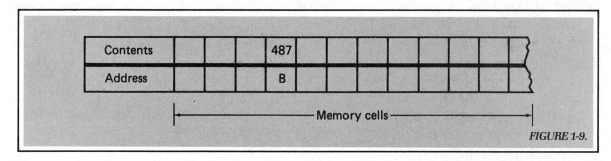

FIGURE 1-9.

Throughout the execution of a program which processes the individual's savings and deposit transactions:

- The person's current balance is referred to by the letter B rather than the actual value. In general, *a data value is referred to by its address in memory.*

- The memory cell remains labeled B. The contents of memory cell B, however, may change during execution of the program. If the individual has made three deposits, then the processing of each deposit will result in a change in the stored contents of memory cell B. In general, *the address of a memory cell remains the same, although its contents may change.*

Although it has proved helpful, our mailbox analogy fails in at least two important respects. A tenant's mailbox may at the same time hold a variety of unrelated mail items—a magazine, a postcard, a letter, and so on. A computer memory cell, however, can store only a single data item at a time. *When a data item is assigned to a memory cell, it automatically destroys the previous contents of that memory cell, if any.*

A letter carrier may find it easier to reach one particular mailbox than another. For a computer the physical location of the memory cell has nothing to do with the time or effort required to reach (that is, to *access*) the contents of a particular memory cell. Each memory cell may be accessed with equal ease, regardless of its address in memory. We refer to this feature of computer memory by using the term *random access memory.*

THE PROBLEM-SOLVING MYTH

It is somewhat misleading to attribute reasoning or problem-solving skills to a computer. Generally speaking, *people* solve problems, *not* computers. People prepare instructions and computers then follow these instructions.

It is true that computers may supply the answers to problems, but only as a result of following a detailed set of directions, prepared by a programmer, which informs the computer how the problem is to be solved. A computer program tends to represent a *generalized* solution to a specific problem. The computer then "solves" the problem for *particular* values of the program variables. Suppose that the problem at hand is to prepare a program that finds the average of two numbers. By introducing program variables to represent the two numbers, the programmer solves the problem by producing a program that finds the average of *any* pair of numbers, regardless of their values. The computer then "solves" the average problem by following the supplied list of program instructions and determining the average for *particular* pairs of data values that are provided by the user of the program.

The list of instructions must be coded in an appropriate programming language, such as BASIC. Regardless of the programming language used, the set of program statements is prepared as though instructions were being given to a robot. For example, to find the average of two numbers, it would be necessary to provide for the following steps:

1. Input two numbers.

2. Add the two numbers.

3. Divide the sum by 2.

4. Store the result (that is, the average).

5. Print the result.

Regardless of the values of the two numbers, the procedure that the computer must follow, as represented by these five steps, remains the same.

The concepts that have been presented so far are fundamental to an understanding of computers and the nature of the programming process. Our next concern is to become familiar with the syntax (grammatical rules) of a particular language.

A BASIC BASIC PROGRAM

The following four statements represent a BASIC program that determines and prints the sum of two numbers, where program variables A and B are used to represent the two numbers and R represents their sum:

```
10  INPUT A, B
20  LET R = A + B
30  PRINT R
40  END
```

Notice that each statement is preceded by a line number. Every BASIC statement must be given a line number which must be some whole number. (The upper limit depends on the machine.) Program instructions are then executed in line-number order. Let us analyze each statement.

▪ *Line 10.* This statement corresponds to the input phase. During the execution of the program, the computer is instructed to "request" that two data values be entered by displaying a question mark (?). The user must supply two data values in order for program execution to resume. The first data value is assigned to memory cell A, and the second data value entered is assigned to memory cell B.

- *Line 20.* This statement corresponds to the processing and storage phases. The sum of the values represented by variables A and B is calculated, and the result is assigned to R. In memory, the contents of memory cells A and B are added, and the result is stored in memory cell R. The contents of memory cells A and B remain unaffected by the addition operation. If, for example, the original data values entered are 3 and 5, then:

3	5	8
A	B	R

- *Line 30.* The output phase of a data processing operation is represented by this statement. The contents of memory cell R is displayed on the CRT screen. It may be helpful to think of this statement as "duplicating" the contents of memory cell R on the CRT screen since the contents of storage location R remains unaffected by the output operation.

- *Line 40.* As a result of this statement, the computer is instructed to halt processing.

The symbols used to denote the arithmetic operations in BASIC are summarized in the following table:

Operation	Arithmetic Symbol	Basic Symbol
Addition	+	+
Subtraction	−	−
Multiplication	×	*
Division	÷	/

EXAMPLE

The BASIC program to the right is designed to determine and print the difference, product, and quotient of two numbers:

```
10  INPUT A, B
20  LET D = A - B
30  LET P = A * B
40  LET Q = A / B
50  PRINT D
60  PRINT P
70  PRINT Q
80  END
```

If the values entered for A and B are 12 and 3, then the contents of the different memory cells would be as follows:

12	3	9	36	4
A	B	D	P	Q

The output of the program illustrated would appear on three separate lines. In order to get the answers (D, P, and Q) to appear on the same line, the following program could be used:

```
10  INPUT A, B
20  LET D = A - B
30  LET P = A * B
40  LET Q = A / B
50  PRINT D, P, Q
60  END
```

LINE NUMBERS IN A BASIC PROGRAM

Suppose that the following program to find the sum of three numbers has been keyed in and is stored in memory:

```
10   INPUT A, B, C
20   LET R = A + B + C
30   PRINT R
40   END
```

If we now wish to find the *product* of the three numbers rather than their sum, we have two choices: either start over or modify the existing program. It would be silly to retype the entire program when only a single statement of the original program (line 20) has to be changed. We can substitute a line simply by retyping the new line after the last line of the original program. By assigning it the same line number as the one it is to replace, we direct the computer to make the substitution automatically in memory, destroying the previous statement that had the same line number:

```
10   INPUT A, B, C
20   LET R = A + B + C
30   PRINT R
40   END

20   LET R = A * B * C
```

Although two statements that have the same line number may appear on the screen, only the last line 20 is stored in memory.

Suppose that in typing a program, a statement was inadvertently omitted:

```
10   INPUT A, B
20   LET R = A / B
30   END
```

Notice that the print statement has been omitted. To insert it, all we need do is to type it in after line 30, but assigning it a line number that corresponds to its *logical* position in the program. Since it must be executed after line 20, but before line 30, we may assign it a line number between 20 and 30:

```
10   INPUT A, B
20   LET R = A / B
30   END
25   PRINT R
```

Thus, numbering program statements in multiples of 10 gives us the flexibility of inserting additional line numbers without renumbering any of the original program statements. Since the computer executes statements in line number sequence (and not necessarily in the order in which they appear on the screen), the program will yield correct results.

Note: These *editing* features of BASIC assume that the programs are being entered in the so-called *interactive* mode, as with a personal micro-computer in which the computer gives the user immediate feedback.

REVIEW EXERCISES

Fact Recall

1. A document that may serve as both an output and an input document is called a _____ document.
2. A group of similar records is called a _____ .
3. A _____ document is usually produced as the result of a summarizing operation.
4. A(n) _____ field may include both digits and letters.
5. *Origination* refers to how and from what source the raw set of facts and figures are derived. The origination phase of data processing should immediately precede the _____ phase.
6. Numeric field data are _____ -justified.
7. Arranging a set of Social Security numbers in numerical order is called _____ .
8. Records containing summary type information or information that remains relatively constant are called _____ records.
9. Raw data are entered on a _____ document for subsequent processing.
10. Separating employment applications according to sex is called _____ .
11. Entering the most current information on a record is called _____ .
12. The grouping of similar transactions for processing during regular time intervals is called _____ processing.
13. A group of related fields is called a _____ .
14. Alphanumeric data are _____ -justified in their fields.
15. A group of related transaction records is called a _____ .
16. Another name for a detail record is a _____ record.
17. The maximum number of characters that may be entered in a given field is called the field _____ .
18. The processing operation that determines whether one number is less than, equal to, or greater than another number is called _____ .
19. During master file updating the _____ record gets changed.
20. In contrast to output that appears in a light-emitting diode (LED) display of a pocket calculator, output that is printed on paper forms is called _____ _____ .

Multiple Choice

21. Which of the following fields would contain alphanumeric data?
    a. Zip-code field   c. age field
    b. car license plate   d. day-of-the-week field
       number field
22. Which BASIC statement corresponds to the processing phase?
    a. INPUT   b. LET   c. END   d. PRINT

23. Which of the following represents a report document?
   a. employee time card
   b. savings account deposit slip
   c. student academic transcript
   d. canceled check
24. Which data concept does *not* encompass any of the other three?
   a. field   b. character   c. record   d. file
25. Which of the following statements are *false*?
   a. The basic phases of any data processing system are: input, processing, output, and storage.
   b. A file may include information in addition to the information contained in the individual records.
   c. The primary difference between a customer master record and a customer transaction record is that the master record usually contains additional information relating to the customer's personal background and purchase/payment history.
   d. A data processing system does *not* require a computer.
   e. A file may *not* contain more than a single type of record.
26. Which of the following statements are *true*?
   a. As a result of a summarizing operation a source document is generated.
   b. A computer is essential to the smooth functioning of any data processing system.
   c. The purpose of master file updating is to sort the master records within the file.
   d. A textbook publisher receives orders from several different book stores. The set of all such unprocessed orders during a given time period forms a transaction file.
   e. A person's credit rating would most likely be found in a customer transaction file.
27. Which of the following statements are *true*?
   a. A programmer is free to select symbolic variable names.
   b. A computer always executes program instructions in the order in which they appear in the program.
   c. The address of a memory cell never changes.
   d. The contents of a memory cell never change.
28. What would be the output of the BASIC program given below?

```
10  LET A = 5
20  LET B = 4
30  LET C = A + B
40  PRINT C
50  END
20  LET B = 2
```

   a. 9   b. 1   c. 7   d. 0

29. What would be the output of the BASIC program given below, assuming the value inputted for A is 10?

```
10   INPUT A
20   LET S = A * B
30   PRINT S
40   END
15   LET B = 4
```

a. 14 **b.** 6 **c.** 10 **d.** 40

30. The following data set represents a customer account master file.

Name field	Account number field	Account balance field
Green, Bob	3298	15.67
Brown, Susan	9802	1.09
Blue, Carol	1872	75.48
Lavender, Louis	0599	66.00
Coral, Mike	4133	295.76
Grey, Simon	2426	35.90

a. How many fields are in each record?
b. How many records are in the file?
c. A *key* field is a field that uniquely identifies a record. If we wish to sort a file, the key on which the file is to be sorted must be specified.
  (1) Sort the given file, using the name field as the key field.
  (2) Sort the file in ascending order, using the account-balance field as the key field.
  (3) Sort the field in descending order, using the account-number field as the key field.

EXCURSION INTO BASIC

In this section, we shall briefly take a closer look at the input, output, and processing operations as implemented in the BASIC programming language. Each subsequent chapter will close by developing some additional aspects of BASIC. At the end of our last Excursion Into BASIC, you will not only be able to write your own BASIC programs, but you will have a greater appreciation of the joys, challenges, and frustrations that a programmer experiences.

THE READ AND DATA STATEMENTS

We have briefly discussed the fact that the INPUT statement may be used to supply the program with specific data values *while the program is executing*. When the data that are going to be operated on by the BASIC program are known at the time the program instructions are being prepared, it is often convenient to build the data into the program by including within the body of the program a statement that provides the actual data values. A DATA statement is used to list the data items, while the READ statement is used to indicate the BASIC variables that will be assigned the data values. The following programs compare the use of the INPUT and the READ and DATA statements in supplying data to a program.

```
10  INPUT A              10  READ A
20  LET B = 30 * A       20  LET B = 30 * A
30  PRINT A, B           30  PRINT A, B
40  END                  40  DATA 4
                         50  END
        (a)                      (b)
```

When program (a) is executed, the program stops at line 10 and waits, and waits, and waits . . . until a number is entered at the keyboard by the user of the program. The program is executing in an *interactive* mode. In program (b), no such human interaction is required. When line 10 is executed in program (b), it automatically searches for the DATA statement and assigns the value in the DATA statement (here 4) to the variable A. Line 30 in both programs prints the value of **A** followed by the value of B on the same horizontal line of output. In program (b), the output would be 4 followed by 120; in program (a), the output would depend on what data value was entered after statement 10 was executed.

The DATA statement supplies values to the program—it doesn't instruct the computer to do anything. It is a nonexecutable statement and may therefore be placed anywhere in the program. Some programmers prefer to place the DATA statement immediately preceding the END statement; others prefer to place the DATA statement at the beginning of the program, immediately preceding or following the READ statement. Sample programs that appear in this book will have the DATA statement immediately before the END statement.

In the next sample program, *two* variables are to be read and assigned values:

```
10  READ A, B
20  LET Q = A / B
30  PRINT A, B, Q
40  DATA 36, 4
50  END
```

Notice that the variables listed in both the READ and the DATA statements are separated by commas, without any punctuation mark following the last variable or data item. In order to analyze the effect of each program instruction, we may use the following variable chart:

	Contents of Cells		
Line	A	B	Q
10	36	4	
20	36	4	9

As a result of the execution of line 30, the numbers 36, 4, and 9 are outputted across the same horizontal line. A semicolon (;) may also be used to separate variables in the PRINT statement:

```
30  PRINT A; B; Q
```

On most machines, this will have the effect of printing the values of the variables more closely together, eliminating extra blank column spaces. In general, punctuation marks are used in the PRINT statement to control the horizontal column spacing of the output. Since the effect of punctuation in the PRINT statement may vary from machine to machine, the manual for the particular machine being used should be consulted.

BASIC Exercises

Determine the output for each of the following programs.

```
1.  10  READ L , W
    20  LET P = 2 * (L + W)
    30  PRINT P
    40  DATA 14 , 6
    50  END
2.  10  READ B , E
    20  LET M = B - E
    30  LET R = M / 2
    40  PRINT R
    50  DATA 10 , 4
    60  END
3.  10  READ X , Y , Z
    20  LET A = (X + Y + Z) / 3
    30  PRINT A
    40  DATA 7 , 17 , 6
    50  END
```

PROCESSING: THE LET STATEMENT

Arithmetic operations are usually accomplished using the LET statement. Consider the following program:

```
10  INPUT N
20  LET C = N / 4
30  PRINT C
40  END
```

When the LET statement of line 20 is executed, two actions are taken:

■ The expression on the right-hand side of the equal sign is evaluated. If the value inputted for N in line 10 were, for example, 12, then the right-hand side of the LET statement would be evaluated as 3.

■ The result of the evaluation is *assigned* to the storage location (memory cell) named by the BASIC variable that appears on the left-hand side of the equal sign.

Thus, the letter C refers at once to the value 3 and to the address of the storage location to which the value has been assigned. For this reason, the LET statement is sometimes referred to as an *assignment* statement. Consequently, in a LET statement there may be only a single variable with no arithmetic operators $(+, -, *, /)$ on the left-hand side of the equal sign.

<table>
<tr><td>Legal LET Statements</td><td>Illegal LET Statements</td></tr>
<tr><td>10 LET A = B + 3</td><td>10 LET A - 3 = B</td></tr>
<tr><td>40 LET P = R * S</td><td>40 LET R * S = P</td></tr>
</table>

What would be the output of the following program?

```
10  LET A = 2
20  LET A = 5
30  PRINT A
40  END
```

The output would be 5. The LET statement is *destructive* in the sense that when a value is assigned to a memory cell, it destroys the cell's previous contents. When A is assigned the value of 5, the previous value of A (namely, 2) is wiped out.

In many versions of BASIC, the keyword LET is optional. For example, the statement

```
20  LET C = N / 4
```

may be written as

```
20  C = N / 4
```

To make things as clear as possible, the sample programs that appear in this book will use the keyword LET.

Determine the output of each program.

1.
```
10  READ N
20  LET N = 7
30  PRINT N
40  DATA 4
50  END
```

2.
```
10  READ T
20  LET T = T - 2
30  PRINT T
40  DATA 8
50  END
```

1. After line 10 has been executed, the contents of memory cell N is 4. After line 20 has been executed, the value 7 is assigned to memory cell N, destroying its previous contents. The output is 7.

2. After line 10 has been executed, the contents of memory cell T is 8. When statement 20 is executed:
   a. 2 is subtracted from the current contents of memory cell T: $8 - 2 = 6$.
   b. The result (6) is assigned back to memory cell T, destroying its original contents.
   The output is 6, the current contents of memory cell T.

Determine the output for each of the following programs.

```
4.  10  READ P
    20  LET P = P + 2
    30  PRINT P
    40  DATA 13
    50  END

5.  10  READ L
    20  LET L = 3 * L
    30  LET B = L - 1
    40  PRINT B
    50  DATA 8
    60  END

6.  10  LET A = 7
    20  READ M
    30  LET M = A * M
    40  PRINT A, M
    50  DATA 4
    60  END
```

RESPECTING THE ORDER OF OPERATIONS

Peter asked Clara and Charlie to evaluate the expression

$$4 + 2 * 3$$

Clara obtained 10 as an answer, while Charlie explained that the answer must be 18, since $4 + 2$ is 6 and 6 multiplied by 3 is 18. Clara, on the other hand, said she prefers to multiply *before* adding. Clara explained that she multiplied 2 by 3 to obtain 6, and then added 4 to 6, which gives the result 10. While Charlie and Clara scratched their heads, Peter explained that in order to avoid this type of confusion, we shall agree to adhere to the following set of rules:

Evaluate arithmetic expressions from left to right in the following order:

1. Perform multiplications and/or divisions, working from left to right.

2. Return to the beginning of the line to perform additions and/or subtractions, working from left to right.

If some of the terms of an expression are enclosed within parentheses, then the expressions in parentheses are evaluated first, taking precedence over those that are not included within parentheses.

According to these rules, Clara was correct:

$$4 + \underbrace{2 * 3}$$ → multiplication is performed first

$$4 + 6$$

10

Peter then explained that if the expression were to be evaluated in the manner in which Charlie evaluated it (first combining 4 and 2 and then multiplying), the 4 and 2 would have to be enclosed in parentheses:

$$(4 + 2) * 3$$
$$6 * 3$$
$$18$$

The following examples illustrate the effect of using parentheses.

EXAMPLES

With parentheses

1. $4 * (3 - 1) = ?$

    $4 * 2 = 8$

2. $20/(2 * 5) = ?$

    $20 / 10 = 2$

3. $7 + 12 / (3 + 1) = ?$

    $7 + 12 / 4 = 7 + 3 = 10$

Without parentheses

1. $4 * 3 - 1 = ?$

    $12 - 1 = 11$

2. $20 / 2 * 5 = ?$

    $10 * 5 = 50$

3. $7 + 12 / 3 + 1 = ?$

    $7 + 4 + 1 = 12$

The formula for converting degrees Fahrenheit into degrees Celsius is $C = \frac{5}{9} (F - 32)$. Suppose we wished to write a BASIC program that inputs a Fahrenheit temperature and prints the equivalent Celsius temperature. We must be able to express the algebraic conversion formula in BASIC.

Program analysis

1. What is the input? F
2. What is the processing required?
    $C = 5 / 9 * (F - 32)$
3. What is the output? C

Coded program

```
10 INPUT F
20 LET C = 5 / 9 * (F - 32)
30 PRINT C
40 END
```

In order to write BASIC programs one has to be able to transform an algebraic formula or expression into an equivalent BASIC expression.

EXAMPLES

Translate into BASIC. (A, B, C, D, and M are BASIC variables.)

1. $M = A + \dfrac{B}{C}$

2. $M = 3(A - B)$

3. $M = \dfrac{A + B}{C}$

4. $M = \dfrac{A}{C} - BD$

1. LET M = A + B / C
2. LET M = 3 * (A - B)
3. LET M = (A + B) / C
4. LET M = A / C - B * D
   or
   LET M = (A / C) - (B * D)

BASIC Exercises

7. Evaluate.
   a. 11 − 3 * 2
   b. 36 / 9 + 3
   c. 18 / (2 * 3)
   d. (10 + 1) * 3
   e. 12 − 6 / 2 + 4
   f. (12 − 6) / (2 + 4)
8. Translate into BASIC. (R, S, T, and W are BASIC variables.)

   a. $W = \dfrac{R}{ST}$

   b. $W = \dfrac{RS}{R + T}$

   c. $W = \dfrac{T - S}{T + S}$

   d. $W = \dfrac{RS}{T} - T$

   e. $W = (R + T)(S + R)$

   f. $W = \dfrac{R}{S} + \dfrac{S}{T}$

PLANNING THE OUTPUT

The output of a BASIC program is controlled by the PRINT statement. In displaying the results of a processing operation, we may like to attach an explanation or in some way label the output. The computer will print any expression exactly as written, provided it is enclosed by quotation marks within a PRINT statement. For example, the result of executing the statement

        10 PRINT "expression"

would simply be the word *expression* itself.

EXAMPLES

Program	Output
1. 10 PRINT "HAVE A NICE DAY" 20 END	HAVE A NICE DAY
2. 10 LET A = 5 20 PRINT "A="; A	A = 5

Note: semicolon

3. 10 READ X
   20 PRINT "X="; X
   30 DATA 9
   40 END
	X = 9

Program	Output

```
4.  10   READ P                                   TAX = $8.25
    20   LET T = .0825 * P
    30   PRINT "TAX=$"; T
    40   DATA 100
    50   END

5.  10   PRINT "FAHRENHEIT", "CELSIUS"      FAHRENHEIT        CELSIUS
   ┌20   PRINT
   │30   READ F
   │40   LET C = 5 / 9 * (F - 32)           212               100
   │50   PRINT F, C
   │60   DATA 212
   │70   END
   └►
```

►*Note:* skips a line

CHAPTER

2

COMPUTER SYSTEM COMPONENTS

INTRODUCTION

Clara has had a difficult day at the office. As she drives home on a highway, she switches on the computer-controlled automatic cruise control. She has to stop for gas. Realizing that she is short on cash, Clara pays by credit card. When she checks the accuracy of her receipt, she notices that the letters and numerals printed are of a special shape. The gas attendant advises her that the letters and digits are printed that way so that they can be read by a machine when the credit slip is processed. Since the banks have already closed, Clara stops at her local 24-hour ready cash window. She inserts her charge card, punches in her ID number and the amount, and, almost magically, cash appears!

Clara arrives home and empties her mailbox. She finds a punch-card bill from the local telephone company and a computer-generated bill from her favorite department store. She grins because she also finds a tax refund check from the IRS, printed on a punch card. Clara enters her apartment and turns on the evening news. She learns that the United States has successfully launched an outer-space probe whose on-board computers are navigating its course as well as gathering and transmitting valuable scientific data. As she is listening to a computer-formulated weather forecast, the telephone rings. Bad news. Her best friend has suffered a heart attack; but she is in the best of hands—a computer is monitoring her vital signs in a hospital recovery room.

With her vacation approaching, Clara telephones her travel agent in order to make an airline reservation. Her travel agent keys in some information to a computer keyboard terminal sitting atop her desk. The travel agent is able to verify that a suitable flight has room and makes the reservation. After dinner, Clara's fourteen-year-old daughter asks for help with her homework. When Clara finds out that the assignment is to write a BASIC computer program, Clara says "Goodnight!"

There isn't a day which goes by that a computer doesn't affect our lives; sometimes for the better, and sometimes for the worse. It should always be remembered, however, that a computer is a *tool* which may be used to improve the quality of life or which may be abused by allowing it to intrude on our lives. How it is used is the decision of people, not of the machine. In order to form intelligent opinions concerning computers, it is essential to know something about what computers are and how they work. In order to be able to control computers, we must understand something about how to communicate with a computer. With these two goals in mind, we begin in this chapter to explore the nature of larger computer systems.

WHAT CAN A COMPUTER DO?

Is a computer faster than a speeding bullet? Yes. Is a computer capable of performing more work in the same amount of time as all the people working in a tall office building? Yes. Can a computer *think*? There is much about the architecture of a computer system that invites comparison with the human brain. Both respond to stimuli, called *input;* both can remember instructions and data by storing them in *memory* centers; both can *process* data by performing calculations and by making logical comparisons; both are equipped to communicate or *output* information. In short, both the human mind and the computer are information processors, capable of performing the four basic functions characteristic of all data processing systems: input, processing, storage, and output. Computers, however, are capable of learning and performing only by rote methods, being inflexibly directed by a set of program instructions that must be placed in memory before processing can begin. The program, of course, must be developed by a person.

THINKING VERSUS FOLLOWING INSTRUCTIONS

In order to assemble a model airplane or a "knocked down" piece of furniture, the accompanying list of instructions (that is, the directions) must be strictly followed. Such a list of step-by-step instructions is an example of an *algorithm.*

An algorithm is a straightforward "recipe" method for solving a particular type of problem. More formally stated, an algorithm is a planned list of procedures or operations that, if strictly followed, will lead to a solution in a finite number of steps. Algorithms can be devised for baking a cake, for explaining how to travel to a friend's house, or for solving an algebraic equation, to name just a few examples.

Is there an algorithm for winning at chess? No, since an algorithm cannot be stated in *advance* that will always guarantee that a given player will win. One can, however, develop general strategies and approaches that may clarify the path to a solution, although they cannot guarantee success. This type of approach is characterized by "educated" guessing performed in some systematic fashion and is referred to as *heuristics.* Algorithmic and heuristic approaches may be considered to be opposites. Algorithms are specified in advance and clearly define the steps necessary to reach a solution to a given problem. In a heuristic approach, the exact method of solution is not known at the outset; only a general approach is known which may be refined as the solution process begins, yet may or may not ultimately prove successful.

People are capable of devising and following both algorithmic and heuristic processes—the latter we tend to associate with creative thinking, problem-solving, and the ability to make leaps in drawing logical inferences. Computers, on the other hand, must follow instructions in robot-like fashion. That is, in order to solve a problem, computers must be provided in advance with the precise method for solving it. A computer program is used to instruct a computer not only in what must be done, but how it is to be accomplished. The computer used to solve a problem or perform a processing task must specify the algorithm to be followed which will lead to the desired result. It is the job of a programmer to devise the necessary algorithm and then code it in an appropriate computer language (for example, BASIC, COBOL, or FORTRAN) so that it can be communicated to the computer.

There is much productive research currently being conducted in the area of *artificial intelligence.* Artificial intelligence is a specialized branch of computer science devoted to exploring methods by which computers can be programmed to engage in heuristic processes. Although much of this work is presently confined to the research laboratory, Texas Instruments has designed a general-purpose "natural language interface," a commercial product that is a direct result of their research efforts in this area. A natural language interface is a sophisticated group of programs that encourages a computer user to ask the computer questions *naturally* by making available to the user selected *English* phrases which he or she then uses to construct a valid English-language question or command that the computer understands.

USES OF COMPUTERS

If computers are not capable of "thinking," why do we depend so heavily on them? One reason is *speed.* Computers can catalog, store, and retrieve information with incredible speed. Many tasks that would take a person years to accomplish, a computer can complete in a matter of seconds or fractions of a second. A large modern computer, for example, can perform in excess of 10 million arithmetic operations per second. Computers have made space exploration a reality. The calculations necessary to design, launch, and monitor the flight of a spacecraft would take one or more lifetimes if performed manually. The mass storage capacity of computer systems has allowed businesses and other large organizations to manage successfully the huge volumes of information that they must maintain. Computer speed also helps to account for our increasingly "cashless" society. Computers permit an individual's credit account to be kept current so that it is possible to walk into a store and complete a credit purchase in a matter of minutes, including the time it takes for the store clerk to receive authorization from the credit card company. As many of us know only too well, they are also relentlessly persistent in sending us bills.

Accuracy is another major factor in using computers. Whereas people's efforts are subject to careless or "human" error, computers process information with uncompromising accuracy. In general, computers do not make mistakes, they merely follow instructions. Erroneous computer results are invariably due to faulty logic on the part of the human programmer. An incorrect computer-generated bill is usually caused by the negligence of an office worker who fails to initiate an appropriate action or who submits inaccurate data to the computer.

A third factor of importance in working with computers is *reliability.* While the quality of people's work may suffer as a result of distraction, fatigue, or illness, computers do not become bored and are extremely reliable. Computer installations are often operated on a 24-hour basis with little *downtime.* Downtime is the time interval in which a computer is nonoperational; when a computer is not working it is said to be "down." The use of modern solid-state (integrated circuit) components, preventive maintenance checks, and built-in electronic self-checking circuits help minimize the chance of a computer malfunction or breakdown.

Interestingly, computers are often used to perform relatively simple processing tasks, but are asked to repeat the tasks a great number of times. For example, in calculating a payroll, the *method* of calculation for each individual worker is the same; what may vary is the number of hours worked, hourly wage, and number of deductions. In processing customer credit account purchases and payments, the related computations and methods of updating a person's account are the same, regardless of the identity of the person and the actual items and dollar amounts involved. The speed and accuracy of computers make them particularly well suited to performing repetitive types of calculations and operations.

To summarize, we use computers because of their speed, accuracy, and reliability. Computers are particularly useful in executing long chains of calculations; performing tasks of a repetitive nature; and storing large volumes of data and selectively retrieving data necessary to accomplish a particular processing task, which may range from satisfying a single inquiry to updating a file or producing a comprehensive set of report documents.

COMPUTER SOFTWARE: AN OVERVIEW

The term *software* refers to the computer programs that direct the activities of the computer. There are different types of computer software. Some programs are designed to solve user problems while other types of software are needed to ensure the smooth operation of the computer itself. Generally speaking, software may be classified as follows:

- *Applications software.* These are the types of programs that most people think of when discussing computer software. Applications programs are designed to meet the data processing needs of a particular user or group of users. Programs that process payrolls, update customer credit accounts, perform the necessary calculations in the design of an aircraft, or are written by a student in a college course in computer programming are all examples of applications programs.

- *Systems software.* These are the types of programs that are of particular interest to the computer professional and design engineer. *Systems programs* are the programs designed to make the computer system operate more efficiently, and are typically supplied by the computer manufacturer. An example of systems software is the *operating systems programs.* Operating systems software is indispensable to the operation of a computer, and is found in personal microcomputers as well as in large multimillion-dollar computer systems. Operating systems software has the overall responsibility of supervising and coordinating the internal activities of the computer, while seeking to minimize the need for human intervention. Operating systems software is considered to be almost an intrinsic part of the computer; indeed, if the operating system programs of a computer are removed, then all internal computer processing will quickly cease.

- *Language translators.* Language translators are programs that serve a function similar to that of the foreign-language interpreters at the United Nations. Most computer programs are written in an English-oriented language, such as BASIC, FORTRAN, or COBOL. These languages are "foreign" to the computer. A computer understands only one language—its own internal machine language code. A special computer program is used which converts the original program that is written in a user-oriented programming language (called the *source* program) into the equivalent machine language code (called the *object* program). The language translation process is an internal machine activity, with each source language requiring its own special language translator program. Typically the language translator program is stored on disk and brought into memory when needed. (See Figure 2-1.)

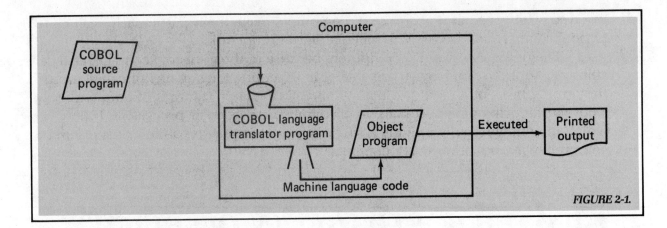

FIGURE 2-1.

TYPES OF PROGRAM INSTRUCTIONS

Programs written in different programming languages, such as BASIC, FORTRAN, and COBOL, will vary considerably in appearance, with each conforming to a different set of syntactical (grammatical) rules. All of these languages, however, share a number of common features that reflect the basic capabilities of computers. A computer language will generally include specific types of program statements designed to do the following:

Perform an input and output operation. In an input operation, program instructions and/or data are brought into the computer and stored in computer memory. In an output operation, stored information is copied from main memory and transmitted out of the computer. In BASIC, the INPUT and the READ and DATA statements accomplish an input operation, while the PRINT statement effects an output operation.

> *Note:* There are special commands in BASIC which transmit instructions and data to and from the computer and an auxiliary storage device such as a disk drive.

Assign a constant or variable data value to a memory cell. The LET statement in BASIC is an example of an assignment statement. It may be used to place a constant in a memory location. For example, LET A = 9 stores the constant 9 in memory location A. The assignment statement is also used to assign a variable value to a memory location as a result of performing a calculation. The statement LET P = 3 * B multiplies the current value (that is, stored contents) of B by 3 and then assigns (stores) the result in a memory location named P. In a *move* operation the contents of one memory cell are copied into another storage location. The statement LET A = B will assign the value stored in B to variable A. If, for example, the contents of memory cell B is 5, then after the LET statement has been executed, the value of A will also be 5. Thus, we have "moved" 5 into memory cell A. Although this is referred to as a move operation, after the statement LET A = B has been executed, *both* A and B will store the same value. Hence, the term *copy* more accurately describes the effect of this type of program language statement.

Compare data. Computers have the ability to compare the magnitudes of a pair of data values. For example, a computer can determine whether data value X is equal to data value Y, less than data value Y, or greater than data value Y.

■ *Transfer program control.* Program statements are normally executed either in the order in which they are written or in line-number sequence. Program language statements are available that can alter the order in which statements are executed by directing the computer to jump to a program statement which may be out of sequence. Comparison operations typically involve a transfer of program control. For example, in a program which processes checking account transactions, the program compares the amount of each check with the current account balance. If the account balance is greater than the amount of the check, then the check is processed. However, if the account balance is not greater than or equal to the amount of the check, then the program will bypass the program language statements which accomplish the normal processing activities, and jump to a statement that terminates the processing because of "insufficient account funds." For this reason comparison operations are sometimes referred to as *compare* and *branch* operations. It is this ability of computers to compare and then branch (depending on the result of the comparison) which gives computers their "decision-making" ability. The IF/THEN statement accomplishes the compare and branch operations in BASIC and will be discussed in our Excursion Into BASIC at the end of this chapter.

■ *Halt a data processing operation.* In BASIC the END statement signals the end of a data processing cycle.

All data processing tasks, regardless of how complex, must ultimately be reduced to the five types of operations represented by the program language statements presented above.

We have pointed out that computers are often called upon to perform repetitive tasks. In translating these processing tasks into a set of computer program instructions, it would be inefficient to rewrite the same set of instructions each time that they will be repeated. Consider the following program in BASIC, in which the same set of instructions, line numbers 10, 20, and 30, is executed repeatedly:

```
┌►10   INPUT N
│  20   LET A = N / 2
│  30   PRINT A
└─ 40   GO TO 10
   50   END
```

■ *Line 10.* A number will be entered by the user.

■ *Line 20.* The number inputted will be divided by 2 and the result assigned to A.

■ *Line 30.* The contents of A will be printed.

■ *Line 40.* The program will automatically be sent back to line 10. The GO TO statement unconditionally transfers control of the program back to line 10. The set of instructions given in lines 10, 20, and 30 will be executed repeatedly, creating a *loop*. How many times will this loop be executed? According to this program, indefinitely—we have not provided a means by which the computer can "escape," or exit, from the loop. Line 50 will never be executed.

Consider the next program in which the INPUT statement is replaced by the READ and DATA statements. What will be the output?

```
10  READ N
20  LET A = N / 2
30  PRINT A
40  GO TO 10
50  DATA 10, 7, 52
60  END
```

Program Execution	N		A		Output
1		10		5	5
2	~~10~~ 7		~~5~~ 3.5		3.5
3	~~7~~ 52		~~3.5~~ 26		26
4			? OUT OF DATA IN 10		Control is transferred back to line 10, which attempts to read another value for N. When it doesn't find one, the program abruptly terminates with an OUT OF DATA warning message.

Exercises

Determine the output for each program.

1.
```
10  LET S = 0
20  READ X
30  LET S = S + X
40  PRINT S
50  GO TO 20
60  DATA 3, 18, 5
70  END
```
2.
```
10  READ A, B
20  LET M = (A + B) / 2
30  PRINT A, B, "AVERAGE" = "; M
40  GO TO 10
50  DATA 7, 9, 4, 6, 13, 8
60  END
```

THE NATURE OF A COMPUTER

A computer *system* includes three major types of components: an input device, the computer, and an output device. An input device communicates previously prepared program instructions and data to the computer. The computer operates on the data by following the supplied list of instructions. When the computer encounters an instruction which tells it to show its work to the "outside" world, it transmits a copy of the appropriate information to an output device. In smaller computer systems (for example, some microcomputers) the input and output (I/O) devices may be housed in the same box as the computer. For example, a typewriter-like keyboard would represent an input device, and a television-like (CRT) display monitor would represent an output device. In larger computer systems, I/O devices are usually physically separated from the computer but attached to it by special cables. Larger computer systems will in general have several different input and output devices attached to them.

The computer itself (that is, the computer minus any I/O devices) is sometimes referred to as the *mainframe* or *computer mainframe*. The computer mainframe consists of two distinct units: a *main memory* unit and a *central processing unit* (CPU). Picture a college professor of mathematics solving a problem on the chalkboard in a classroom. The classroom would be analogous to the computer mainframe box, the chalkboard, which temporarily stores information, may be likened to the memory unit, and the professor who provides the "brains" would represent the CPU.

Throughout program execution, the memory unit does not perform any processing functions. It passively stores instructions and data that are required during processing. It is the CPU that takes charge. The CPU interprets the stored program of instructions and performs the required data manipulations. In addition, the CPU coordinates all input and output operations, making certain that each device connected to the computer works in harmony with the other components so that the individual devices function smoothly as an integrated system. (See Figure 2-2.) Note that before data and program instructions can be operated on by the CPU, they must be stored in main memory. Any information that is to be routed to an output device must be **present** in memory.

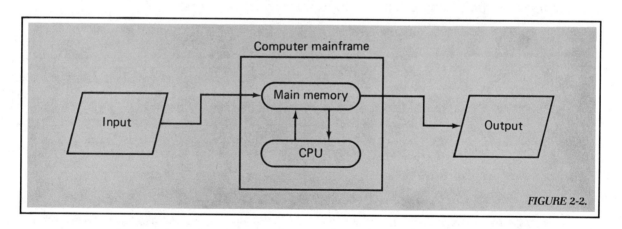

FIGURE 2-2.

The CPU itself is made up of two distinct units: a *control unit* and an *arithmetic-logic unit* (ALU). The control unit controls the execution of the program. It fetches from the memory unit each program instruction and interprets it. The complex flow of data within the computer is coordinated by the control unit in much the same way that a traffic police officer directs automobile and pedestrian traffic at a busy intersection.

Neither main memory or the control unit are capable of performing processing tasks such as arithmetic operations. The control unit delegates these chores to the ALU. All arithmetic calculations and logical comparisons are performed by the ALU which, under the supervision of the control unit,

- fetches data from memory

- performs the necessary data manipulations in temporary work areas called *registers*

- transmits the results back to main memory where they are stored and remain available for a subsequent processing operation or for an output operation.

The relationships between the various units are illustrated in Figure 2-3.

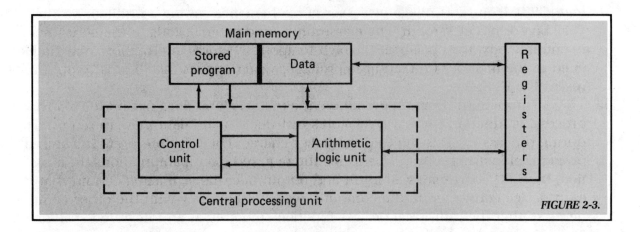

FIGURE 2-3.

It may be helpful to think of a computer as a business office: the *control unit* corresponds to the office supervisor, the ALU represents an office worker, and the *memory unit* can be likened to a file cabinet:

Manual Processing	*Computer Analogy*
When data must be processed, the office supervisor might request that an office worker fetch the data contained in a file folder stored in an office file cabinet.	In order for the computer to process data, the control unit instructs the ALU to fetch data from the appropriate storage locations in main memory.
When an office worker processes the data taken from the file folder, the worker must often use scrap paper to help perform the required data manipulations.	Registers are the computer's "scrap paper." Data values are copied from memory into registers, where they are operated on by the ALU.
After the processing is finished, the results may be recorded in the appropriate file folder; the folder must then be returned to its proper location in the file cabinet.	When the ALU completes its data manipulations, it transmits the data from the register locations back to main memory.
The office worker then receives the next instruction from the office supervisor.	The ALU then receives its next instruction from the control unit.
The office supervisor receives directions from a superior—the boss.	The control unit receives its instructions from a "higher authority"—the programmer who has supplied the set of program instructions that is stored in main memory and which the control unit is obligated to follow.

So far the computer may not seem much different than a hand-held calculator. A calculator has an input device in the form of its keyboard. The LED display screen or paper output tape serves as an output device. Most calculators cannot only perform arithmetic operations but, like a computer, they are able to "remember" a data value. A MEMORY key on the calculator permits the user to store a data value temporarily and then recall it when needed. A computer, however, differs from a calculator in several important respects:

■ In order to effect each individual calculator operation, an appropriate set of keys must be pressed. To repeat the process, the same sequence of keys must be pressed by the user. A computer has the ability to store internally a list of program instructions and then to *direct its own operation* by implementing each stored instruction, thereby eliminating the need for human intervention. As long as the program remains stored in memory, it may be executed repeatedly by the computer (CPU) at electronic speeds.

■ A computer has the ability to compare two data values and, based on the results of the comparison, to execute a specified instruction or group of instructions found within the stored program of instructions.

■ The speed of a computer also distinguishes it from other types of calculating devices. The most powerful computers have operating speeds that are measured in terms of *nanoseconds* (billionths of a second) and are capable of executing as many as 200 million instructions per second.

BACK TO BASIC: MEMORY

Determine the output for the following program:

```
10   READ A
20   PRINT B
30   DATA 5
40   END
```

Observe that the variable A, not B, is assigned the value 5. The PRINT statement in line 20 instructs the computer to display the contents of storage location B. The output of the program, however, is *not* nothing: it's the number 0. "Nothing" and zero are not the same thing; nothing implies emptiness, while zero is a number. Memory cells (storage locations) which have not been assigned values by the program are *not* empty, they contain the number zero.

Next consider the output of the following program:

```
10   LET A = 3
20   LET A = 4
30   READ A
40   PRINT A
50   PRINT A
60   PRINT A
70   DATA 8
80   END
```

In order to determine the output of the program, a variable chart is used to indicate the contents of each memory cell at the end of the execution of each program statement, that is, we "walk through" the program line by line.

Line	Cell Contents	Comment
10	3	
20	3̸ 4	LET is a "destructive" statement.
30	4̸ 8	READ is a "destructive" statement.

Thus the output would be the number 8, printed three times (on separate lines) since there are three separate PRINT A statements (lines 40, 50, and 60). Observe that when program line numbers 20 and 30 are executed, the previous contents of memory cell A is destroyed. However, we may print the contents of any memory cell, any number of times, without destroying its contents.

To summarize:

■ A memory cell is never empty. All memory cells which have not been assigned values by the program contain either the number 0 or "garbage" left over from a previous program.

> Note: Since memory cells may contain values from a previous program, some programmers will begin a BASIC program by initializing appropriate program variables. The statement LET S = 0 initializes the variable S by ensuring that it contains a 0 and not some other value entered by a previous program.

■ A data value assigned to a memory cell destroys the previous contents of that storage location, if any. As a result of the destructive nature of a READ operation (as it affects memory), it is common to find the expression "write *to* memory" used to refer to an input operation.

■ A memory cell's contents may be printed any number of times without destroying the contents of the cell. As a result of the nondestructive nature of a PRINT operation (as it affects memory), it is common to find the expression "read *from* memory" used to refer to an output operation.

These three principles are universal. They are true regardless of the programming language used.

Exercises   **Determine the output for each of the following programs.**

```
3.  10  READ A
    20  LET A = A + 1
    30  LET B = A * A
    40  PRINT A, B
    50  DATA 9
    60  END

4.  10  READ A
    20  LET B = B + 2
    30  LET A = A + B
    40  PRINT A, B
    50  GO TO 10
    60  DATA 5, 13
    70  END
```

INPUT/OUTPUT DEVICES

If one would "knock down" a computer and examine what's inside, one would find a bunch of wires, electronic circuit boards, various solid-state (transistor) devices, and other such related electronic and magnetic parts. It seems reasonable that if a computer is to "understand" program instructions and data, these must first be converted into an electronic form. We have just described the major function of an input *device:* to capture data from an input *medium* and then reduce them to electronic impulses that are suitable for computer consumption. The distinction between device and medium is an important one. A *medium* on which music and songs are recorded, for example, is the familiar platter-like long-playing vinyl record disk; the *device* that plays the record (interprets the information encoded on the record grooves) is the phonograph stylus/player. In preparing a computer program, a programmer might write it on an ordinary piece of paper. The coded program, however, must then be prepared for computer input using a suitable medium. If a typewriter-like data entry device is being used, then all that need be done is to type the instructions and data using a prescribed format. If a punch card system is being used, then each language instruction must be typed onto an "IBM" punch card which serves as the input medium. The cards containing the program would then be read by a card reader which represents the input device. (See Figure 2-4.)

FIGURE 2–4. A card reader. (Courtesy of Digital Equipment Corporation.)

Generally speaking, output devices serve two major functions:

- They represent computer results to the "outside" world in a form readable by a human. A CRT display monitor and a printer, which writes the computer output on a paper medium, are examples of output devices which accomplish this function. The printer produces *hard* copy output (paper) while the CRT screen offers *soft* copy.

- They store information externally in a *machine*-readable form so that it may be used as computer input at some later date. Magnetic tape and magnetic disk are routinely used for this purpose. A payroll program, for example, may be stored on tape until it is needed for producing a payroll during the next payroll period.

Any I/O device that is part of a computer system so that it is able to communicate directly with the CPU is said to be *on-line*. A computer *terminal* is an on-line I/O device that is capable of both sending and receiving data from a computer. A device which has a keyboard for data entry and an attached CRT display screen to show output is a common type of terminal. An I/O device that is not under the direct control of the CPU is said to be *off-line*.

SECONDARY STORAGE

Although a person may have a very good memory, there is a limit to how much information that person can recall accurately. People therefore often rely on external media, such as paper or books, to store information that is not currently needed or is of such great volume that it exceeds the memory capacity of the brain. Due to economic and other practical considerations, the main memory unit of a computer is also limited in its storage capacity. A computer, therefore, requires access to an auxiliary or secondary storage device that supplements the storage capacity of main memory. Tape and disk drive units are two of the most widely used secondary storage devices.

Secondary storage devices serve two major functions:

- To provide for the *temporary* storage of data that may be needed in a *current* processing operation.

- To provide for the permanent storage of data that may be required in a *future* processing operation. Because of their enormous storage capacities, secondary storage devices are sometimes referred to as *mass* storage devices.

To illustrate the need to have access to a secondary storage medium during processing, consider the activity of a person who must telephone 25 people in order to invite them to a party. The people's names and telephone numbers would probably be stored on a secondary storage medium such as a telephone address book or a slip of memo paper. As the party's host prepares to phone each person, she must retrieve the name and telephone number, temporarily storing them in her main memory center, located in her brain. As each person informs the party host whether they will attend the party, the host will probably not want to depend on her memory and will "store" their yes/no responses by writing them next to their names. During computer processing, it is common to find a similar type of ongoing transfer of information between main memory and a secondary storage device. Information that is saved in secondary storage will be transmitted into main memory when requested by the CPU. In order to make room in main memory for new information, the CPU may transfer information that must be saved, but is not currently required, to secondary storage.

Although tape and disk drive units are referred to as secondary (auxiliary) storage devices, they are also considered to be I/O devices. Data may be read from tape or disk and *loaded* (copied) into main memory or they may be transmitted from main memory and written to (saved on) tape or disk. A secondary storage device typically offers from 10 to 100 times the storage capacity of main memory. Secondary storage devices offer a lower cost per unit of stored data than main memory. Main memory, however, offers faster data *access* times, that is, data stored in main memory can be located by the CPU much more rapidly than data stored on tape or disk.

A larger computer system will typically have a variety of I/O devices attached to it, including:

- one or more punch card readers
- several on-line terminals which the central computer "hosts"
- one or more hard copy printers
- a device which can read optical character recognition (OCR) documents
- several tape drive units
- an array of disk drives

In addition, there are other types of secondary storage devices in use, including the magnetic drum and the mass storage (cartridge tape) device. Some computer systems also include provision for producing computer output microfilm (COM). The banking industry depends heavily on magnetic ink character recognition (MICR) document readers.

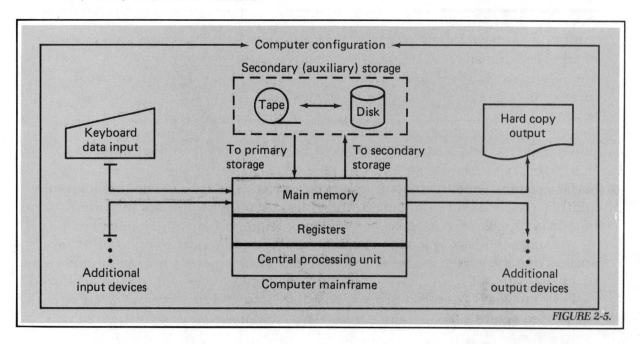

FIGURE 2-5.

FIGURE 2–6. *A very large computer installation which features eight interconnected Control Data Cyber class computers. This computer complex is capable of processing 24 million instructions per second.* (Courtesy of Control Data Corporation.)

A computer mainframe and its externally connected devices, called computer *peripherals*, is referred to as a computer *configuration*. A computer configuration tends to reflect the needs of the particular organization that is being serviced and will generally vary from one computer installation to another. (See Figures 2-5 and 2-6.)

TAPE AND DISK STORAGE

Until now we have largely avoided discussing some of the distinguishing features of tape and disk storage. Although both tape and disk devices are widely used and are both magnetically based storage media, they are fundamentally different in a number of respects. Some of their distinguishing features will be presented in this section.

A tape drive unit is similar in appearance and operation to the familiar reel-to-reel tape recorder/player used to record and play music in the homes of many hi-fi enthusiasts. (See Figure 2-7.) The tape itself has a Mylar plastic base and a surface coating which permits it to be magnetized. The tape is one-half inch in width, typically 2400 feet in length, and is usually supplied on $10\frac{1}{2}$-inch reels. A reel of tape is capable of storing large amounts of data, yet is relatively inexpensive.

Magnetic disks enjoy the distinction of being the most popular of the available secondary storage media. A standard hard disk is a metal platter 14 inches in diameter, with both sides having a surface coating that allows it to be magnetized. Disks are typically packaged in sets consisting of from 4 to 20 disks, called *disk packs*. (See Figure 2-8.)

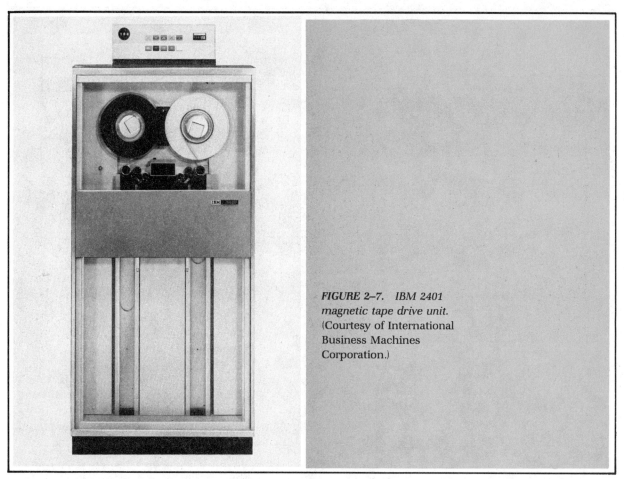

FIGURE 2–7. *IBM 2401 magnetic tape drive unit.* (Courtesy of International Business Machines Corporation.)

(a) (b)

FIGURE 2–8. (a) *Disk packs and disk cartridges (standing upright). Disk cartridges are usually found in minicomputer systems and consist of a single disk which is capable of storing data on both upper and lower disk surfaces.* (b) *An inside look at a disk pack in which a portion has been removed in order to see the central drive shaft.* (Courtesy of Dysan Corporation.)

The disks in each disk pack are arranged vertically, one above the other. In the disk drive unit (see Figure 2-9) the disk pack is mounted on a rotating drive shaft, just as a record would be placed on the center spindle.

Although disk storage is more expensive than tape storage, it offers faster data access times, with a disk pack having the potential of storing more data than

FIGURE 2–9. *Disk drive units.* (Courtesy of Digital Equipment Corporation.)

a reel of tape. In comparison with a reel of tape, a disk pack is relatively heavy, making it somewhat less convenient to mount and dismount.

In both tape and disk formats, information is encoded on the surface by a *write head* and represented as a pattern of magnetized spots. A *read head* is used to decode information stored on the tape or disk surface. In main memory, information is reduced to individual characters, with each character having an assigned storage location. Data stored on tape and disk, on the other hand, are stored as units of information called *records.* Storage locations in main memory refer to characters, while storage locations on tape and disk refer to records. As a result of the different arrangements of the read/write head and drive mechanisms, records are organized quite differently in a tape file than in a typical disk file. During an input/output operation, tape travels under the read/write heads in one direction, from left to right. Records must therefore be written to and read from the tape in a sequential fashion, one following the other. (See Figure 2-10.) There is no way of identifying a particular record in a tape file so that the tape drive mechanism can immediately locate it without sequentially examining each preceding record of the file. That is, in order to locate a given record, the tape must be read from the beginning of the file and each record examined in sequence. Records that are not needed are passed over, one by one, until the desired record is found. Thus in

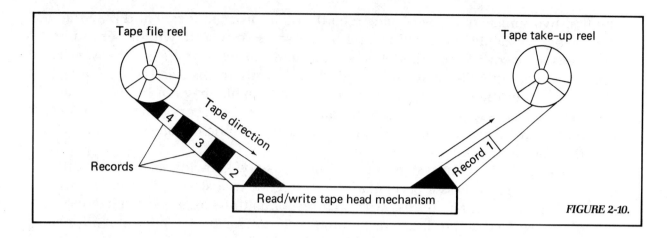

Tape file reel

Tape take-up reel

Tape direction

Records

4

3

2

Record 1

Read/write tape head mechanism

FIGURE 2-10.

order to access the 50th record in a tape file, the first 49 must be examined. Such a system for finding a stored record is called *sequential access.* This type of file organization can be a disadvantage when only a small number of records contained in the file must be processed.

A disk surface is divided into concentric circles called *tracks* on which information may be stored. Each track is further subdivided into *sectors,* and each sector may contain one or more records. Disk surfaces typically contain 100, 200, or 400 tracks. The greater the number of tracks per surface, the greater the storage capacity of the disk. (See Figure 2-11.) The design of the disk drive mechanism is such that information may be written to and read from any segment of a particular track. In order to visualize this concept, it might be helpful to think of playing a record disk. It is possible to play any song on the record disk without playing the songs immediately preceding it. All that is required is that the phonograph arm be lifted and positioned on the desired groove or track. It is not necessary to listen to

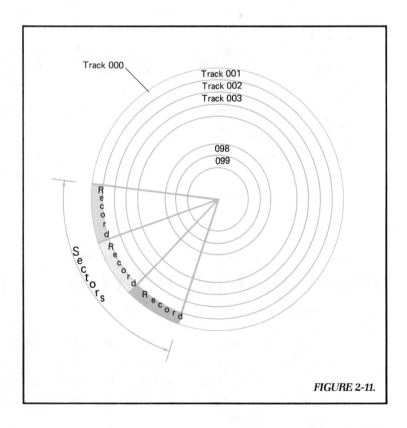

Track 000

Track 001

Track 002

Track 003

098

099

Record

Record

Record

Sectors

FIGURE 2-11.

the first two songs on a long-playing record disk in order to locate and play the third song. This ability of reaching a particular song (or record) without examining the songs (or records) preceding it is referred to as *direct or random accessing*. Records stored on a disk may be located directly, without the need to examine other records in the file. In contrast, records in a tape file may *not* be directly accessed. Direct access is sometimes referred to as random access since each record in the file may be located with equal ease, regardless of the physical location of the stored record in the file.

Just as we find our way to a particular house by knowing its address, in order to be able to access a particular record directly in a stored disk file, each record must be given an address which corresponds to its assigned storage location on the surface of the disk. One common method for determining the address of a record is based on selecting a numeric field of the record as a *key* identifying field. In a payroll file containing employee records, the employees' social security numbers may serve as key fields, uniquely identifying each record in the file. A mathematical formula is then applied to the value of each key field, which translates into the record's address on the disk surface. The physical design of the disk drive unit allows the read/write head mechanism to write data to and read data from the calculated address of the stored record. For this reason, we say that disk is an *addressable* storage medium, tape is a *non-addressable* storage medium. Recall that the main memory is also an addressable storage medium, with each stored data item being referenced by the address of the memory cell to which it has been assigned.

Table 2-1 summarizes some of the important features of main and secondary storage as represented by tape and disk. A more complete discussion of I/O devices will be found in Chapter 4.

TABLE 2-1

Medium	Addressable	Access Method	Access Time[a] (1 = fastest)	Cost per Stored Character (1 = least expensive)
Main memory	Yes	Random	1	3
Magnetic disk	Yes	Random[b]	2	2
Magnetic tape	No	Sequential	3	1

[a]Access time *refers to the time necessary to locate and transfer stored data.*
[b]*A variety of file organizations are possible using the disk medium, including sequential. (See Chapter 7.)*

PROGRAM LIBRARIES

Programs which are frequently used are *not* normally written anew each time they are needed. Instead, they are maintained on tape or disk and stored in program libraries, much as reference books are maintained on library shelves. When the particular program is needed, the tape or disk on which the program is saved must be located. Typically this is accomplished by a special software system which catalogs, maintains, and retrieves the program from an on-line secondary storage device. Less frequently needed programs may be stored off-line on tape or disks which are appropriately labeled and stored on a library shelf. When they are needed, they are physically pulled off the shelf and mounted on the appropriate storage device. (See Figure 2-12.)

Source programs and data may also be keyed directly onto a tape or disk and then used as input. This is accomplished by means of special keyboard data entry devices, called key-to-tape or key-to-disk, which are attached to a disk or tape drive unit. These input devices have made card-punch data entry systems almost obsolete.

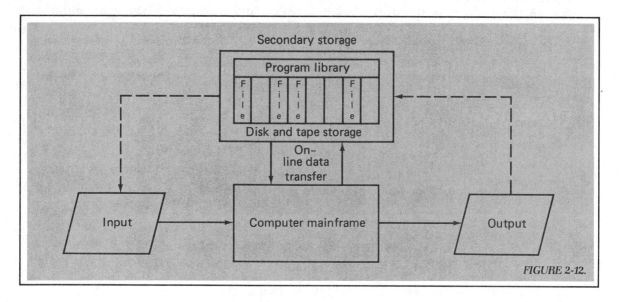

FIGURE 2-12.

UTILITY AND CANNED PROGRAMS

Programs that satisfy a specific processing need, but that are of general usefulness to programmers regardless of the application area of the source program, are called *utility* programs. In preparing programs in diverse application areas such as payroll, inventory control, accounts receivable, and student academic transcripts, each program may have a need for a program that first sorts and/or merges the records in the file before the file maintenance or updating procedure begins. A program that is designed to sort (or merge) records in a file according to some given key field, regardless of the nature of the file or the type of file activity that will follow, is an example of a commonly used utility program.

Computer "housekeeping" operations are often accomplished using utility programs. Such operations may include:

- readying a secondary storage unit to read or write data

- creating a file on a secondary storage medium

- cataloging a program into a library

- copying information from one storage medium to another, for example, transferring a file from tape to disk or vice versa

Sometimes businesses find it economically advantageous to purchase or lease complex programs designed for a general type of application. The alternative would be to invest huge amounts of time, money, and effort in writing a program that already exists and is guaranteed to work. After all, why "reinvent the wheel?" Such programs are called *canned* or *service* programs. Statistical package programs, which are able to apply a wide variety of statistical measures to any supplied data set, are commonly purchased canned programs.

A popular microcomputer-based canned service program is the Visi*Series* software that is offered by VISICORP. VisiCalc,* for example, is a program with extensive "number crunching" capabilities. VisiCalc creates a formatted cell-like electronic worksheet with up to 63 columns in width and 254 rows in length. The worksheet can be designed to accommodate any numerical-based application—inventory control, budgeting, economic forecasting and planning, and so on—and can be used to generate summarizing report documents. VisiCalc's recalculation feature permits the user to ask "what if?" type questions. The variables affected by a change in formula or in a data value will be adjusted immediately and the updated statistics displayed.

VIRTUAL MEMORY

Often large complex programs that operate on large volumes of data will exceed the available storage capacity in main memory. One approach to this problem would be to build computers with ever-larger memory capacities. Economically, this is not a practical solution. An alternative approach is based on making use of a computer's on-line secondary storage facilities. Disk storage, for example, has a greater storage capacity and is cheaper per unit of stored data than main memory. Why not split the program so that the part that is needed is stored in main memory and the part that is not immediately required is stored on an on-line disk device? We can then provide special software so that when a segment of a program is not needed, it is moved to disk storage while active parts of the program reside in main memory. The programmer is then free to write a program assuming that the available storage capacity is the sum of the available capacities of main (real) memory and secondary storage (virtual memory).

The segments of the fragmented program are referred to as *pages*. Most larger computer systems come equipped with a virtual memory capability that permits large complex programs to be divided into pages. The initial pages of the program are stored in main memory while the remaining pages are found in virtual memory (usually on disk). As the program begins to execute, pages in main memory complete execution and are exchanged on an ongoing basis for pages in virtual memory. In this way, the entire program is executed, yet is never stored in main memory in its entirety. It is the job of the CPU, guided by special software, to supervise this paging activity. (See Figure 2-13.)

Virtual memory systems seek to combine optimally the advantages of both main and secondary memories: the speed of main memory with the higher storage

*VisiCalc is a trademark of VISICORP.

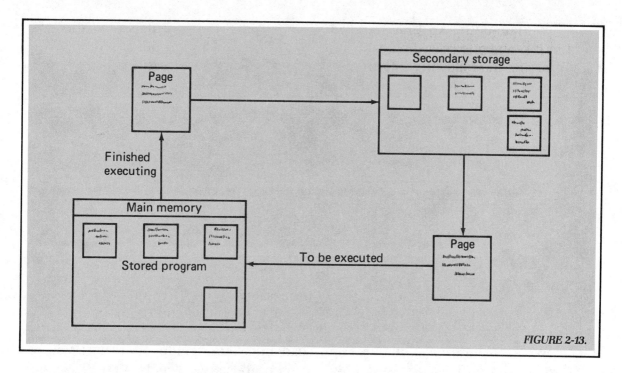

FIGURE 2-13.

capacity and lower cost per stored character of the secondary storage. From a programmer's point of view, virtual memory effectively expands main memory. On the other hand, virtual memory systems have two obvious disadvantages:

- The system software required to supervise the paging activity occupies valuable storage space in main memory.

- The paging activity consumes time, resulting in a program execution time that is greater than if the entire program were to reside in main memory.

Although originally found only in larger computer systems, many smaller computer systems now offer a virtual memory capability.

THE RECORD AND FILE CONCEPT REVISITED

In order for a computer to be able to process data, the data must be organized and maintained in some systematic fashion. In most data processing environments, this means that data must be organized in the hierarchical arrangement field → record → file. In general, the computer reads records from a given file and *writes to memory* (storage). The data within each record (fields) are manipulated or processed according to the instructions of a program that has been previously stored in memory. The computer then *reads from memory* (retrieval) and outputs the desired result. Chapter 7 will discuss various file organizations and file processing. In this section, we shall briefly look at an example which illustrates how data might be organized in anticipation of computer processing.

State-of-the-Art University (SAU) has decided to computerize all the information it maintains regarding each student enrolled in the school. Currently, SAU maintains the following information (stored in various university offices):

- Student name

- Address

- Current and past courses taken

- Tuition payment history

- Birth date

- Course grades

- Terms in which enrolled

A graduate student in the data processing department of SAU, Sam by name, is asked to assist in the computerization of all student information. Sam observes that the student data that are maintained by the university fall into two general categories: biographical-financial and academic. Sam decides that there will be two student master files corresponding to each of these two general categories. Each file will contain individual records, one record for each student enrolled in the school. If the school enrollment is 5,000 students, then each file will contain 5,000 records. The general scheme for how the data will be organized is illustrated in Figure 2-14.

Sam advises University officials that since it is possible for two different students to have the same first and last names, it will be necessary to assign each student a unique identification number (student ID). Sam then displays the format of a sample student record in the biographical-financial file. (See Figure 2-15.)

Any additions or changes in grades would require that the academic history file be updated. Recall that this type of file is called a *master file*. The set of all records that contain information on how a corresponding master record is to be modified is called a *transaction* or *detail* file. Sam suggests that the following format be adopted for individual student transaction records. (See Figure 2-16.)

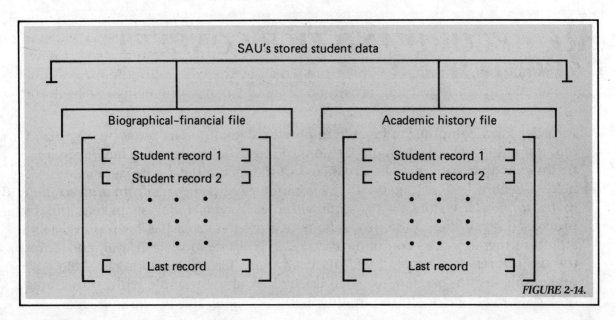

FIGURE 2-14.

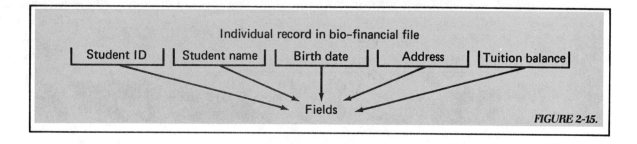

Individual record in bio-financial file

| Student ID | Student name | Birth date | Address | Tuition balance |

Fields

FIGURE 2-15.

Sam then reminds university officials of some of the advantages of computerizing student information. He mentions that under the control of the appropriate computer program, it will be a relatively simple matter to produce reports such as:

- A roster of the school enrollment sorted in any desired sequence, for example, in alphabetical order

- A complete academic transcript for each student

- A listing of students who have overdue tuition balances

- An honor roll listing

- A listing of all students whose grade point averages fall below a specified number

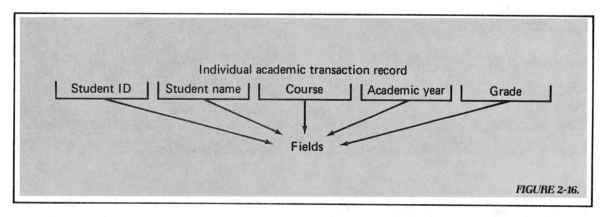

Individual academic transaction record

| Student ID | Student name | Course | Academic year | Grade |

Fields

FIGURE 2-16.

Admittedly this example is considerably oversimplified. It should, however, give the reader a grasp of how the field–record–file concept may be capitalized on in organizing data for subsequent computer processing. It also hints that when preparing programs that will have to be read by the computer, the programmer must take into account the format of the input (such as the fields involved and their positions and widths).

EXAMPLE

In a COBOL program the term *data division* includes the definition of all program files and the descriptions of their records. For each record, a listing of the included fields is given. The *picture* clause defines the type and width of each field. Alphabetic, numeric, and alphanumeric field types are distinguished by the characters A, 9, and X, respectively. A(5), for example, represents an alphabetic field whose width is 5.

Let us represent a typical layout for the individual academic transaction record illustrated in Figure 2-16. Assume the fields are defined as follows:

Field Name	Field Width	Field Type	Picture Clause
Student ID	8	Numeric	9(8)
Student name	24	Alphabetic	A(24)
Course code	6	Alphanumeric	X(6)
Academic year	4	Numeric	9(4)
Course grade	1	Alphabetic	A(1)

The transaction file will be named ACA-TRANSACT-FILE; each record (corresponding to a particular student) will be called STUDENT-TRANSACT-RECORD. These names are determined by the programmer, but must conform to the rules for assigning COBOL variable names. In forming variable names, COBOL allows greater flexibility than BASIC, permitting up to 30 characters to be used (but no blank spaces). The appropriate segment of the COBOL program is given below:

```
DATA DIVISION.
FILE SECTION.
FD ACA-TRANSACT-FILE
    LABEL RECORDS ARE OMITTED.
01 STUDENT-TRANSACT-RECORD.
    05 STUDENT-ID          PICTURE 9(8).
    05 STUDENT-NAME        PICTURE A(24).
    05 COURSE-CODE         PICTURE X(6).
    05 ACADEMIC-YEAR       PICTURE 9(4).
    05 COURSE-GRADE        PICTURE A(1).
```

Level numbers indicate the hierarchical structure of the data, level number 01 representing the most encompassing grouping. The choice of 05 is arbitrary, provided it is greater than 01.

REVIEW EXERCISES

True or False

1. The ALU of the CPU coordinates internal computer activity.
2. Virtual memory increases the effective memory capacity of main memory.
3. A comparison operation will be performed by the control unit.
4. A disk surface is composed of concentric circles called sectors.
5. The location of a particular record will typically take less time if the file is stored on disk rather than on tape.
6. Registers are storage boxes which store magnetic tape reels.
7. The main memory includes registers and the ALU.
8. Algorithmic and heuristic methods may be considered to be opposites.

9. Program instructions and data may be stored either internally or externally with respect to the computer mainframe.

10. The mainframe includes both main memory and the CPU.

Multiple Choice

11. Computers are used to:
    a. store and retrieve information
    b. manipulate data
    c. perform routine repetitive operations
    d. all of these

12. The major advantage of secondary storage compared to primary storage is its:
    a. speed
    b. reliability
    c. storage capacity
    d. flexibility and ease of operation

13. When compared to a business office, which component of the computer is analogous to a clerical worker?
    a. main memory
    b. control unit
    c. arithmetic-logic unit
    d. secondary storage device

14. The major advantages of computers include:
    a. accuracy, reliability, downtime, and speed
    b. accuracy, reliability, speed, and their universal language
    c. accuracy, declining cost, speed, and reliability
    d. accuracy, reliability, speed, and ability to engage in heuristic processes

15. In which type of storage can data be the most quickly accessed (located)?
    a. main memory   b. disk   c. tape   d. all about the same

16. Which of the following is a nonaddressable storage medium?
    a. main memory   b. tape   c. disk   d. tape and disk

17. Which BASIC language statement is most closely associated with repetitive processing?
    a. READ   b. GO TO   c. PRINT   d. LET

18. Which of the following statements are *false*?
    a. Program libraries may be maintained both on-line and off-line.
    b. In an input operation data are written to memory, and in an output operation data are read from memory.
    c. Computers generally solve problems only after having been provided with the method of solution.
    d. The control unit of the CPU decodes and executes program instructions.
    e. None of these.

19. Which of the following statements are *true*?
    a. Data received from an on-line secondary storage device must first be stored in main memory before they can be operated on.
    b. All data manipulations must be reduced to either move, arithmetic, or yes/no comparison operations.

  c. A program executing in virtual memory takes longer than if the program were able to execute without using the virtual memory capability of the computer.

  d. Records on a tape file are read in the same order in which they are written.

  e. All of these.

20. The partitioned components of a program in virtual storage are called:

  a. segments **b.** leaves **c.** pages **d.** blocks

21. In which of the following is the unit of stored data the record rather than an individual character?

  a. main memory **b.** tape **c.** disk **d.** tape and disk

22. Per unit of stored data, which type of storage tends to be the least expensive?

  a. main memory **b.** tape **c.** disk **d.** all are about the same

23. Which is *not* a function of the control unit?

  a. fetching program instructions

  b. coordinating I/O operations

  c. decoding program instructions

  d. transmitting data to and from registers

24. Which is an example of an applications program?

  a. a program that generates bills for a department store's credit account customers

  b. a program that translates a COBOL program into machine language

  c. a program designed to copy information from one type of storage medium to another

  d. all of these

25. Which of the following statements are *false*?

  a. A disk drive device may serve either as an input or as an output device.

  b. The smallest addressable unit of data stored on disk is the record.

  c. Disk storage is faster and less expensive per stored character of data than tape.

  d. Data stored on disk may be randomly accessed.

 # EXCURSION INTO BASIC

In every problem in which a computer solution is being designed, there are two fundamental considerations: the data structure and the control structure. Data structure refers to the manner in which a related set of variables are grouped and organized in order to facilitate a data processing task. The design of a new record and file system involves the planning and selection of an appropriate data structure, which will be reflected in the record contents and format. Control structure refers to the logical organization of the program instructions: Does the computer solution call for a simple sequence of statements to be executed in a linear fashion, one after the other, from the lowest statement line number to the highest statement line number? Does the solution involve a comparison and branch operation? Will it be necessary to execute the same set of program instructions repeatedly? For example, in designing a computer program which processes credit account transactions, the program must include provision for the repeated processing of different customer transactions. In addition, the action the system will take if a person's credit account balance exceeds a certain critical value (the person's credit limit) will have to be specified, that is, a comparison will have to be made between the account balance and the person's credit limit.

In this appendix we look at an aspect of structuring data—the processing of nonnumeric data. A fundamental type of control structure, the IF/THEN decision statement, will also be presented.

STRING VARIABLES

Until now we have restricted our attention to BASIC programs that process numeric data. Many problems involve alphanumeric data. For example, we may wish to write a program that involves people's names and addresses. We now consider how to input alphanumeric data.

In BASIC the computer must be "alerted" to the fact that a variable may represent alphanumeric data (a letter, digit, special character, or some combination of these). A BASIC variable that ends with a dollar sign ($) is used to represent alphanumeric data. Alphanumeric data are sometimes referred to as character strings. The BASIC variable names C$, A1$, and X$ each represent a character string and are referred to as (character) *string variables.** There are three general methods for introducing alphanumeric data into a BASIC program: through the LET statement, the INPUT statement, and the READ and DATA statements. These techniques are illustrated in the following set of examples. Note that the actual alphanumeric data values must be enclosed within quotation marks.

EXAMPLES

Program

```
1.  10  LET A$ = "JOHN"
    20  PRINT "MY NAME IS"; A$
    30  END
```

Output

```
MY NAME IS JOHN
```

*The rules for naming BASIC variables may vary from machine to machine. If you have access to a computer, it is suggested that you consult the manual for that machine.

```
2.  10  PRINT "WHAT IS THE DAY OF THE WEEK?"
    20  INPUT D$
    30  PRINT "TODAY IS"; D$
    40  END
```

Output

```
WHAT IS THE DAY OF THE WEEK?
TUESDAY                              ( = D$, entered by user)
TODAY IS TUESDAY
```

Program

```
3.  10  READ N$
    20  PRINT N$
    30  GO TO 10
    40  DATA "PASCAL", "BABBAGE", "IBM"
    50  END
```

Output

```
PASCAL
BABBAGE
IBM
? OUT OF DATA IN 10
```

Program

```
4.  10  READ P$, R, H
    20  LET S = R * H
    30  PRINT P$, "SALARY = $"; S
    40  GO TO 10
    50  DATA "BOB", 4, 35, "MARY", 5, 40
    60  END
```

Output

```
BOB     SALARY = $ 140
MARY    SALARY = $ 200
? OUT OF DATA IN 10
```

THE IF/THEN DECISION STATEMENT

In addition to performing arithmetic operations, the computer is capable of comparing two data values and, based upon the result of the comparison, taking an action that has been specified by the programmer. The following relational symbols are used in forming comparisons:

To Compare A With B Use	Read as . . .
$A > B$	A is greater than B
$A > = B$	A is greater than or equal to B
$A = B$	A is equal to B
$A < B$	A is less than B
$A < = B$	A is less than or equal to B
$A < > B$	A is unequal to B

Program statements in a BASIC program are executed in sequence, from the lowest line number to the highest line number. If the computer encounters a GO TO statement, however, the flow of the program is interrupted, and the program *must* jump, out of sequence, to the line number specified in the GO TO statement. For this reason the GO TO statement is sometimes called an *unconditional transfer* statement. If the computer encounters a statement of the form

IF   *comparison*   THEN   *line number*

the program may or may not be required to branch out of line number sequence. If the result of the comparison made in the IF clause of the statement is true, then the program will branch to the line number specified in the THEN clause. If the comparison is not true, the IF/THEN statement will be ignored, and the next program statement in line number sequence will be executed. For this reason, the IF/THEN statement is sometimes called a *conditional transfer* statement.

For example, in the program segment

```
20  IF A > B THEN 50
30  PRINT B
```

if the value of A is, in fact, greater than the value of B, the program will branch (jump) to line 50, bypassing any program instruction having a line number between 20 and 50. If the value of A is *not* greater than B (that is, A is less than or equal to B), the program will "drop through" and execute the statement that has the next highest line number. In this example, line 30 would be executed if A is *not* greater than B.

If you consider a computer program to be a road, the IF/THEN statement represents a fork in the road. The computer may take one of two alternative paths, depending on the result of the comparison in the IF clause. Each path represents a different alternative action. Thus it is the IF/THEN statement that activates a computer's "decision-making" capability. The IF/THEN statement represents an extremely powerful programming structure. The sorting of data, for example, is based on a systematic comparison of data values. More complicated programs might require the use of multiple IF/THEN statements. The IF/THEN statement is sometimes referred to as a logical decision or branch operation; the term *selection sequence* is also applied to the IF/THEN structure.

Let us now analyze a complete program which includes a decision statement (or selection sequence). The sample program determines and prints the larger of two given numbers.

```
10  READ A, B
20  IF A > B THEN 50
30  PRINT B; "IS GREATER THAN"; A
40  GO TO 10
50  PRINT A; "IS GREATER THAN"; B
60  GO TO 10
70  DATA 10, 5, 1, 4
80  END
```

Line	Comments
10	Two numbers, A and B, are inputted. Assume A and B are never equal.
20	A is compared with B. If the current value of A is greater than the current value of B, the program branches to line 50.
30	This statement is reached only if A is *not* greater than B. Hence we print the indicated result.
40	Program control is now transferred to line 10 so that another pair of data values may be read in.
50	This statement is reached only if the condition in the IF clause of line 20 is true. Hence we print the indicated result.
60	Program control is transferred to line 10 so that another pair of data values may be read in.
70	Sample data are chosen so that both paths of the program are tested. For the first pair of data values, A is greater than B; for the second pair, A is not greater than B:

A	B	Output
10	5	10 IS GREATER THAN 5
1	4	4 IS GREATER THAN 1
		? OUT OF DATA IN 10

EXAMPLE

A number may be either positive, negative, or zero. In order to identify a number as one of these types, more than one decision statement must be used. The following program performs a different operation on each of these different types of numbers. Determine the output.

```
10    READ N
20    IF N < 0  THEN 60
30    IF N > 0  THEN 90
40    PRINT N
50    GO TO 10
60    LET A = N / 2
70    PRINT A
80    GO TO 10
90    LET B = N * N
100   PRINT B
110   GO TO 10
120   DATA -6, 5, 0
130   END
```

SOLUTION

N	A	B	Output
-6	-3	0	-3
5	-3	25	25
0	-3	25	0
			? OUT OF DATA IN 10

Determine the output for each of the following programs.

```
1.  10   READ X, Y
    20   LET Z = X / Y
    30   IF Z < 1  THEN 70
    40   PRINT Z
    50   GO TO 10
    60   DATA 6, 2, 8, 1, 2, 4, 45, 5
    70   END
2.  10   READ N$, H
    20   IF H > 40  THEN 50
    30   PRINT N$; "NO HOURS OVERTIME"
    40   GO TO 10
    50   LET OT = H - 40
    60   PRINT N$; OT; "HOURS OVERTIME"
    70   GO TO 10
    80   DATA SMITH, 43, JONES, 35, BROWN, 40
    90   END
```

3. Write a program which:
   a. reads in two data items at a time: a person's last
      name (say, N$) and his checking account balance
      (say, B)
   b. prints the names and balances of only those people
      who have a negative balance
   c. uses the following representative sample test data:

```
DATA SMITH, 134.50, JONES, 0.78, BROWN, -2.95
```

CHAPTER

3

COMPUTER MEMORY AND TECHNOLOGY

INTRODUCTION

The trend in computer hardware is to offer the user more computing power for a smaller dollar investment. Advances in transistor technology account, in large part, for this welcomed phenomenon. The internal "organs" of a modern computer are based on *microelectronics*, which refers to the dense packing of solid-state (transistor) circuit components on chips having a silicon base, called an *integrated circuit* (IC) chip. In *large scale integration* (LSI) several thousand circuit components are etched on a silicon wafer. With the technology represented by *very large scale integration* (VLSI) it is not unusual for an IC chip to include in excess of 64,000 discrete circuit components on a square chip of silicon measuring no more than one-quarter inch on a side. (See Figure 3-1.)

From the manufacturer's point of view, the expensive aspect of computers lies in the initial design and testing of circuit components. Once designed, however, IC chips can be mass-produced, realizing enormous economies in production.

FIGURE 3–1. *"Computer on a dime." The Motorola MC68000 microprocessor chip which corresponds to the CPU. The tiny silicon chip houses the equivalent of nearly 70,000 individual transistors interconnected in a microprocessor configuration.* (Courtesy of Motorola Inc.)

DATA REPRESENTATION AND MEMORY

There is an obvious problem in understanding how we communicate with computers, which we have largely avoided. In executing a BASIC program, for example, how does the computer recognize the difference between the numbers 89 and 98? or the BASIC keywords READ and PRINT? Computers are, after all, merely an integrated collection of electronic circuits held together by wires and circuit boards. These electronic components must, in some fashion, uniquely represent and store data.

Electronic circuit components are *two-state* devices in the same sense that a light bulb is a two-state device: it is either *on* or *off*; current flows or current does *not* flow. It seems reasonable, therefore, that computers must use sequences of *on* and *off* circuits to represent data. Unfortunately the number system that we are most familiar with, the decimal system, is not consistent with the two-state nature of electronic circuits. The decimal number system uses *ten* distinct digits (0, 1, 2, ..., 9) to represent numeric values. There is, however, a number system that parallels the two-state operating condition of electronic circuits. This number system is based on *two* digits, 0 and 1; no other digits are permitted. Using this scheme, it is possible to represent any number as a sequence of ones and zeros. (See Chapter 9.) Such a number system is referred to as the *binary* number system. Each digit, 0 and 1, is referred to as a *bit* (*bi*nary dig*it*). All information that is to be stored in memory must ultimately be represented as a unique string of bits (0s and 1s).

We have previously indicated that a program written in a user-oriented language, such as BASIC, COBOL, or FORTRAN, cannot be understood by the computer until it is translated into the computer's native language, called machine language. Machine language is an all numeric binary code, which is determined by the electronic design of the particular computer. In translating individual characters into machine language the computer is guided by a predetermined translation code that is intrinsic to the design of the computer, and which will vary from machine to machine. This code assigns to each character (letter, digit, punctuation mark, etc.) a unique pattern of binary digits. It might be helpful to compare this translation process with looking up the meaning of a word in a dictionary. Each computer is provided with its own machine language dictionary. When it is given an English character it "looks up its meaning in its dictionary" and finds the equivalent binary representation of the character. The binary-coded definitions of each character are determined by the electronic design of the particular computer. The letter H, for example, may be translated by one computer dictionary as 1100 1000, while in another computer dictionary H may be coded as 1010 1000.

Regardless of the particular "dictionary" used, a character will typically be represented by eight consecutive bits, called a *byte*. Thus 1 byte equals 8 bits. The particular sequence of 1s and 0s that will fill up these eight bit positions will depend on the character being represented and the particular translation code that the computer manufacturer has adopted. The translation code used by IBM, for example, is called *EBCDIC* (*extended binary-coded decimal interchange code*). (See Figure 3-2.)

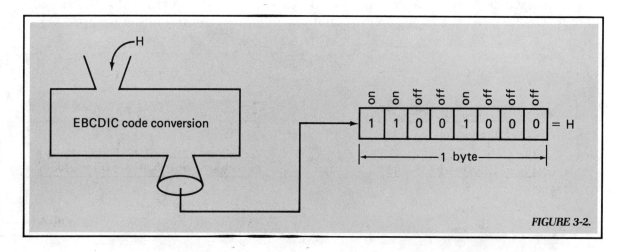

FIGURE 3-2.

Since a byte typically represents a single character, it is common to find these terms used interchangeably, that is, one byte equals one character. We again stress that the byte representation of a character will not be the same for every computer, being dependent on the electronic design of the machine and the translation code used by the manufacturer. While IBM uses EBCDIC, other manufacturers may use other established codes. Another popular translation code which represents characters as a sequence of 8 bits is *ASCII-8* (American *s*tandard *c*ode for *i*nformation *i*nterchange). *BCD* (*b*inary-*c*oded *d*ecimal) is a 6-bit code that is sometimes used to represent data stored on magnetic tape.

MEMORY CAPACITY

The memory capacity of a computer is usually expressed in terms of how many characters it can store. The unit of measurement commonly used is 1K bytes, which equals "one thousand" bytes of storage. Actually, 1K = 1,024 bytes, where 1,024 is the power of 2 (2^{10}) that is closest to 1,000. A computer which has a stated memory capacity of 64K is capable of storing 64 $\times$ 1,024 bytes = 65,536 bytes (characters). At one time the storage capacity of a computer was a useful criterion in helping to distinguish between different "sizes" of computers. Many of today's micro and mini (small) computer systems have main memory capacities that were found a decade ago only in large computer systems. It is now possible to purchase a microcomputer system having a main memory capacity of 64K for several hundred dollars. It used to take a full-sized room housing several tons of heat-generating hardware to offer the same level of computing power.

MEMORY ORGANIZATION

Computer memory is typically organized so that a byte corresponds to our familiar memory cell concept, except that a byte can only store a single character. A byte is identified by a number, which represents its address in memory. In an IBM computer, for example, byte addresses are sequentially numbered in memory, with the first byte having an address of 0, the second byte having an address of 1, and so on. If the computer has a main memory capacity of 64K, then the bytes (that is, the memory cells) would be numbered from 0 to 65,535. As usual, a stored character is located by referring to its address (byte number) in memory. (See Figure 3-3.)

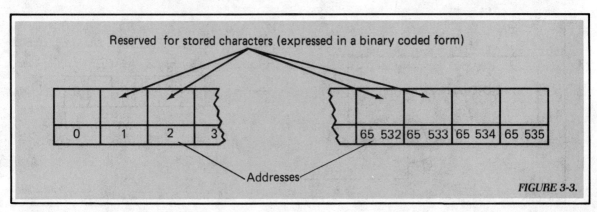

FIGURE 3-3.

A maximum of one character can be stored in each byte. Since each byte has an address in memory (in this example, a number between 0 and 65,535), the smallest data item that can be addressed (that is, referenced) is the character; individual bits *cannot* be addressed. Clearly, a data item consisting of several characters would need to be represented by a group of consecutive bytes.

Fortunately, most programming languages free the programmer from the task of keeping track of the individual characters of data and their numeric byte addresses. All the programmer need do is introduce symbolic (alphanumeric) variable names, and the computer will automatically assign and label byte storage locations with these variable names. The programmer, however, must remain aware of the demands the program places on the available storage capacity of the machine on which the program is to be run.

The interested reader will find a more complete discussion of binary numbers, data representation, and memory organization in Chapter 9.

REPRESENTING A PROGRAM INSTRUCTION

In the preceding section we stressed that each individual character is given a unique byte representation consisting of a block of 1's and 0's. In this section, we briefly look at the form a complete instruction takes when stored in memory.

An instruction that is stored in memory looks quite different than a programmer-prepared instruction. A stored program instruction typically consists of a long string of bits which specifies the *type* of operation to be performed and indicates which data values are involved in the operation. As part of the program translation process, each type of operation is represented by a unique binary code called the *operation code*, or *op code*. Thus the computer is able to distinguish an addition operation from a comparison operation by examining the op code.

In addition to specifying the op code, a stored program instruction must also indicate the *operands*, which are the data values that are being operated on. For example, if the operation is addition, the computer must know which two numbers are to be added together. These two numbers are referred to as the operands.

Stored Program Instruction	
Op code	Operands

Actually the operand does not state the actual data values that are to be operated on. Instead, the operands give the *addresses* of the storage locations of the data values that are to be operated on. The op code answers the question: What is to be done? The operands answer the question: Where do we find the data values to be operated on? Figure 3-4 illustrates a typical format for an instruction having two operands. In reality both the op code and the operands are represented as a consecutive (and long) string of 1s and 0s.

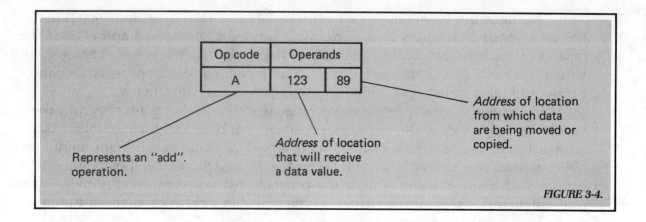

Represents an "add". operation.

Address of location that will receive a data value.

Address of location from which data are being moved or copied.

FIGURE 3-4.

For example, suppose that before the instruction illustrated in Figure 3-4 is executed, the contents of the memory cells are as follows:

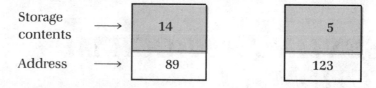

Storage contents $\longrightarrow$

Address $\longrightarrow$

After this instruction has been executed, the contents of the memory cells would be as follows:

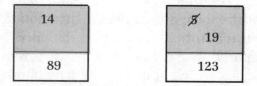

Recall that a program instruction such as the one illustrated in Figure 3-4 resides passively in memory much as a book remains on a library shelf. Both must be fetched and interpreted by someone or something. In a computer, this is the responsibility of the control unit section of the CPU. In order to execute a stored program of instructions, the control unit will:

1. fetch a single program instruction at a time from main memory

2. keep track of the current instruction as well as the next program instruction to be executed

3. examine the op code and interpret the instruction

4. transfer control to the ALU in order for the instruction to be implemented

It is the ALU that actually moves the data in order to perform the required operations. Figure 3-5 identifies an instruction and an execution cycle as the components of a *machine cycle*. A machine cycle represents the machine activity necessary to initiate and complete the execution of a single program instruction so that the computer is ready to execute the next stored program instruction. Computer speed is often expressed in terms of the number of instructions a computer can execute in one second, with MIPS (million instructions per second) represent-

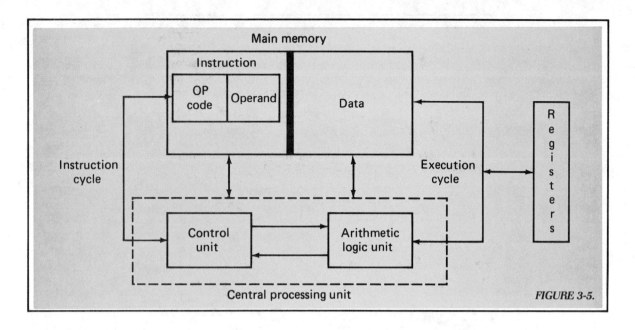

Main memory

Instruction

OP code | Operand

Data

Instruction cycle

Execution cycle

Registers

Control unit

Arithmetic logic unit

Central processing unit

FIGURE 3-5.

ing a common unit of measurement. A computer having a rating of 2.0 MIPS, for example, is capable of executing an average of 2 million instructions per second. A rating of 0.25 MIPS translates into 250,000 instructions per second (one-quarter of a million). A medium to large computer will typically feature a rating in excess of 1.0 MIPS.

EXAMPLE

In the BASIC program instruction 50 PRINT H, which part corresponds to:

1. the op code
2. the operand

SOLUTION

1. The op code refers to the type of operation. Therefore the PRINT command would represent the op code.
2. The operand refers to the location of the data item that is represented by the variable name H.

A BRIEF LOOK AT THE ANATOMY OF A MICROCOMPUTER

The compactness, relatively low cost, and considerable power of microcomputers are largely due to modern microelectronic technology. A typical microcomputer configuration is shown in Figure 3-6. The major internal components of a microcomputer include the following:

■ A *microprocessor chip* which includes all the circuits that constitute a CPU etched on a square silicon wafer typically no more than one-quarter inch on a side.

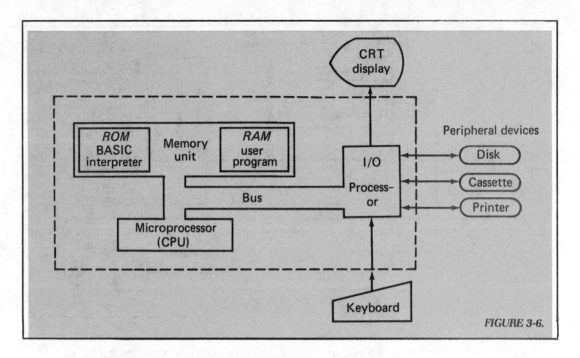

FIGURE 3-6.

■ *Memory chips.*   There are two distinct types of memory:

1. *Random access memory* (RAM) corresponds to the main memory in that it is the section of memory that is addressable by the programmer. It is used for the temporary storage of program instructions and data. RAM is *volatile* in the sense that when the power is turned off, its contents are destroyed.

2. *Read only memory*.(ROM) is that section of memory whose contents are determined and fixed by the manufacturer, and which the programmer cannot alter. A ROM chip typically includes a BASIC language interpreter, which takes the BASIC language instructions entered by the programmer and stored in RAM, and translates them into machine language so that they can be executed. In addition, a ROM chip includes special utility and system operating programs. ROM is nonvolatile; its contents remain intact even when the power is turned off.

■ *Input/output processors* that serve as an interface ("go-between" or common boundary) between an I/O device and the microprocessor.

■ *Buses*, which are the electronic wires and circuit boards that connect the previous three types of devices so that they may communicate with one another.

The main logic circuit board of the Apple IIe featuring the 8-bit 6502 microprocessor, eight 64K RAM chips, and two custom LSI devices is shown in Figure 3-7. Only 31 integrated circuits are required to run the computer.

TYPES OF ROM MEMORY CHIPS

In addition to ROM memory chips whose contents are unalterably fixed during the manufacturing process (sometimes referred to as *mask* ROMs), there are some types of ROMs that can be reprogrammed through the application of special techniques.

ROM Type	Explanation	Typical Application Area
Fuse PROM	The memory of a PROM (programmable ROM) comes to the user "blank." Each memory cell in a PROM contains a minuscule fuse. The PROM is programmed by sequentially storing in each memory cell either a binary 1 or a binary 0. In order to store these logical states, a fuse is either blown or left intact. A cell having a blown fuse stores one binary state, while a cell whose fuse is intact stores the opposite binary state. Once the contents of a PROM memory chip are written, the PROM cannot be reprogrammed.	The storage of operating system control programs.
EPROM	The contents of an erasable PROM (EPROM) can be wiped clean through the application of ultraviolet light. The EPROM can then be reprogrammed.	The storage of operating system control programs, particularly in environments in which the software being written must be tested and possibly modified.
EEPROM	Electrically erasable PROMs (EEPROMs) can have their stored contents electrically changed. Unlike EPROMs, EEPROMs do not have to be removed from the system during the reprogramming process.	Same as EPROM, but is even better suited to those application areas in which ROM memory chips may require periodic modification.

The general term applied to the process by which the end user of a computer "burns in" his own special operating control instructions is referred to as *microprogramming*. The special instruction codes that are permanently stored in ROM memory are referred to as *firmware*. Firmware is somewhat of a hardware and software hybrid. Software is usually interpreted as programs that are stored in memory (that is, in RAM) only when needed. Hardware, on the other hand, refers to physical components without regard to whether the devices have a logical capability. Loosely speaking, firmware may be thought of as software that is permanently "wired into" the machine. The built-in software that enables a hand-held scientific pocket calculator to evaluate trigonometric, logarithmic, and exponential functions is an example of firmware.

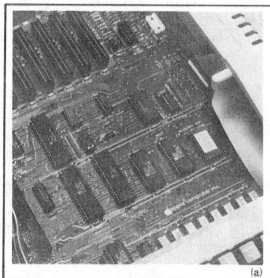
(a)

(b)

FIGURE 3–7. (a) Closeup of main logic board of Apple II e. (b) Apple II e exposed. (Courtesy of Apple Computer, Inc.)

MEMORY TECHNOLOGIES

Of central importance in the design of a computer is the physical device that will be used to store and represent data. Design and selection considerations include the following:

- Speed and random access capability
- Reliability, ease of maintenance
- Storage capacity
- Size
- Cost
- Volatility (whether the storage contents are lost when the power is withdrawn)

Often the achievement of one or more of these design goals will be at the expense of another. For example, main storage capacity can often be increased, but only at the expense of size and cost. To refine existing technologies and develop new ones so that improvements are realized in one or more of these categories, without suffering a trade-off in the other areas listed, remains an ongoing research goal of the highest priority. In this section, we shall survey some of the more popular types of memory devices.

MAGNETIC CORE MEMORY

With the growth of microelectronics and semiconductor technology, magnetic core memory has declined in importance to the point where it is primarily of historical interest. Nevertheless, it is worthwhile discussing since it will help the reader to conceptualize how a two-state physical device can represent and store information.

A magnetic core is a tiny doughnut-shaped ferrite core, less than a millimeter in diameter. Each core is strung on a wire. As a controlled electric current is passed through, the core will be magnetized in one of two possible directions (clockwise or counterclockwise), depending upon the direction of the current. Either direction may be designated as 1, with the other becoming 0. Let us assume that a clockwise rotation represents a 1. (See Figure 3-8.)

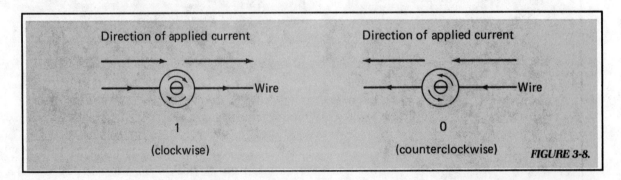

FIGURE 3-8.

By stringing thousands of these cores on a grid of wires, the controlled application of current can be used to induce desired directions of magnetism or sequences of 1s and 0s. (See Figure 3-9.)

For example, in storage location 00, the binary number 11010011 is stored, which is the EBCDIC byte representation for the letter L. Memory address 01 stores a different character (the EBCDIC representation for the digit 5). One of the desirable characteristics of magnetic core memories is its nonvolatility, that is, it will retain its magnetized states should there be a power interruption.

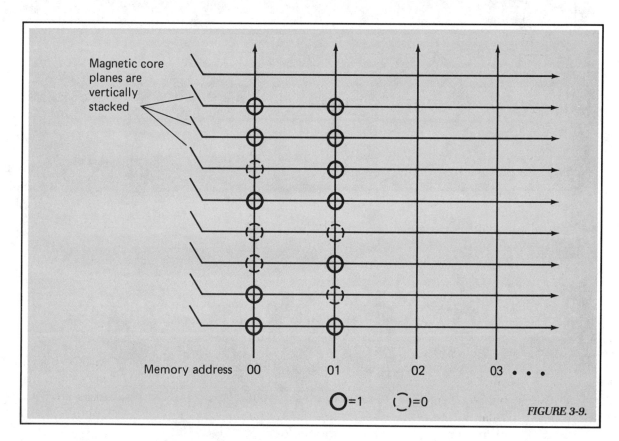

FIGURE 3-9.

SEMICONDUCTOR MEMORY

Most computers, regardless of their size and price, feature main memory units that are based on semiconductor technology. Semiconductor memory is fabricated on a silicon chip with the emplacement of thousands of transistors and related circuit components. Each transistor functions as a two-state device, either conducting a current or not conducting a current. (See Figure 3-10.) As a result of economies achieved by LSI, semiconductor memory is cheaper, faster, and smaller than core memory. A chip smaller in size than a fingernail is capable of storing in excess of 64,000 bits. A major deficiency of semiconductor storage is its volatility, since it is unable to maintain its storage contents should the power fail or be withdrawn. One of the most widely used methods for fabricating semiconductor chips is based on "growing" a transistor on a silicon base using successive layers of material. This type of semiconductor is called a *metal-oxide semiconductor* (MOS). Most LSI chips use MOS technology.

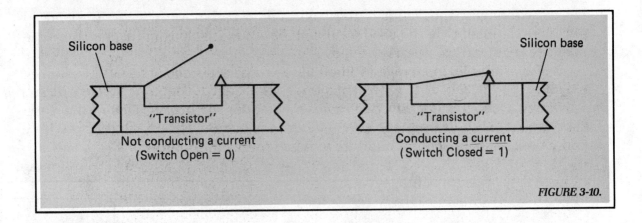

Silicon base

Silicon base

"Transistor"

Not conducting a current
(Switch Open = 0)

"Transistor"

Conducting a current
(Switch Closed = 1)

FIGURE 3-10.

MAGNETIC BUBBLE MEMORY

A still-developing technology is based on externally applying a magnetic field over a magnetic film having the opposite polarization (e.g., north–south versus east–west magnetization). The result is to create localized regions which, having the opposite polarization, form minuscule "bubbles" on the surface of the magnetic film. Bubble memory is also a two-state device. The presence of a bubble at a particular location represents a 1, while the absence of a bubble represents a 0. By applying a rotating magnetic field, patterns of circulating bubbles may be created.

Bubble memory is different from semiconductor storage in at least two fundamental respects:

▪ Bubble memory is nonvolatile; semiconductor memory is volatile.

▪ Loosely speaking, memory cells in semiconductor storage are stationary, with 1s and 0s being "deposited" in each cell. Data are then randomly accessed. In bubble memory, the memory cells (bubbles or no bubbles) rotate as if on a circular conveyor belt. Stationary read/write devices then write to memory, read from memory, or delete from memory. (See Figure 3-11.)

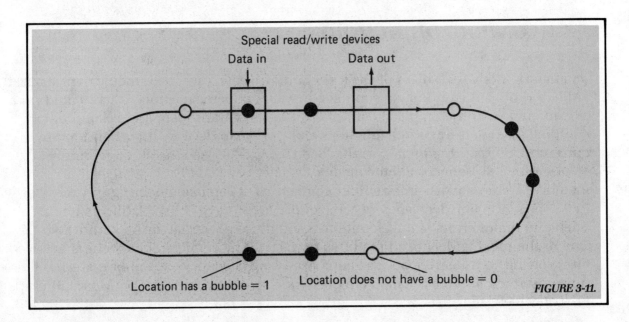

Special read/write devices

Data in

Data out

Location has a bubble = 1

Location does not have a bubble = 0

FIGURE 3-11.

In bubble storage devices, data cannot be accessed by going directly to the particular storage location. Instead, data must be accessed *serially* with the stationary read/write device "waiting" for a particular storage location to pass in order to write to it or read from it. Consequently access times for bubble storage are considerably slower than for random access semiconductor memory. Bubble memory, however, has a slight economic advantage over semiconductor memory. Magnetic bubble memory technology is being applied to secondary storage devices which do not require nanosecond speed capability but can benefit from its nonvolatility, compactness, and ruggedness. (See Figure 3-12.)

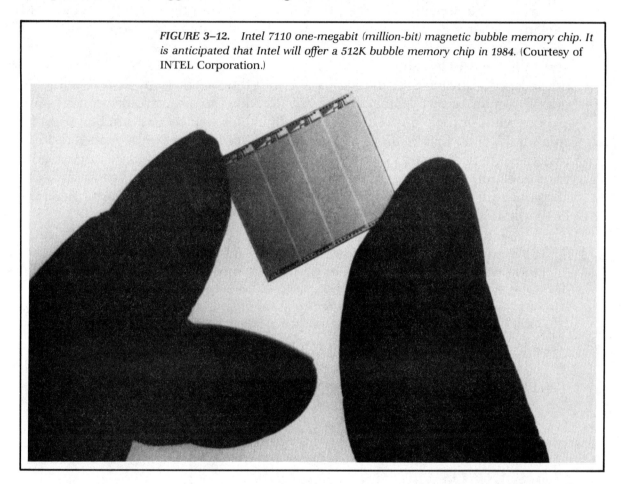

FIGURE 3–12.   *Intel 7110 one-megabit (million-bit) magnetic bubble memory chip. It is anticipated that Intel will offer a 512K bubble memory chip in 1984. (Courtesy of INTEL Corporation.)*

OTHER MEMORY TECHNOLOGIES

Another type of serial access storage device is the charge-coupled device (CCD), which uses a stored electric charge to represent binary information. CCDs can access data faster than magnetic bubble memory, but are slower than MOS devices. CCDs, like MOS, are volatile. With respect to the storage cost per bit, CCD and bubble memory lie between MOS memory and disk memory, MOS being the most expensive.

The technology that may deliver a new generation of computers is based on superconducting circuitry using the Josephson tunnel junction device. Recall that a computer is an electronic device and that the contents of a memory cell may be changed by switching its state from *on* to *off* and vice versa. The faster the switch, in general, the greater the potential operating speed. The Josephson tunnel junction is the fastest switch yet developed. It is able to change states in several picoseconds. (One picosecond is one trillionth of a second.) The Josephson tunnel junction is based on two phenomena of quantum mechanics: electron tunneling and superconductivity. Tunneling is the ability of electrons to overcome energy barriers provided certain conditions are present. In order to achieve a superconducting state, the tunneling device must be cooled to within a few degrees of $-273°$ Celsius (absolute zero). For this reason, this memory technology is sometimes referred to as *cryoelectronic* memory. As a result of the low operating temperature and low power consumption, it is possible to decrease the signal path by packing the circuits more closely together. In conventional technologies this circuit packing would create heat dissipation problems. By decreasing switching times and reducing the length of the signal path, operating speeds of memories based on the Josephson tunneling junction can exceed the speed of the fastest semiconductor memories by a factor of 10 to 100. Needless to say, cryoelectronic memories are not without their problems. Certain difficulties related to manufacturing the insulating films and fabricating the related circuitry have yet to be resolved. In order to achieve temperatures close to absolute zero, the device must be immersed in liquid helium. The change from room temperature to temperatures approaching absolute zero subject the device to mechanical stresses resulting from differences in thermal expansion coefficients.

For the foreseeable future, however, it appears that main memory units will be based on high-speed semiconductor devices with their proven reliability and declining cost. The trend in the design of large modern computers is to optimize the performance of semiconductor-based circuit design. For example, the Cray-2 supercomputer, scheduled for a 1985 delivery date, will be based on custom designed and manufactured semiconductor devices. The length of the signal path, compared to the Cray-1, will be shorter. The mainframe will stand 2 feet high by 3 feet long. It will have a 32-million-word memory and be capable of completing a machine cycle in 4 billionths of a second (that is, 4 nanoseconds).

SUMMARY OF MEMORY DEVICES

Table 3-1 summarizes the characteristics of the different memory devices.

TABLE 3-1

Type	Volatile	Access	Speed Ranking	Primary Application
Core	No	Random	2	Not used
Semiconductor	Yes	Random	1	Main memory
CCD	Yes	Serial	3	Main memory
Bubble	No	Serial	4	Secondary storage

CLASSIFYING COMPUTERS BY TECHNOLOGY

Computers are a relatively recent phenomenon. The first *electronic* computer in operation was designed and built by John Mauchly and J. Presper Eckert at the University of Pennsylvania. Their computer, called *ENIAC* (Electronic Numerical Integrator And Calculator), was completed in 1946. It was an immense machine, occupying about 1500 square feet and weighing in excess of 30 tons. ENIAC was based on vacuum-tube technology. It used 18,000 vacuum tubes and was capable of performing 5000 additions per second. (See Figure 3-13.)

Considerable physical effort was required to program ENIAC, since the program instructions needed to be set externally by throwing a complex series of switches on a wired control panel. John Von Neumann, a leading mathematician, proposed that if the instruction set could be stored internally in digital form, it could then be decoded, executed, and modified if need be, at electronic speeds. *EDVAC* (Electronic Discrete Variable Automatic Computer) was a project begun by a team which included Mauchly and Eckert. It was the first computer designed to use Von Neumann's stored-program concept. EDVAC was completed in 1952. During the same period, *EDSAC* (Electronic Delayed Storage Automatic Computer) was engineered at Cambridge University, England, and in 1949 it became the first operational computer to employ the stored-program approach.

Soon after the EDVAC project began, Mauchly and Eckert left to organize their own computer company. In 1951 they sold the *UNIVAC I* (UNIVersal Automatic Computer) to the U.S. Census Bureau. It was the first commercially available computer designed to accommodate business applications. (See Figure 3-14.)

CLASSIFYING COMPUTERS BY TECHNOLOGY

Using design technology, speed, and physical size as criteria, computer advances can be grouped into computer *generations*. *First-generation* computers (1950–1959) were characterized by vacuum-tube technology, bulky size, and programming that was performed in cumbersome machine language. The unit of time used to express the speed of computer operation was the millisecond (1 millisecond = one thousandth of a second = 0.001 second). Secondary storage was restricted to magnetic tape.

Second-generation computers (1960–1965) were based on transistor technology with a consequent reduction in size and improved reliability and increased speed. Computer speed was now expressed in terms of microseconds (1 microsecond = 1 millionth of a second = 0.000 001 second). During this generation, tiny magnetic cores were used for main memory storage, resulting in greater access speed and storage capacity. Random access magnetic disk storage was introduced in this generation and adopted as an alternative to sequential access magnetic tape storage. Some programming was now being performed in user-oriented programming languages, such as COBOL and the scientifically based FORTRAN (*fo*rmula *tran*slation).

FIGURE 3–13. ENIAC. (Courtesy of Sperry Corporation.)

FIGURE 3–14. UNIVAC I. (Courtesy of Sperry Corporation.)

FIGURE 3–15. Three generations of electronics: vacuum tubes, transistors, and integrated circuits. (From IBM archives; courtesy of IBM Corporation.)

Third-generation computers (1965–?) incorporated solid-state and integrated circuit (IC) technology, leading to further improvements in component reliability and operating speed. (See Figure 3-15.) The time required to execute an instruction is now expressed (for large modern computers) in terms of nanoseconds (1 nanosecond = one billionth of a second = 0.000 000 001 second). To appreciate what an astounding achievement this represents, consider that in 1 nanosecond light travels approximately 11.8 *inches.* This implies that a large modern computer is operating at speeds approaching the speed of light. By comparison, first-generation machines operated in the millisecond range; in 1 millisecond light travels approximately 186 *miles.*

In this generation, MOS and other technologies have replaced magnetic core memories. Improvements have been made in I/O devices. Virtual memory and multiprogramming (the concurrent execution of two or more programs) were also introduced in this generation. This generation witnessed increased emphasis and use of high-level programming languages (rather than machine language) with industry-wide efforts to standardize versions of each language. The marketing of powerful mini- and microcomputers, at relatively low cost, also distinguished this generation. In fact, some people would argue that these machines and the very large scale integration (VLSI—more than 10,000 circuit components etched on a single silicon chip) that has made them possible, have signaled the beginning of the fourth generation of computers. (See Figure 3-16.) Others contend that we are merely experiencing refinements of third-generation technology, and only a major technological breakthrough can propel us into the next computer generation. Table 3-2 compares the computer generations.

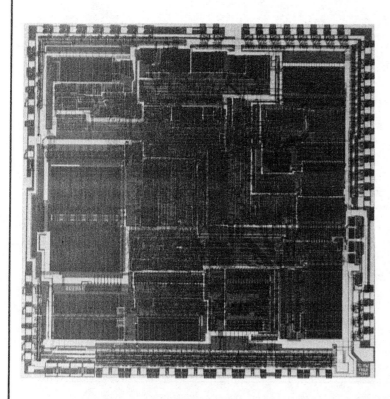

FIGURE 3–16. *Intel 80286 microprocessor, incorporating 128,000 transistors on a single square chip of silicon that measures only one-third of an inch on a side. By itself the 80286 can directly address up to 16 million bytes of memory space.* (Courtesy of INTEL Corporation.)

Discuss the significance of the stored-program approach.

A stored program, entered with data and represented internally in the machine in digital form, permits a sequence of computer operations to be controlled and performed automatically, *without the need for human intervention*. This results in greater overall processing efficiency, speed, and accuracy, and further distinguished first generation computers from their earlier electronic and electro-mechanical predecessors.

TABLE 3-2

Generation[a]	Technology	Key Features	Speed (units)
First (1950–1959)	Vacuum tubes	Large and bulky size; programming in machine language; magnetic tape secondary storage	Millisecond (0.001 second)
Second (1959–1965)	Transistors	Magnetic core memory; early use of COBOL and FORTRAN; use of magnetic disk as a secondary storage medium	Microsecond (0.000001 second)
Third (1965–1975?)	Integrated circuits LSI (large scale integration)	MOS memory devices; ongoing improvements in I/O devices; minicomputers; standardization and greater dependence on high-level user-oriented programming languages; increased emphasis on utility and operating system programs; introduction of virtual memory and multiprogramming[b]	Nanosecond (0.000000001 second)
Fourth (?) (1975?–. . .)	VLSI (very large scale integration) Newer memory technologies: bubble, CCD, superconducting circuitry.	Marketing of increasingly powerful, yet low-cost mini- and microcomputers; remote terminals and improvements in data communications technology and systems which have promoted the growth of distributed data processing networks[c]	Picosecond (0.000000000001 second)

[a]*Dates are approximate.* [b]*Multiprogramming refers to the concurrent execution of two or more programs that are stored in the same memory unit. (See Chapter 6.)* [c]*In distributed data processing, information processing within a large business organization is decentralized so that the branch offices are given specific data processing responsibilities, but have the need and ability to communicate directly with the main computer installation located at the geographically distant home office via telecommunications systems. (See Chapter 8.)*

CLASSIFYING COMPUTERS BY TYPE

In addition to classifying computers by the state of technology that they incorporate, computers may also be categorized by *type*. There are two general types of computers: digital and analog. *Digital* computers work with numbers. They accept data values as input, and using standard arithmetic and comparison operations, they grind out results. *Analog* computers, in contrast, measure and accept as input physical signals that vary over time, such as voltage, temperature, speed, and angle of rotation. The analog computer processes the signal, making an analogy between the actual signal and a physical quantity (often current) in order to arrive at the result. One of the simplest analog devices is the familiar body-temperature thermometer found in most household medicine chests. The thermometer accepts body warmth as input. The processing is reflected by the rise in the mercury column. An analogy is made between the body temperature and the height the mercury reaches, as interpreted by the engraved numerical scale on the side of the thermometer. Computers that have features found in both digital and analog computers are called *hybrid* computers. Analog and hybrid computers are frequently used to monitor and control changes in some fluctuating quantity so that if the change either exceeds or drops below a certain predetermined amount, the computer initiates an action that stabilizes the change, bringing the value being measured to within some acceptable range. This type of computer is commonly found in automated flight control and missile guidance systems.

Digital computers tend to be *general-purpose computers*, while analog computers tend to be *special-purpose computers*. A general-purpose computer may be used in a variety of application areas, for example, to perform complex arithmetic calculations, process a payroll, update customer credit accounts, produce student academic transcripts, ..., each application performed on the same machine but with a different set of user-supplied program instructions and data. A special-purpose computer, on the other hand, is internally wired so that it is dedicated to performing a single function or a very limited number of related processing functions. Unlike a general-purpose computer which can be programmed, a special-purpose computer is nonprogrammable. The processing capability of a special-purpose computer can be modified only by internally rewiring the machine. Special-purpose computers are commonly found in modern manufacturing facilities where they are used to monitor quality control, record production levels, and supervise the mixing of ingredients.

Exercises

1. Classify each of the following computer devices as digital or analog.
   a. a personal microcomputer
   b. a computer that controls the automatic cruise control found in many automobiles
2. Which computer tends to give more accurate results, an analog or a digital computer?
3. Which type of memory chip, ROM or RAM, allows a microcomputer to function as a general-purpose computer?

REVIEW EXERCISES

True or False?

1. Digital computers tend to be general-purpose computers.
2. In a stored-program instruction, the op code identifies the quantities that are involved.
3. In a microcomputer, the BASIC language interpreter would be contained in the memory chip referred to as ROM.
4. Bubble memory is nonvolatile.
5. UNIVAC I was the first electronic computer.
6. A byte is a single binary digit.
7. All memory devices, regardless of the computer generation that produced them, depend on their ability to function in one of two possible states.
8. An important practical limitation of the Josephson tunneling device is that it requires extreme operating temperatures.
9. EBCDIC is only used to convert numeric data into binary form.
10. Once converted into binary form, the byte representation of a character will be the same from computer to computer.
11. Data values are always referenced by their address in memory.
12. The smallest addressable unit in memory is the bit.
13. The first computer generation was based on simple transistor technology.
14. A data item may be stored in several adjacent bytes.
15. A byte may be considered to be a memory cell that is able to store a single character.

Multiple Choice

16. The person most closely associated with the introduction of the stored-program concept is:
    a. Einstein   c. Mauchly
    b. Von Neumann   d. Honeywell
17. When compared with a microcomputer, the CPU of a large computer is analogous to the:
    a. RAM chip   c. microprocessor chip
    b. ROM chip   d. CRT
18. In which of the following storage media is the method by which data are accessed fundamentally different from that in the other three?
    a. RAM   c. disk
    b. tape   d. main memory
19. Which type of memory features serial access of data?
    a. semiconductor   c. CCD
    b. magnetic bubble   d. magnetic bubble and CCD

20. Which of the following technological advances do some people believe is responsible for bringing us into the fourth computer generation?
    a. VLSI
    b. virtual memory
    c. multiprogramming
    d. fast disk storage

21. Which of the following statements are *true*?
    a. Analog computers are generally more accurate than digital computers.
    b. The operand section of a program instruction specifies the addresses of storage locations rather than their actual contents.
    c. A machine and an instruction cycle constitute an execution cycle.
    d. The address of a storage location may change during the execution of a program.

22. Which of the following would be a typical speed rating for a medium-size computer?
    a. 0.1 MIPS
    b. 1 MIPS
    c. 10 MIPS
    d. 100 MIPS

23. Which of the following memory technologies is particularly well suited to a secondary storage device?
    a. semiconductor
    b. bubble
    c. CCD
    d. magnetic core

24. Which type of memory offers the slowest speed capability?
    a. semiconductor
    b. bubble
    c. CCD
    d. cryoelectronic

25. Which pairs of terms are *not* synonymous?
    a. *volatility* and *loss of storage contents*
    b. *byte* and *character*
    c. *auxiliary* and *secondary* storage
    d. *serial* and *random* access

26. With respect to cost per stored bit, which of the following sequences indicates the relative ranking of the devices listed, from lowest cost to highest cost?
    a. MOS, CCD, disk, bubble
    b. disk, MOS, CCD, bubble
    c. disk, bubble, CCD, MOS
    d. MOS, disk, bubble, CCD

 # EXCURSION INTO BASIC

ILLUSTRATING THE STORED PROGRAM CONCEPT

In order to illustrate further the stored-program concept, let us consider how to enter and run the following BASIC program on a typical microcomputer:

```
10  READ A, B
20  LET S = A + B
30  PRINT A, B, "SUM="; S
40  DATA 2, 3
50  END
```

Using a computer keyboard is very similar to using a typewriter: the key bearing each character of each statement must be located on the keyboard and pressed. The pressing of a key will result in the corresponding character appearing on the CRT display screen. One character will be printed in each column space, with a blinking square of light, called a *cursor*, indicating the current column position. The column width of a line will vary from machine to machine, but is usually between 40 and 80 columns. Correcting or *editing* a line is possible without having to retype the entire line. There is usually a BACKSPACE key, which will move the cursor to a previous position to allow a character to be retyped. The reference manual for the particular machine being used should be consulted in order to determine procedures for the insertion and deletion of text.

After typing the letter B in line 10 of the program given above, a key must be pressed in order to move the cursor to the next line. With most computers this is accomplished by pressing a RETURN or ENTER key. Not only does this bring the cursor to the first column position of the next line, but it also stores the contents of the line from which it exits in computer memory. This process continues with each line of the program, including the last line (line 50), terminating with pressing the RETURN or ENTER key.

If you are typing this program on a microcomputer, you will notice that when you exit from the last line, the cursor will move to the next line and nothing else will happen. You have simply *stored* this program in main memory. To illustrate, the typing of the command LIST (followed by hitting the RETURN or ENTER key) will produce on most microcomputers a listing of the program instructions currently stored in memory.

Now that the computer has the program instructions stored in memory, it may execute the program, but only at your command. To command the computer to execute a stored program, it is necessary on most microcomputers to type the system command RUN (followed by hitting the RETURN or ENTER key). In the blink of an eye, the output of the program should appear on the screen:

```
2    3    SUM = 5
```

Suppose that you now wished to run the same program, but with different data. Since the program is stored in memory, all that need be done is to modify line 40.

SOME BUILT-IN COMPUTER FUNCTIONS

As a convenience to the user, a number of built-in "library" functions, which the user may reference in a program, are stored in ROM memory. Many of the functions are mathematically oriented. Consequently only a small sampling of those available are in Table 3-3.

In addition to those functions listed, most versions of BASIC also include trigonometric functions, logarithmic and exponential functions, and additional functions which facilitate the manipulation of alphanumeric data.

TABLE 3-3

Function	Syntax	Effect	Example
Absolute value	ABS(X)	The unsigned value of a numerical value X is returned.	ABS(3) = 3 ABS(−5) = 5
Square root	SQR(X)	Returns one of two equal numbers whose product is X.	SQR(25) = 5 SQR(ABS(−4)) = 2
Greatest integer	INT(X)	Returns the largest integer that is less than or equal to X.	INT(5.99) = 5 INT(4) = 4 INT(0.76) = 0
Random number generator	RND(X)	Returns a *random* number between 0 and 1. Random numbers are generated following *no* predictable pattern. In some systems the choice of X, called the seed value, affects the "randomness" of the numbers.	RND(1) = 0.139807653 RND(1) = 0.900086004
String length	LEN(X$)	Returns the number of characters in a string variable. Spaces and punctuation marks are counted as characters.	LET X$ = 'BOB SMITH' LEN(X$) = 9

EXAMPLE 1

Determine the output of the following program:

```
10   READ N$, X
20   LET F = LEN(N$)
30   IF F = 4 THEN 80
40   LET Y = ABS(X)
50   PRINT Y, INT(Y), SQR(Y)
60   GO TO 10
70   DATA "FINISH", 16, "END", −100,
     "TERMINATE", 1.44, "STOP", 49
80   END
```

SOLUTION

N$	X	F	Y	*Output* INT(Y)	SQR(Y)
FINISH	16	6	16	16	4
END	−100	3	100	100	10
TERMINATE	1.44	9	1.44	1	1.2
STOP	49	4		Program terminates	

EXAMPLE 2

Determine the output of the following program:

```
10   READ X
20   LET R = 10 * INT(X / 10 + 0.5)
30   PRINT X, R
40   GO TO 10
50   DATA 184, 237, 4925
60   END
```

SOLUTION

X	10 * INT(X / 10 + 0.5)	R	Output	
184	10 * INT(18.9)	180	184	180
237	10 * INT(24.2)	240	237	240
4925	10 * INT(493.0)	4930	4925	4930
			? OUT OF DATA IN 10	

CHAPTER

4

INPUT/OUTPUT

SOME HISTORICAL FOOTNOTES IN THE EVOLUTION OF DATA PROCESSING

In the late 1800's, the United States government recognized that based on the number of years it had taken to complete the population census of 1880, there would be a problem in completing the 1890 census before the initiation of the next scheduled census in 1900. The 1880 census required more than seven years to complete, and it was feared that with subsequent increases in population, the completion date of the 1890 census would extend into the twentieth century, thus rendering it obsolete. In an effort to accelerate the census tabulation process, the United States government secured the services of a statistician, Dr. Herman Hollerith. In order to process the census data efficiently, Hollerith developed a punch card and code to record the data and the related hardware necessary to process the punch cards. (See Figure 4-1.) Hollerith's ingenuity enabled the 1890 census to be completed in less than three years, some seven to eight years less than had been anticipated if the previously used tabulation methods had been implemented. Hollerith's success encouraged him to organize his own company which manufactured and distributed punch card equipment. The company Hollerith formed later evolved into a larger company, the International Business Machines Corporation (IBM).

Hollerith was just one person in a long succession of individuals who made significant contributions in advancing the state of data processing. Some of these individuals and their contributions are highlighted in Table 4-1.

FIGURE 4–1.
Hollerith's tabulator/sorter.
(From IBM archives; courtesy of International Business Machines Corporation.)

THE HOLLERITH CODE

For many years the 80-column "IBM" punch card dominated the data processing field as the primary means for encoding input data for subsequent computer processing. Although it has declined significantly in importance, it is still used to

TABLE 4-1

Individual	Contribution	Date	Significance
Not known	Abacus	2000 B.C.	First hand-held calculating device consisting of rows of movable beads.
Blaise Pascal	Mechanical calculator	Mid-1600s	First mechanical calculator based on combinations of rotating gears.
Gottfried Leibniz	Mechanical calculator	Late 1600s	Improved upon Pascal's machine by adding the capability to perform multiplication, division, and the extraction of a square root.
Joseph Jacquard	Punch card	Late 1700s	Use of a punch card to control weaving patterns, making this the first example of a "stored program." The punch card concept was later capitalized on by Hollerith as a means of encoding data for subsequent processing.
Charles Babbage	Difference engine	Early 1800s	The prototype of a machine that would perform arithmetic calculations without human intervention. Concept was ahead of the technology of the time, which was not able to supply the required precision parts in sufficient quantities.
	Analytical engine	1833	The design of this machine anticipated modern computer design by including provision for input/output, memory, control, and arithmetic operations. Again, technology and financial support lagged behind the ideas of this genius, preventing the machine from being manufactured.
John Atanasoff	Atanasoff-Berry computer	1942	Conceived and designed the first electronic computer, at Iowa State University, preceding the work of Mauchly and Eckert (ENIAC).
Howard Aiken	Mark I computer	1944	With the financial support of IBM, Harvard professor Aiken elaborated on Babbage's ideas and produced the first automatic electromechanical computer capable of performing long chains of calculations.

some extent in many data processing installations. We therefore shall briefly discuss how data are coded on a punch card.

The standard punch card is made from a very thin and flexible cardboard-like material; it is $7\frac{3}{8}$ inches in length and $3\frac{1}{4}$ inches in width. The card itself is divided into 80 vertical columns, each column consisting of 12 rows. The top three horizontal rows are called the *12, 11, and 0 zone rows*; the remaining nine rows are called the *digit rows*. (See Figure 4-2.)

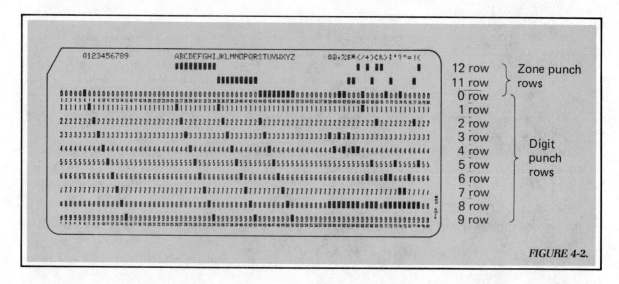

FIGURE 4-2.

Data are recorded onto the punch card by inserting the card into a typewriter-like machine called a *keypunch* machine. Each character key that is depressed on the keypunch represents that character by punching one, two, or three hole punches in a column of the card. At the same time, the character is printed on the top of the card in the same column number. The printing of the character is for the benefit of the keypunch operator or the programmer who, while handling the card, must interpret it. Each coded character is defined by the number and positions of the hole punches appearing in a given column. The hole punches are interpreted according to the following standardized Hollerith code:

- *Numeric characters* (0–9) are coded by a single-column punch appearing in the digit row that corresponds to the value of the digit. A 5, for example, would be represented by a hole punch in the 5 digit row.

- *Alphabetic characters* (A–Z) are coded by two punches in a single column: one is a zone punch (a punch in the top 12, 11, or 0 row) and the other is a digit punch (a punch in the 1–9 digit rows). Specific letters are identified as follows:

	Letter	Punches		
		Zone	and	Digit Rows
	A–I	12	and	1–9
	J–R	11	and	1–9
	S–Z	0	and	2–9
Note	/	0	and	1

- *Special characters* (e.g., punctuation marks) are coded by three punches in a single column.

Determine the Hollerith code for the characters:

1. 8 **2.** C

1. 8 is represented by a punch in the 8 digit row.
2. C is represented by two punches: a punch in the 12 zone and a punch in the 3 digit row.

DATA ENTRY

A *card reader* is the hardware device used to interpret punch card data. Different models of card readers will offer different rates at which cards are processed. Typical rates are in the range of 250 to 1000 cards per minute. The two most common methods for interpreting the column hole punches are sensing brushes and photoelectric means in which the hole punches permit light to pass through, striking photoelectric cells that decode the data. The preparation and input of card data via a keypunch and card reader is a relatively slow and cumbersome process. (See Figure 4-3.) Furthermore, with frequent handling, punch cards are mutilated easily, while being difficult to store. There are, however, two advantages to working with punch card data:

- The encoded data are also printed on the top of the card in a human-readable form.

- Punch cards can serve as turnaround documents, as discussed later in this chapter.

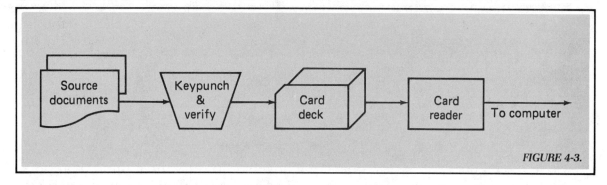

FIGURE 4-3.

THE UNIT RECORD CONCEPT

As a result of the limitations of the early hardware used to process punch card data, and the convenience inherent in having all the data related to a single transaction fitting within an 80-column card boundary, the concept of a unit record evolved. The 80-column card was used as a unit of measure in the same sense that the inch is a unit of measure of length. Thus a single punched data card that contains data representing a single transaction or master record is referred to as a *unit record*.

In order to overcome the weaknesses of punch cards as well as the limitations inherent in the unit record concept, key-to-tape and key-to-disk(ette) data entry systems have been developed. Indeed, key-to-*magnetic-medium* and keyboard CRT terminal devices are at present the dominant modes of data entry in business data processing. (See Figure 4-4.)

FIGURE 4–4. *A key-to-tape data entry system.* (Courtesy of Mohawk Data Sciences.)

PRINTERS

Once the computer processes data, the finished product must often be represented in a form a person can read. Computer output may be represented as either soft copy (CRT display) or hard copy. Hard copy output in the form of some type of printed paper output is accomplished by a printer, a variety of which are in common use. Although special forms will often be used in printed computer output, the most widely used general-purpose output paper is the 11- by $14\frac{7}{8}$-inch page that comes in continuous reams in which the pages are fan folded one on top of the other. The page will typically contain 132 print column positions per line, with a maximum of 66 lines of print per page.

Printers generally fall under two categories: impact and nonimpact. *Impact* printers form a character image on a page by the printing mechanism making physical contact with the page through an inked ribbon. *Nonimpact* printers form character impressions by using thermal, chemical, electrostatic, or photographic techniques, some of which may require the use of specially treated paper. As a result of fewer moving parts and a lack of physical contact being made with the paper, nonimpact printers are generally quieter, tend to require less maintenance, and are capable of achieving higher printing speeds and sharper images than impact printers. Nonimpact printers also offer greater flexibility in the choice of typeface. Impact printers, however, allow multiple copies of a report to be printed through the use of carbon or pressure-sensitized paper.

For jobs involving a large volume of printed output, laser printers are particularly appropriate. Printers based on laser technology are capable of printing speeds in excess of 21,000 lines per minute of letter-quality print. Although the laser printer is a nonimpact printer, its speed makes the printing of multiple copies of a report practical by executing successive print runs of the same job. (See Figure 4-5.)

FIGURE 4–5. *The DatagraphiX model 9820 laser printer, an off-line page printer which operates at speeds up to 21,000 lines per minute.* (Courtesy of DatagraphiX, Inc.)

IMPACT PRINTERS

Three of the most commonly used impact printers are the chain, drum, and wire matrix printers. In a *chain printer*, the character slugs which are used to make the impression are located on a continuous gear train (similar to a bicycle chain) that rotates past 132 print hammers, each hammer corresponding to one of 132 column print positions. As a character passes the appropriate hammer/column position, the hammer is engaged and strikes the character slug, impacting the ribbon and page, thus making the character impression on the page.

A *drum printer* has the character slugs engraved on the surface of a cylindrical drum. Each horizontal row of the drum contains the same character in each print position. The drum's printing mechanism permits the simultaneous printing of more than one character on a line. To print a line of output, the drum revolves printing all the A's on a given line, followed by all the B's on the same line, followed by all the C's on that same line, and so on. One complete revolution of the drum is necessary in order to print a complete line of output.

Rather than printing a solid character impression, a *wire-matrix printer* selects particular wires from a rectangular array of wires to impact an inked ribbon, thus forming a *dot-matrix* image pattern. Figure 4-6 shows the dot-matrix printing of the numeral 4 using a 7 × 9 pattern of dots. Dot-matrix printers that form alphanumeric characters using a greater concentration of dots are widely available and offer significantly sharper print images.

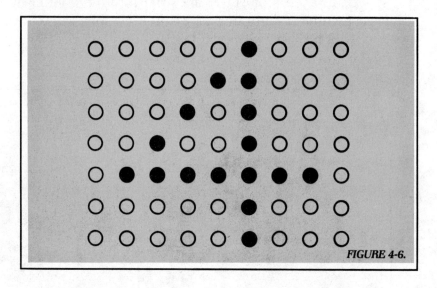

FIGURE 4-6.

Another popular printing mechanism is the spoke-like daisy wheel with each spoke terminating with a character slug. Daisy-wheel printers are known for their sharp letter-quality print. An increasing number of relatively low cost dot-matrix printers now offer a quality of print that approaches the print quality of a daisy-wheel printer. These dot-matrix printers typically form characters by means of a "square" 9 × 8 or 9 × 9 dot-matrix pattern. Some of these printers use a special film ribbon which further enhances the quality of the print.

SERIAL VERSUS LINE PRINTERS

Printers may also be categorized by the amount of information printed. A *serial* printer forms a single character at a time with speed usually expressed in terms of characters per second (chs). A common type of serial printer is based on a print mechanism consisting of an array of wires that can be heated selectively. Dot-matrix images are formed by using this print head in conjunction with thermal sensitive paper, which blackens when heat is applied. Another popular type of serial printer uses ink-jet technology to discharge electronically charged ink through a nozzle, forming a dot-matrix character pattern on the page. As many as 500 dots are used per character, resulting in a high print quality. This type of nonimpact printer is capable of forming images at the rate of from 50 to 300 characters per second. Daisy-wheel and wire-matrix printers also print characters serially.

A *line* printer produces an entire line of output in a single printer machine cycle. (See Figure 4-7.) Speeds of line printers are usually expressed in terms of lines per minute (lpm), with a line generally consisting of 132 print positions. A drum printer is a common type of line printer.

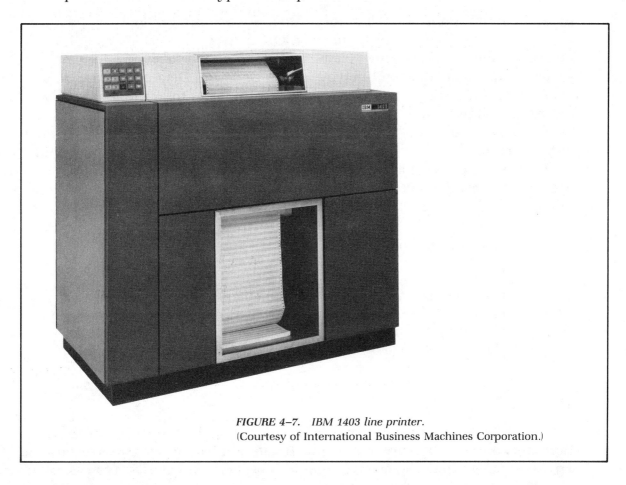

FIGURE 4–7.   IBM 1403 line printer.
(Courtesy of International Business Machines Corporation.)

For large volume printing, printers which are capable of printing a complete page at a time may be used. Page printers are based on some type of electro-photographic technique. Table 4-2 compares the printing speeds of several different types of printers.

TABLE 4-2

Printer	Type	Typical Printing Speed[a]
Chain	Impact	1000–3000 lpm
Drum	Impact	400–1600 lpm
Wire matrix	Impact	2–15 chs
Daisy wheel	Impact	25–50 chs
Thermal	Nonimpact	100–2000 chs
Laser	Nonimpact	4000–21,000 lpm
Ink-jet	Nonimpact	50–300 chs

[a]*lpm = lines per minute; chs = characters per second.*

SECONDARY STORAGE

In addition to routing computer output to a printer, information may be transferred to and from a secondary storage medium. In Chapter 2 it was pointed out that data stored on a secondary storage medium may be accessed in one of two general ways, depending on the type of storage device. Data are written to and read from magnetic tape in *sequential* fashion. In order to locate a particular record on a tape file, the tape must be read from the beginning, with each record being examined until the desired record is found. In magnetic disk storage data may be accessed (located) directly, the retrieval process being essentially independent of the physical location of the record on the surface of the disk. This type of storage is called *direct* or *random access*. In this section, we compare some of the more popular secondary storage devices and media in terms of:

- access *method* and *times*

- storage *capacity* and *density*

- the *rate of data transfer*, which refers to the speed with which data can be transmitted between the main memory and an I/O device, such as a tape or disk drive unit, the limiting factor being the mechanical design characteristics of the peripheral device

MAGNETIC TAPE

Tape *density* is the measure of how much data can be packed into a given tape length. Although there are several tape densities in common use, typical densities are 800, 1,600, and 6,250 bytes (characters) per inch (bpi). The *data transfer rate* depends on two factors: the tape speed and the tape density. The tape speed refers to the rate at which the particular tape drive unit's transport mechanism moves the tape past the electromagnetic read/write head mechanism. The data transfer rate is calculated by multiplying the tape speed by the tape density.

EXAMPLE

A common tape speed is 112.5 inches per second. Given a tape density of 1,600 bpi, find the data transfer rate.

SOLUTION

data transfer rate = 112.5 inches / second × 1,600 bpi
= 180,000 bytes / second

Data transfer rates for magnetic tape typically range between 60,000 and 800,000 bpi. Assuming a standard 10½-inch reel of 2,400 feet of tape, the tape storage capacity may also be calculated easily. The maximum storage capacity is found by multiplying the tape density by 2,400 feet expressed as an equivalent number of inches.

Assuming a tape density of 800 bpi, determine the maximum storage capacity of a standard reel of magnetic tape.

storage capacity = 800 bpi × (2,400 feet/reel × 12 inches/foot)
$$= 800 \text{ bpi} \times (28,800 \text{ inches/reel})$$
$$= 23,040,000 \text{ bytes/reel}$$

It is interesting to note that this reel of tape can store an amount of data equivalent to more than 275,000 punch cards having entries in each of the 80 columns. Clearly, tape is a more compact storage medium. Furthermore, while the use of punch cards imposes a limit of 80 characters on the length of a record, the length of records stored on tape may vary, having an essentially "unlimited" length.

MAGNETIC DISK

Disk storage represents the most commonly used *direct access storage device* (DASD). Disks normally come stacked in a disk pack which can be removed from the disk drive, stored off-line, and replaced by another disk pack. Removable disk packs offer therefore an essentially unlimited off-line storage capacity.

A typical disk pack has from 10 to 12 disks (fewer or more are not uncommon) and may weigh from 10 to 20 pounds, which tends to discourage its frequent removal. Each disk surface is divided into a number of concentric tracks along which data are encoded magnetically. The greater the number of tracks on a disk surface, the greater its storage density. In a *dual-density* disk data may be stored on both sides of the disk.

The on-line storage capacity of a disk drive unit will depend on the number of disks in the mounted disk pack and on the storage density of each disk. The IBM 3330 disk system, for example, accommodates 12 disks per pack, with a storage capacity of 100 megabytes (mega = 1 million).

A medium or large modern computer system will typically feature a bank of disk drive units, each with its own removable disk pack, thereby increasing the effective on-line storage capacity of the disk facility significantly. (See Figure 4-8.) Data transfer rates generally fall in the range of 150,000 bytes to 1.5 megabytes per second, although some units are capable of rates as high as 3 megabytes per second.

FIGURE 4–8. The Sperry 1100/60 large scale computer system. An array of disk drives is located in the background. (Courtesy of Sperry Corporation.)

Figure 4-9 illustrates a disk pack and its read/write heads. Each disk surface has its own read/write head (except for the two outermost surfaces, which are not used since they are susceptible to scratches). In order to locate data it is usually necessary for the disk pack to rotate and for the entire read/write head assembly to be moved either forward or back until it is positioned over the desired track. The appropriate read/write head is then activated. If you can imagine a record player with several long-playing albums stacked on the spindle and one phonograph arm/ stylus for *each* of the stacked records, you will have a rough idea of what's involved

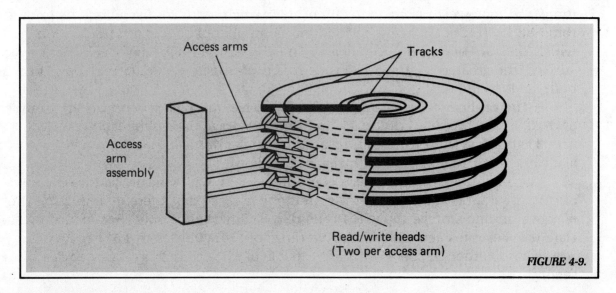

Access arms

Tracks

Access arm assembly

Read/write heads
(Two per access arm)

FIGURE 4-9.

in reading from and writing to a particular disk surface. An important difference in our analogy is that while most phonograph arms are able to be pivoted and sweep out an arc in playing back an album, the read/write heads of a disk drive unit can only be moved radially as a unit, either inward or outward, maintaining a straight-line path with the center drive shaft.

The actual means of zeroing in on (i.e., addressing) a particular record on a stored disk file will not be discussed until Chapter 7.

In order to minimize access time, some disk drive units are designed with nonremovable disk packs. One read/write head is provided for each *track* (rather than each recording surface), eliminating the need for the access arm assembly to move the read/write heads in or out in order to position them over a particular track. These designs offer faster access times than removable disk drives, but at the expense of sacrificing an off-line storage capability in the form of a removable disk pack. The higher storage densities that are typically found with nonremovable disk drive units offset, to some extent, this loss of off-line storage capability. Those installations that use nonremovable disk drives must also rely on removable disk drive units. For example, consider the problem of processing a file that is stored off-line on a removable disk pack. If the contents of the disk are to be read into main memory from the on-line nonremovable disk drive, then the disk pack must first be loaded into a backup removable disk drive unit and its contents "dumped" onto the nonremovable disk.

The increase in the number of heads and the close engineering tolerances required increase the cost of nonremovable disk drives. As a result of their higher cost and loss of an off-line storage capability, nonremovable disk drive units are not as widely used as removable disk drives.

A compromise approach is offered by a *disk data module*, which houses both the disks and the associated read/write head mechanism in a portable sealed unit. In general, the permanent sealing of disks within a disk drive unit for the purpose of optimizing certain performance characteristics is referred to as *Winchester technology*. The performance advantages attributed to a Winchester design approach include faster data access times and greater storage densities compared to removable disk packs. In addition, the sealed unit protects the disk components from scratches and air contaminants. Although the data module is not lightweight, it can be removed from on-line storage and replaced by another data module. This performance and flexibility come at a greater financial cost than disk packs that have comparable storage capacities but do not incorporate Winchester technology. (See Figure 4-10.)

FIGURE 4–10. A disk pack data module that contains both disks and the read/write head assembly. (Courtesy of BASF Systems Corporation.)

While the sequential record search process gives the tape medium average access times which are expressed in terms of minutes (or parts of a minute), access times for direct access disk storage typically range between 10 and 150 milliseconds. Nonremovable fixed-head designs offer the fastest access times, typically between 10 and 25 milliseconds. Access times for a particular disk drive unit are stated as *average* figures, since the actual access times are influenced by several physical considerations that depend upon the preceding read/write operation. For example, the access time (actually its *seek time* component) will depend upon the number of tracks that the read/write head assembly must be moved from its previous position to the new read/write position. Furthermore, there is a certain amount of *rotational delay time* experienced when the disk pack rotates from its previous position to the position that aligns the read/write head over the desired portion of the track that will sustain the read/write operation.

MAGNETIC STORAGE DEVICES FOR MICROCOMPUTERS

A flexible (floppy) magnetic disk provides most microcomputers and minicomputers with a direct access storage capability. A typical floppy disk drive unit can store from 100K to 500K bytes on a $5\frac{1}{4}$-inch diameter floppy disk. Microcomputer compatible Winchester disk drives are available, which feature the sealing of a *hard* disk within the disk drive unit, enabling faster data access times and higher storage densities to be achieved. A Winchester disk drive typically features a storage capacity ranging between 5 and 20 megabytes, which tends to compensate somewhat for the disk being nonremovable.

Some newer disk drives are designed to accept a removable Winchester disk *cartridge* measuring $5\frac{1}{2}$ inches square and $\frac{3}{4}$ inch in thickness. A hard disk is housed in the protective cartridge casing, which insulates it from the environment. Only after the cartridge has been seated in place inside the disk drive unit does a sliding door open, giving access to the disk. The storage capacity of the Winchester disk cartridges typically ranges from 5 to 16.5 megabytes. A single 5-megabyte removable cartridge offers a storage capacity equivalent to over 30 floppy disks.

Another recent development is the "microfloppy" disk with a diameter of $3\frac{1}{2}$ inches (or less) and a proposed storage capacity in the megabyte range.

Cassette drives provide microcomputers with a relatively inexpensive (albeit slow) means for sequential access storage. Cassette drive units are adequate for most student use as well as for beginning hobbyists, but provide unacceptably slow access times and low data transfer rates when used by the advanced student or serious hobbyist. Furthermore, much of the quality commercial software tends to be available exclusively on disk; a limited selection of recreational and educational software is available in both disk and cassette formats.

MAGNETIC DRUM

A magnetic drum storage device is a direct access storage unit that offers very fast data access times (generally faster than the disk), very high data transfer rates (1.0 to 1.5 megabytes per second) but somewhat limited storage capacity (typically 4 to

15 megabytes). Its operating principle is relatively simple. A small cylindrical drum is coated with a series of magnetic strips, called tracks, which completely encircle the drum surface. Data are accessed by revolving the drum about a shaft at a very high constant speed, with a series of read/write heads, one per track, reading and writing data to the appropriate tracks on the drum surface. Since the introduction of the fixed-head disk, the magnetic drum has declined in importance. Fixed-head disks offer comparable data access times and transfer rates while providing significantly greater storage capacity.

While tape and disk can normally be removed from their respective drive units and stored off-line, a magnetic drum is nonremovable. The long-term storage cost using the magnetic drum would therefore be high compared to that for tapes or disks. The long-term storage cost associated with tape is significantly lower than that for disk storage.

MASS STORAGE SYSTEMS

Each time a tape that is stored off-line is needed, it must be manually located, pulled, and then carried to the tape drive unit where it is loaded. The purpose of a mass storage system is to replace tape libraries by an on-line storage device capable of storing the corresponding large volumes of data. In a mass storage system, such as the IBM 3850, hexagon-shaped cell compartments arranged in a honeycomb pattern store small cylindrical cartridges, approximately 2 inches in diameter and 4 inches in length (similar in appearance to photographic film cannisters). Each data cartridge stores a rolled strip of magnetic tape approximately 64 feet in length, which is capable of storing up to 50 million characters of data. (See Figure 4-11.) An access arm mechanism automatically locates a particular data cell and

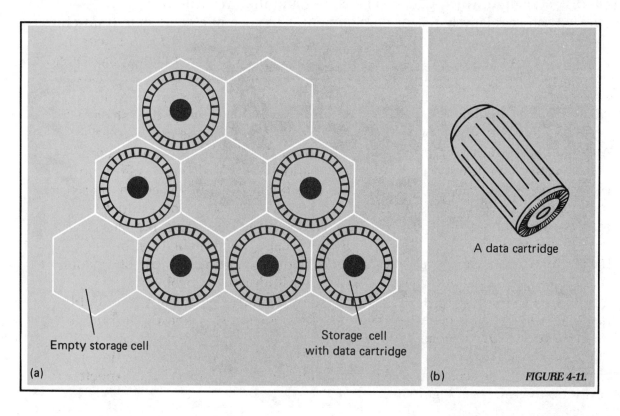

Empty storage cell

Storage cell
with data cartridge

A data cartridge

(a)

(b)

FIGURE 4-11.

then fetches the cartridge from the cell in much the same way that a record would be located and removed for play from a jukebox whose records are stored in horizontal rows, one on top of the other. The cartridge is then brought to a special tape device for a read/write operation. After this process has been completed, the tape is placed back into its cartridge and then returned to its storage cell. The storage capacity of this mass storage system is as great as 472 billion bytes, the equivalent of the storage contents of more than 175,000 reels of magnetic tape. The average access time is in the range of 3 to 5 seconds. Although this is considerably slower than access times experienced with disk storage, it represents significant time savings compared to the time needed to locate and mount a reel of tape.

SOME NEWER TECHNOLOGIES

Optical disks based on laser technology offer faster access times and significantly greater storage capacities compared to more conventional design approaches. In one approach data are written to an optical disk by a laser burning a pattern of microscopic holes on the surface of a transparent disk coated with a metallic film. Data are read from the disk by a laser beam having diminished intensity. The presence of a hole, interpreted as a 1 bit, will be indicated by light being transmitted by the hole. A 14-inch optical disk has a storage capacity of 10 billion holes. An important limitation of optical disks is that once data are written to the disk surface, they cannot be erased or changed. Optical disks are therefore suitable only for archival storage. Current research is being directed toward trying to design an optical disk system in which data can be erased and then rewritten.

Another relatively recent development is the use of a solid-state RAM chip as the basis of a secondary storage device. A RAM card is available for many of the popular brand microcomputers; it expands the microcomputer's memory considerably in general by as much as 256K bytes. With the insertion of a RAM card, the additional memory may be used in the same fashion as disk storage, yielding a "disk access" capability that is some 50 times faster than that of disk storage. The extra memory capacity provided by the RAM card, however, is of the volatile type. A continuous power source is required in order to maintain its storage contents.

In the late 1970s some companies abandoned their research efforts in exploring the potential applications of magnetic bubble memory. (See Chapter 3.) The mid-1980s, however, promise to deliver an increasing number of products which incorporate bubble memory technology. The renewed interest in bubble memory is largely due to dramatically lower production costs, the availability of bubble chips having increased storage densities, and the continued attractiveness of its ability to retain its stored contents when the power is withdrawn (nonvolatility).

Due to the faster data access times, nonvolatility, and reliability of bubble memory, some people believe that secondary storage devices based on bubble memory technology may soon be used in addition to a floppy disk drive, with the floppy disk drive being reserved for archival storage of data. Certainly the use of bubble memory devices in portable computers and terminals can be expected to continue to grow. (See Figure 4-12.)

FIGURE 4–12. *Megabytes of nonvolatile storage can be made available in a small printed circuit board area based on the Intel 7110 one-megabit bubble memory and related support components. Bubble storage systems lack moving mechanical parts, which makes them much more rugged and reliable compared to other technologies offering similar capacities of nonvolatile storage.* (Courtesy of INTEL Corporation.)

ADDITIONAL INPUT DEVICES

Card-oriented input devices are *batch* type data entry devices. The card decks representing different processing tasks (jobs) are accumulated and, for efficiency reasons, processed as a job stream at regular time intervals. Another type of batch-oriented input device is based on *optical character recognition* (OCR). Optical document readers are capable of reading typed documents, often by measuring the pattern of reflected light, where the characters conform to some standardized type face. The American National Standards Institute (ANSI) has issued a standardized OCR character set. (See Figure 4-13.) Some OCR machines are capable of reading certain types of hand printing.

ABCDEFGHIJKLMNO
PQRSTUVWXYZ♩♪⅄⊣¦
0123456789.⌐:⌐=
+/*″{}%?&'–$∧[]
<>()!#∂\ .⌐?'–

ÜÑÄØÖƐ𝑅£¥

FIGURE 4-13.

A related method of data entry uses a *mark sense* bubbling sheet or card to capture data. To record data, an oval in a particular location is shaded using pencil. The presence or absence of a mark is then detected by a machine, which measures the intensity of reflected light at each of the oval positions. A similar technique is used in some supermarkets, which take advantage of the black and white striped *universal product code* (UPC) bars that appear on the wrappings of packaged goods. The product is then passed over a bar code scanner, and when this is used in conjunction with a cash register/computer, the price is automatically tallied on the cash register. At the same time, inventory records are automatically updated by the store's computer. (See Figures 4-14 and 4-15.)

FIGURE 4-14.

FIGURE 4–15. NCR supermarket scanning system. Grocery items are placed over the criss-crossed scanning device which optically reads the bar code on the labels. (Courtesy of NCR Corporation.)

In order to facilitate the processing of bank checks, the banking industry adopted *magnetic ink character recognition* (MICR) based methods in 1959. Items such as bank identification number and customer account number are preprinted on checks using characters selected from the MICR character set. During the processing of a check, the amount of the check is also printed using MICR, usually being added to the lower right portion of the check. Special MICR machines automatically read these data directly from the check. (See Figures 4-16 and 4-17.)

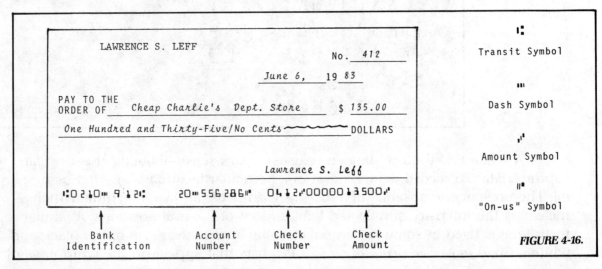

FIGURE 4-16.

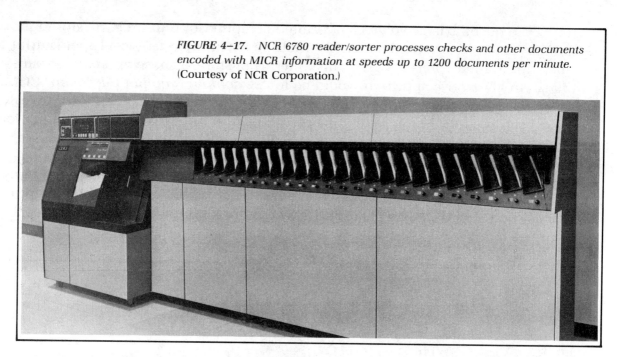

FIGURE 4-17.   NCR 6780 reader/sorter processes checks and other documents encoded with MICR information at speeds up to 1200 documents per minute. (Courtesy of NCR Corporation.)

A consideration in the use of mark sense documents is that stray marks may be misinterpreted by the machine reading process or, in fact, lead to the rejection of documents by the machine. A weakness of all document reading machines (including mark sense, OCR, and MICR) is that if the input document is torn or mutilated, it may not be processed. The limited variety of MICR characters restricts the use of MICR methods to a small number of processing applications. Mark sense, OCR, and MICR input documents, however, share a very desirable feature: they represent data in *both* machine readable and human comprehensible form. In addition, each of the three documents serves both as a source document and as an input document, eliminating the need to code from the source document onto an appropriate input medium. For example, mark sense forms capture original source data; the *same* form is then used as a machine input document.

Much research is being directed in the area of developing data-entry voice terminals. Current technology permits a user to "train" a computer to recognize a limited vocabulary set. Such devices require that each input data word be punctuated by a pause of a fixed duration.

ADDITIONAL OUTPUT DEVICES

It is sometimes convenient to base a data processing cycle on punched card *output*. Some utility and credit companies, for example, may include in their customer billing a machine generated punch card that includes information related to the customer account ID and the billing amount. The card serves as a *turnaround* document, with the customer returning it with the payment. These companies use the card to facilitate the processing of the payment transaction. The machine used to produce the card output initially is called a *card punch* machine. Some data processing machines include both a card reader and card punch facility. Output from a card punch typically ranges between 150 and 500 cards per minute.

Frequently, large volumes of printed computer output must be stored in a human-readable form and be readily available for future reference. Paper output in such applications presents problems in terms of storage space and ease of handling. An alternative approach would be to use *computer output microfilm* (COM). It consists of miniature photographed images of the output that would ordinarily have been produced on a printed page. The COM output may be either in the form of a roll of microfilm or as a series of 4 × 6-inch microfiche cards. In some systems microfiche is produced from computer output off-line by inputting a magnetic tape in a COM device, which then produces microfiche records of the tape's contents. Some COM devices operate on-line, with the desired computer output transmitted directly to the COM device, which then produces the microfiche. (See Figure 4-18.)

FIGURE 4–18. The DatagraphiX ARIS II, which is an advanced remote imaging system featuring a dry heat development process and a laser imaging system. The system records COM output at speeds up to 12,000 lines per minute. (Courtesy of DatagraphiX, Inc.)

Although microfiche is a very compact storage medium, with two microfiche cards storing the equivalent of approximately 100 pages of printed output, it has the drawback that it cannot be read directly by a person. A microfiche reader must be used to project a desired selection from the microfiche card onto a screen. For suitably large volumes of output, microfilm storage tends to be less expensive than the long-term storage of paper output. As a mass storage medium, however, microfilm is not as economical as tape storage.

TERMINALS

Perhaps the most familiar and widely used on-line I/O device is the CRT keyboard terminal, also referred to as a "tube." The name CRT refers to the soft copy television-like screen display. The screen size will vary from machine to machine, although a screen display capacity of 24 lines, with 40 or 80 characters/line, is typical. A "25th" line is printed on the bottom of the screen display by pushing or *scrolling* the screen's contents up one line so that the top line vanishes, thereby making room for the newly added bottom line. This scrolling process is an automatic machine function, which can also be initiated using an appropriate key on the keyboard. A CRT can generate printed screen output at the rate of about 200 to 2,000 characters per second. The rate at which input data are printed on the screen will, of course, depend on the rate at which the operator keys in the data.

In general, the terms *CRT terminal* and *microcomputer* are *not* synonymous. A microcomputer will not only feature a CRT display monitor, but will also include a microprocessor. A CRT terminal is merely an I/O device which provides the means for entering and receiving transmitted data from some mainframe computer located at a geographically remote location. The mainframe computer may be as close as in the same room or as distant as in another city or state. Another type of *remote job entry* (RJE) is possible through a batch-oriented terminal based on using a card reader and printer. Terminals (CRT or batch oriented) may be thought of as satellite computer stations linked through some form of data communications network, often by using telephone lines (telecommunications). Data communications will be discussed in more detail in Chapter 8.

THE CONTROL UNIT INTERFACE

A typical computer configuration in a modern computer installation will include a variety of different types of I/O devices attached to the computer. Two potential problems emerge in the communication between the I/O devices and the computer:

■ Each type of I/O device functions using a different information code. A card reader, for example, uses a different code than a magnetic tape device; an impact printer requires a certain type of electronic signal so that the appropriate hammer mechanism can be engaged in forming the desired character impression. How can a computer accommodate these different information codes efficiently when it is designed to operate internally with a single code such as EBCDIC?

■ Each I/O device is capable of transferring data to the computer at a different rate, with the fastest of these rates being considerably slower than the speed at which the computer can process data. How does the computer avoid the wasteful time that would result in having to "wait" for the input device to read and transmit data, character by character? Or how does it avoid waiting for an output device to write a character before it transmits another character to it from main memory?

A *control unit* (*not* to be confused with the control unit section of the CPU) is an intermediary electronic device that converts electronic information codes during input/output operations, with each I/O device being assigned its own control unit. A control unit situated between an input device and the computer will take an input signal and convert it into the particular information code used by the computer; a control unit positioned between the computer and the output device converts the computer output signal into an electronic signal that can be interpreted by the particular output device. As a result of this code conversion process, the control unit is said to perform a *standard interface* function. The control unit is usually housed within the individual I/O device.

In order to reconcile the speed disparity that exists between the computer and its associated I/O devices, the control unit also performs a *data buffering* function. Rather than the input device transmitting data as they are being read by the input device, character by character, the coded data are stored in a temporary storage location called a *buffer* area. When requested by the computer, the contents of the buffer are transmitted to main memory at electronic speeds which parallel the operating speed of the computer. Idle CPU time is minimized since while an input operation is being performed by the input hardware (with the data temporarily stored in the buffer area), the CPU is free to work on another operation. This concept of staggering processing tasks so that the CPU is kept busy, is referred to as *overlapped* processing. A similar procedure is followed during an output operation. Computer output is transmitted at electronic speeds from main storage to the buffer area that is associated with the selected output device. The output device then writes output at its own speed. This process maximizes computer efficiency since the computer does not have to "wait" while the relatively slow output device completes a character by character write operation. (See Figure 4-19.)

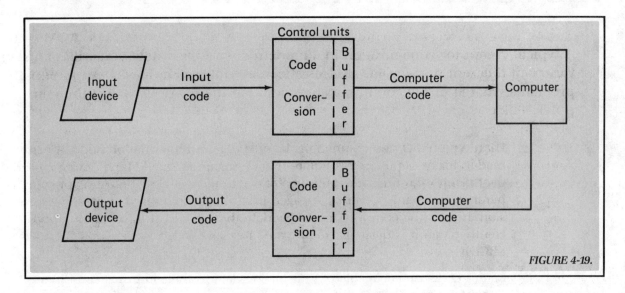

FIGURE 4-19.

CHANNELS

In order to help free the CPU of the responsibility of coordinating the input and output activities of an array of I/O devices, a hardware device called a *channel* is often connected between the control unit and the computer. (See Figure 4-20.) A channel includes the logic capability necessary for it to control the overlapped processing of tasks, whereby the CPU is occupied with internal processing while an input/output operation related to the same or a different job is being performed. Some computers incorporate channels within the physical unit that houses the CPU.

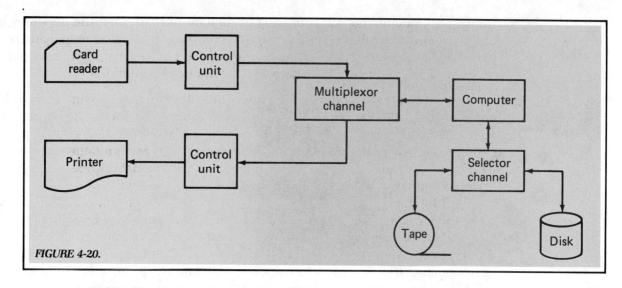

FIGURE 4-20.

Two basic types of channels are found in computer systems. A *multiplexor* channel is used in conjunction with relatively slow-speed I/O devices such as card readers and impact printers. The multiplexor channel allows the computer to service concurrently the I/O devices that it attaches to the computer. The computer, for example, will fetch a character from an input device, transmit a character to a printer, and so on, eventually returning to the first device to fetch another character. The idea is that in the time it takes the computer to complete this cycle, the first device has had sufficient time to read another character. If the device should "get ahead" of the computer, then the character is stored in a buffer area. The multiplexor channel, therefore, increases system efficiency by overlapping input/output operations, giving the impression that these I/O devices are operating simultaneously.

Relatively fast I/O devices, such as magnetic tape, disk, and drum devices, are attached to the computer using a *selector* channel. A selector channel functions as a type of on/off switch, permitting only a single I/O device to communicate with main memory at a time. Only after an input/output operation being conducted with one I/O device is completed, can an input/output operation associated with another selector channel I/O device be initiated.

SUMMARY

In data processing several themes tend to recur:

- Potential increases in processing speed achieved through hardware developments must be measured against cost considerations. Sometimes the speed gained by adopting a new system or switching to a new technology is not judged by a business firm to be worth the corresponding financial expenditure or disruption in operations that might result.

- Technology must be matched to the human user. Input forms (such as OCR documents), report documents, and hardware must be designed with an eye toward the people who will be using them. The usefulness of computer output is directly related to the accuracy of the data used to produce the output. If source OCR documents are confusing or difficult to read, then the accuracy of the data captured will be compromised. If computer generated management reports are not printed in a convenient and easy to read format, then they will be of little use to the people for whom the information is intended.

■ Can *source data automation* be introduced into the data processing system in order to improve accuracy and overall system efficiency? Source data automation is the general term applied to the process of capturing data at their points of origin, so that they are in a machine-readable form. Source data automation tends to improve both the accuracy and the speed of a data processing system since it eliminates a stage in the data processing cycle that is especially prone to error: the transferring of data from the source document onto an appropriate input medium. Also, by eliminating the intermediate step of manually preparing source data for computer input, and the personnel who would normally be needed to accomplish that task, the overall cost of the data processing operation declines. The use of OCR, mark sense forms, MICR encoded documents, and bar code scanning represents efforts to introduce source data automation.

■ How can the *throughput* of an electronic data processing system be maximized? Throughput is a measure of efficiency and expresses the amount of work that passes through a computer, usually in a given interval of time. Batch processing, overlapped processing, and multiplexing tend to increase the throughput of a system. There are other methods in use. Operating system software, to be discussed in Chapter 6, also improves system efficiency.

For the convenience of the reader, some of the important statistics related to the major I/O devices and secondary storage devices discussed in this chapter are summarized in Tables 4-3 and 4-4. The ranges given are *typical* performance figures.

TABLE 4-3

Device	Type	Read/Write Speed (Data Transfer)
Card reader	Input	250–2000 cards per minute
MICR reader	Input	500–2000 documents per minute
OCR reader	Input	100–2500 documents per minute
Card punch	Output	150–500 cards per minute
Line printer	Output	250–3000 lines per minute
Nonimpact printer (electro-photographic)	Output	4000–21,000 lines per minute

TABLE 4-4

Magnetic Device	Access Time (milliseconds)	Storage Capacity (millions of bytes)	Data Transfer Rate (1000 bytes per second)
Tape	Up to several minutes	1–50	60–800
Hard disk	10–100	2–25	150–3000
Floppy disk	75–150	0.1–0.5	10–400
Drum	5–20	4–15	1000–1500

REVIEW EXERCISES

True or False?

1. Permanently sealing a hard disk within a disk drive unit is referred to as Josephson technology.
2. Flexibility in choosing type faces is an advantage most closely associated with impact printers.
3. Multiplexing implies that the associated I/O devices must have a data buffering capability.
4. Microfiche is an alternative to magnetic tape storage.
5. The unit record concept is useful in preparing data for input using a key-to-diskette data entry device.
6. OCR and MICR equipment are batch-oriented devices.
7. Multiplexing and overlapped processing are similar in concept with both improving system efficiency.
8. The first real mechanical calculator was devised by Hollerith.
9. Mass storage systems, such as the IBM 3850, are designed as an alternative to disk storage.
10. More than one I/O device may be attached to the computer using a selector channel.
11. Nonimpact printers tend to offer higher printing speeds than impact printers.
12. Magnetic drum storage has declined in importance because it is not as convenient as disk storage.
13. Impact printers tend to offer greater reliability than nonimpact printers.
14. Disk storage supports both sequential and random data access.
15. Data stored on an optical disk cannot be erased.
16. It would be accurate to describe a channel as a "minicomputer" due to its logic capability and its role in coordinating input/output operations.
17. Disks may be either removable or nonremovable from the disk drive.
18. The greater the tape density, the greater the tape's data transfer rate.
19. One disadvantage of magnetic drum storage is that it offers less storage capacity than competitive types of secondary storage devices.
20. A punch card may be used as both an input and an output medium.
21. A microcomputer system that has a Winchester disk drive must also have a floppy disk drive.
22. DASD refers to a type of printer.
23. A 132-column print line is the one most commonly encountered in business data processing.
24. A Winchester disk drive seals either a hard or a floppy disk in the disk drive unit.
25. Magnetic drum storage does not provide for off-line storage.

Multiple Choice

26. Although each of the following individuals made notable contributions to the development of data processing, which individual's ideas were consistently frustrated by the limitations imposed by the current state of technology?
    a. Pascal   **b.** Leibniz   **c.** Jacquard   **d.** Babbage

27. Which type of printer offers the greatest printing speed capability?
    a. daisy wheel   **b.** wire matrix   **c.** laser   **d.** drum

28. Which storage medium offers the slowest access times?
    a. tape   **c.** drum
    b. disk   **d.** all are about the same

29. Which of the following is *not* considered to be a disadvantage or limitation of the punch card?
    a. its dependence on the unit record concept
    b. its flexible paper-like nature
    c. the effort required in keypunching and handling
    d. its representation of data in both machine and human comprehensible form

30. Which is a direct access storage medium?
    a. magnetic disk   **c.** optical disk
    b. magnetic drum   **d.** all of these

31. Which type of printer requires specially treated paper?
    a. thermal   **c.** daisy wheel
    b. wire matrix   **d.** chain

32. Which individual is credited with the design of the first electronic computer?
    a. Hollerith   **c.** Atanasoff
    b. Mauchly and Eckert   **d.** Aiken

33. Which is *not* an advantage of MICR processing?
    a. MICR has been standardized.
    b. MICR includes an extensive character set.
    c. MICR documents serve as both a source document and an input document.
    d. MICR documents include information in both machine and human readable form.

34. Which of the following functions does a control unit *not* perform?
    a. information code conversion
    b. data buffering
    c. multiplexing
    d. standard interface

35. Data entry based on interpreting bar codes is found in:
    a. supermarkets   **c.** OCR processing
    b. banks   **d.** optical disks

36. Which of the following secondary storage media tends to be the least expensive?
    a. tape   **c.** drum
    b. disk   **d.** all are about the same

37. 1600 bpi is a common:
    a. tape speed   **c.** tape thickness
    b. tape density   **d.** tape length

38. Which is *not* true of data buffering?
  a. It provides for the temporary storage of data.
  b. It is only necessary for batch type processing.
  c. It helps to compensate for the speed disparity between the main memory and the I/O device.
  d. It is found in communicating with input devices and with output devices.

39. Which is *not* true of batch processing?
  a. Transactions are grouped and processed at one time rather than individually as received.
  b. Only punch card data may be used for batch processing.
  c. Disk storage systems are based on batch processing.
  d. Choices b and c

40. A card reader can read cards at a rate of 1800 cards per minute. Assuming that each card contains a character punch in each column, what is the maximum rate of data transfer expressed in characters per second?
  a. 2,400   **b.** 144,000   **c.** 30   **d.** none of these

41. Which of the following may improve computer system efficiency?
  a. multiplexing
  b. overlapped processing
  c. replacing a tape library by a mass storage system
  d. all of these

42. Given a tape density of 800 bpi and a tape speed of 200 inches per second, what is the rate of data transfer expressed in bytes per second?
  a. 4   **b.** 4000   **c.** 160,000   **d.** 16,000

43. Which is *not* a magnetic based medium?
  a. MICR documents   **b.** OCR documents   **c.** tape   **d.** drum

44. Given a tape density of 800 bpi, determine the length of magnetic tape required to store the data on an 80-column punch card, assuming each column contains a character punch.
  a. 10 inches   **b.** 1 inch   **c.** 0.1 inch   **d.** 0.01 inch

45. Which of the following statements is *false*?
  a. A chain printer is an example of a line printer.
  b. Nonimpact printers cannot produce multiple copies of the computer printed output during a single production run.
  c. COM is an example of soft copy.
  d. UPC codes are interpreted by special bar scanner devices.

46. Assuming a tape density of 1,600 bpi, determine the maximum storage capacity of a standard reel of magnetic tape.
  a. 46,080,000 bytes   **c.** 30,720,000 bytes
  b. 3,840,000 bytes   **d.** None of these

47. Which of the following media depends on light intensity for data to be read?
  a. punch card   **c.** OCR documents
  b. optical disk   **d.** all of these

48. Which of the following statements is *false*?
    a. COM devices may operate either on-line or off-line.
    b. A microfiche card stores the equivalent of approximately 50 pages of printed output.
    c. COM is often used because it is the least expensive of the mass storage systems.
    d. A person cannot read a microfiche card directly.
49. Which of the following access times, expressed in milliseconds, is typical for disk storage?
    a. 0.5   b. 5   c. 50   d. 500
50. Which of the following statements is *true*?
    a. A laser printer would be appropriate for use in book printing.
    b. Tape is the most widely used random access storage medium.
    c. Winchester disk drives typically have faster data access times but lower storage densities compared to conventional designs.
    d. The disk is the most widely used sequential access storage medium.

EXCURSION INTO BASIC

ACCURACY OF INPUT AND OUTPUT

A computer is relentlessly accurate. It is also an extremely literal machine which is not capable of interpreting what the programmer had in mind when preparing a list of program instructions. In preparing input for a computer, extreme care must always be exercised. Computers do not tolerate errors in spelling or punctuation, no matter how minor they may appear to the human observer. Any error that violates the grammatical principles of a programming language is referred to as a *syntax error*. The following statement contains two syntax errors:

```
10 REED A, B,
```

The keyword READ is misspelled, and there is an error in punctuation: a comma does *not* follow the last variable in a READ statement. A program that contains a syntax error cannot be executed until the syntax error is corrected. Most computers will in some manner flag or identify the syntax error or the line that contains the syntax error. It is then the responsibility of the programmer to eliminate each syntax error.

The output generated by a computer must also be scrupulously examined. Although a computer program may be free of syntax errors and produce printed results, the output may not reflect what the programmer intended. Invariably such erroneous results are due to some error in the logical planning and organization of the program. This type of error is referred to as an error in *program logic* and is usually more difficult to identify and correct than a syntax error. Any error in a program, syntax or logic, is referred to as a *bug*. The process of identifying and removing program bugs is called *debugging*.

It is the fate of a programming student to spend much of his or her time debugging programs—do not become discouraged! The most effective approach in debugging is to take *preventative* measures to ensure accurate coding. You are urged to resist the temptation of preparing hurriedly a list of program instructions and then rushing to submit the program for computer execution. Thoughtful and patient program planning and coding will yield benefits in terms of reduced debugging time and a less frustrating interaction between man and machine.

SOME EXAMPLES

Neither of the following two programs will give the results that the programmer intended:

```
10   READ A, B              10   READ A, B
20   LET P = A + B          20   LET P = A + B
30   PRINT P                30   PRINT P
40   GO TWO 10              40   GO TO 40
50   DATA 2, 5, 8, 4, 10, 5 50   DATA 2, 5, 8, 4, 10, 5
60   END                    60   END
          (a)                         (b)
```

Each program contains a different type of error. Can you locate the error in each program? Program (a) contains a grammatical error in line 40: GO TO is incorrectly spelled as GO *TWO*. Before a computer will execute a program, it must translate each program instruction into machine language. When it encounters line 40, it doesn't know how to interpret GO *TWO*. The program will *not* execute, but terminate abruptly after displaying an error message, called a *diagnostic*, such as

```
?SYNTAX ERROR
```

Some computers will specify the line number and display the message

```
?SYNTAX ERROR LINE 40
```

Program (b) does *not* have a syntax error. The program will execute, and the first sum 7 (2 + 5) will be displayed. The program will continue to run—and run, and run. As far as the computer is concerned, there is no error! The programmer, however, has made an unintentional error in line 40: the GO TO keeps transferring the control of the program back to line 40, over and over again. This type of error, referred to as a *logic error*, is more insidious than a syntax error since it remains undetected by the computer and does not necessarily result in a diagnostic error message. It is the responsibility of the programmer to identify the error (bug) in the program, and then to correct (debug) the program. Usually a manual "desk check" based on tracing the program with sample data will help locate any errors in program logic. In fact, such a desk check should always precede the keying in and running of a program.

Each of the following BASIC statements contains a *syntax* error. Identify the error and then rewrite the statement so that the error is eliminated. *Note:* The statements are unrelated to one another.

```
1.  10   READ A; B
2.  60   LET L + M = P
3.  40   DATA $5, $3.5, $8.99
4.  50   PRINT "SUM" = S
5.  30   LET P = 2(L + W)
```

```
1.  10   READ A, B
2.  60   LET L = P - M        A single variable name must ap-
    or                        pear on the left-hand side of the
    60   LET P = L + M        equals symbol in a LET statement.

3.  40   DATA 5, 3.5, 8.99    The $ may be included in the
                              PRINT statement within quotation
                              marks if the output is to be in dol-
                              lars and cents.

4.  50   PRINT "SUM =";  S    With some microcomputers the
                              semicolon is optional.

5.  30   LET P = 2 * (L + W)  An arithmetic operator must sepa-
                              rate a constant and a variable or
                              two variables.
```

BASIC Exercises

Debug each of the following programs by identifying the line or lines that contain errors and then writing the correct statements.

```
1.  10   READ L, H
    20   LET E = L + H - 2
    30   PRINT M
    40   DATA 8, 2
    50   END

2.  10   READ A, B
    20   LET P = A * C
    30   PRINT P
    40   DATA 7, 4
    50   END

3.  10   READ X, Y
    20   IF Y = 0  THEN 70
    30   LET A = X / Y
    40   PRINNT "QUOTIENT = A"
    50   GO TO 30
    60   DATA 12, 6, 4, 8, 1, 0
    70   END

4.  10   READ N
    20   PRINT "1 + 1 =";  N
    30   DATA 3
         END
```

CHAPTER

5

FLOWCHARTS AND PROBLEM SOLVING

INTRODUCTION: FLOWCHART SYMBOLS

A suggested strategy for approaching the material contained in this section might be summarized as illustrated in Figure 5-1.

This type of graphic analysis is called a *flowchart*. It is often used in the planning of a computer solution to a problem. In this chapter some standard flowcharting techniques will be examined. These methods are essential to the programming efforts of both the novice and the seasoned programmer.

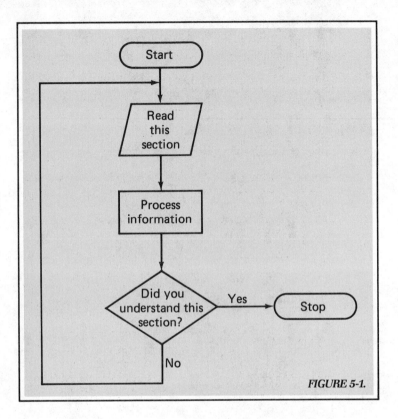

FIGURE 5-1.

WHY FLOWCHARTS?

The preparation of a computer solution to a data processing task often requires much prior thinking and planning on the part of the programmer. After all, any data processing operation, regardless of its complexity, must be reduced to a step-by-step procedure which may only involve:

- input/output operations
- arithmetic operations
- logical comparisons (decisions)
- transferring control from one step in the process to another

Each of these operations has to be performed in a planned sequence. In order to accomplish a processing task, tens, hundreds, or even thousands of program instructions may be needed. In all but the simplest operations it would be ineffi-cient (if not impossible) to plan and write simultaneously the set of language-coded program instructions designed to accomplish the task.

A flowchart provides a convenient pictorial method of planning, organizing, and articulating the computer solution to a given problem in a nontechnical form. It represents a blueprint of the logic and sequence of steps necessary to progress from the given input to the desired output. Flowcharting is based on representing basic processing operations by means of a standardized set of geometric shapes, which are independent of the particular computer or programming language being used. As a result, flowcharts provide a valuable means for describing and communicating the purpose and logic of a program to both programming and management personnel. They are also a useful tool in modifying an existing program as well as in locating a program bug (i.e., an error in program logic). Some of the basic flowcharting symbols are identified in Table 5-1.

TABLE 5-1

Flowchart Symbol	Comments	Related BASIC Keyword
Terminal symbol	Every flowchart begins and ends with this oval-shaped symbol.	END or STOP
I/O symbol	Any input or output operation is indicated using this symbol. For example, reading punch card data or printing hard copy output results would be indicated with this parallelogram-shaped symbol.	INPUT: INPUT or READ OUTPUT: PRINT
Process symbol	This rectangular-shaped symbol defines the assignment of a data value to a memory location named by a variable as a result of some processing operation. Arithmetic calculations, for example, would be represented by this process symbol.	LET
Decision symbol	The comparison of data values is indicated using this symbol. The diamond shape allows alternate program paths to be indicated, based on the results of the comparison.	IF ... THEN
Connector symbol	1. Used to connect parts of a flowchart on the same page separated due to lack of room.	1. Not applicable
	2. Used to connect segments of a flowchart in order to indicate a transfer of program control.	2. GO TO
Flow lines	Indicates the direction of program flow.	Not applicable

ANNOTATING FLOWCHART SYMBOLS

Inside the appropriate flowchart symbols, concise descriptions are written, with the flow lines and arrowheads indicating the sequence in which the tasks are performed. Figure 5-2 illustrates the computation of sales tax for a tax rate of 8%.

Notice that the same symbol, a parallelogram, is used to represent an input and an output operation. The keywords (also called *reserved words*) READ or INPUT are used to define an input operation; the keywords PRINT or WRITE are used to represent an output operation. An oval shaped symbol is used to indicate either the beginning (START) or end (END or STOP) of a processing operation. A diamond-shaped symbol encloses a decision or comparison operation, with two alternative exit paths indicated. All additional types of processing operations are enclosed by rectangles. Typically, these operations involve arithmetic calculations or the copying of data from one memory location to another.

THE DECISION BOX

It is often helpful to phrase comparison operations in the form: IF {a certain condition is true} THEN {take a specified action}; ELSE {take an alternative action}. The general format of this IF ... THEN ... ELSE structure is illustrated in Figure 5-3.

For example, the phrase "IF an item purchased is subject to sales tax THEN compute tax; ELSE tax is zero" appears in flowcharted form in Figure 5-2. The ability to express a verbal expression which involves a comparison operation in an IF ... THEN ... ELSE form will often facilitate the translation of a problem into a flowchart solution.

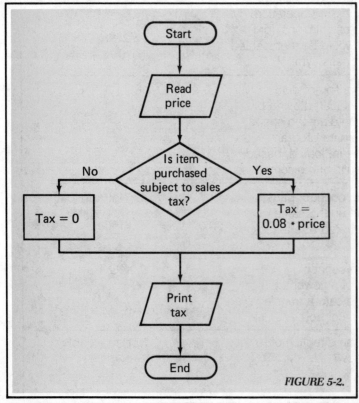

FIGURE 5-2.

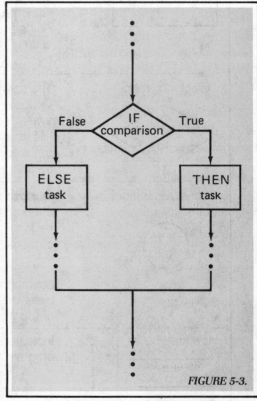

FIGURE 5-3.

THE PROCESSING BOX

All operations represented by this rectangular symbol typically result in the assignment of a data value to a memory location whose address is given by a variable name. For this reason, the process box is sometimes referred to as an *assignment box*, and the statement it encloses is referred to as an *assignment statement*.

In Figure 5-2 there are two assignment statements:

- TAX = 0 assigns the constant value 0 to the variable TAX.

- TAX = 0.08 * PRICE evaluates the expression on the right-hand side of the equal sign and then assigns the result to the variable TAX.

In each case, the previous value of TAX is obliterated by the current value being assigned to TAX. In general, assignment statements are *destructive* in the sense that a value assigned to a variable will wipe out the variable's previous value. Although a statement such as K = K + 2 is an illegal algebraic statement, it is a meaningful assignment statement. Its effect is to add 2 to the current value (contents of memory cell) K and store the result back in K. For example, suppose that before the assignment statement K = K + 2 is executed, the contents of K is 3:

After execution				Before execution
K	K	$\longleftarrow$	K + 2	K
5 ~~3~~				3

With regard to the choice of variable names, the programmer will often choose flowchart variable names which anticipate the programming language to be chosen. This eases the progression from the flowchart to the translated computer program since the same variable names may be used. As a result of this text's emphasis on the BASIC programming language, we will follow this convention by generally choosing variable names that are consistent with the most commonly used versions of BASIC. We stress that the conciseness of BASIC variable names makes the decision to use them in the discussion of flowcharts one of convenience rather than necessity. Indeed, if the flowchart is being designed for nontechnical management personnel, or if the programming language has not been specified, then the use of mnemonics (memory-aiding alphabetic abbreviations) is the logical choice.

Determine the contents of each memory cell after the following set of BASIC program statements has been executed.

```
10  LET T = 3
20  LET A = T * 2
30  LET B = A
40  LET T = 5
```

Note that line 10 stores the value 3 in memory location T; line 20 performs an arithmetic calculation, assigning the result to memory location A; line 30 copies the contents of memory cell A into memory cell B; line 40 assigns the value 5 to memory cell T,

thereby destroying its previous
contents:

Determine the output of the flowcharts illustrated in Figures 5-4 and 5-5.

1.

2.

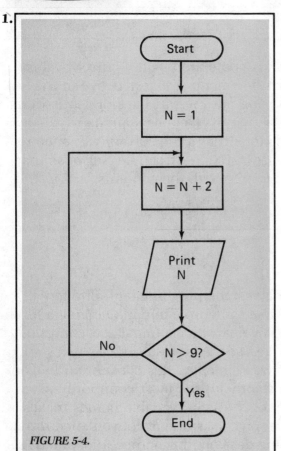

FIGURE 5-4.

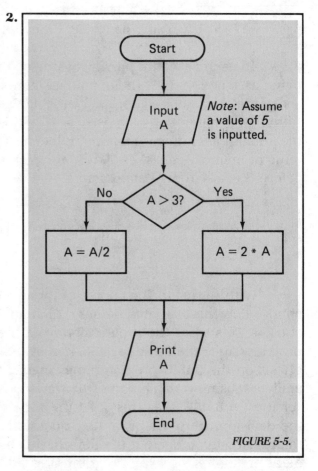

FIGURE 5-5.

1. The flowchart indicates that the value of N is initialized at 1. The assignment statement N = N + 2 adds 2 to the current value of N, which is then printed. A decision is then made: if the value of N is greater than 9 then the processing terminates; else, the flowchart loops back to the assignment statement and again increases the value of N by 2, and so on:

N	Output
1	
3	3
5	5
7	7
9	9
11	11

2. A value is inputted (say, 5). If the value is greater than 3 then the value of A is multiplied by 2 and the result is assigned to A; else, the value of A is divided by 2 and the result is assigned to A. After the value of A has been printed, the processing terminates.

Assuming the data value 5 is inputted, the output would be 10.

1. Which is *not* an advantage of flowcharts?
   a. Flowcharts are language independent and may therefore be used to communicate the purpose and logic of a program to nontechnical personnel.
   b. A flowchart facilitates the process of converting the statement of a data processing task into a set of program instructions designed to accomplish the task.
   c. Since a flowchart is easier to read then a coded set of program instructions, it can be useful in modifying an existing program which has an accompanying flowchart.
   d. A flowchart suggests the programming language that should be used.
   e. A flowchart analysis may be helpful in developing the algorithm needed to accomplish the task.
2. Name the flowchart symbol that would be used to represent each of the following tasks:
   a. to print a checking account statement
   b. to calculate the average of two data values
   c. to read three data values from a punch card
   d. to determine whether a credit account balance exceeds a given limit
   e. to terminate a program

DESIGNING FLOWCHARTS

Recall that in executing a program, the memory unit stores program instructions and data, the control unit directs computer activities so that operations are executed in their correct sequence, and the ALU performs the required data manipulations. In preparing a flowchart it may be helpful to consider the paper as the memory unit or storage area, the programmer's pen or pencil as the control unit, and the individual flowchart symbols that will manipulate the data, the ALU. Thus in designing a flowchart solution to a problem, the programmer simulates the computer activities required in order to progress from the input to the desired output.

In this section, we discuss how to design a flowchart to a programming related problem by presenting a series of examples. Our approach is based on a four-step procedure:

Step 1. *Identify* the input and output variables and assign them variable names.

Step 2. *Plan* the solution by describing the required processing in terms of an appropriate algorithm. Often the algorithm will take the form of the evaluation of a formula or of making one or more comparisons and, based on the results of the comparison, taking a specified action. In addition, variables that must be introduced to represent intermediate results in processing, and which were not identified in step 1, must be defined.

Step 3. *Draw* the flowchart.

Step 4. *Test* the flowchart by "walking" sample test data through the flowchart.

In complex programs it may be difficult to implement step 2 since the required algorithms may not be immediately obvious. In fact, this represents one of the most commonly cited weaknesses of flowcharting as a problem solving tool. Nevertheless, in such situations it is usually possible to frame a tentative outline of the method to be used and then to build the flowchart gradually. The completed flowchart then serves to define the algorithm needed to solve the problem. As one gains more experience with flowcharts, this approach is not as forbidding as it might appear to the novice programmer. Problems of such complexity, however, are beyond the scope of this introductory presentation.

ILLUSTRATIVE EXAMPLES

The following set of examples should be carefully studied. The flowcharting techniques that are illustrated can be used in planning the solutions to a wide variety of problems.

EXAMPLE 1 SOLUTION

Input three student test scores and print the average.

Step 1. Assign variable names:

X1 = 1st test score

X2 = 2nd test score

X3 = 3rd test score

AV = average

Step 2. Devise the algorithm or method by which the given data are to be manipulated systematically in order to arrive at the desired result. In this case, a simple relationship is all that is required:

$$average = \frac{sum\ of\ scores}{number\ of\ scores}$$

Step 3. Draw the flowchart. (See Figure 5-6.)

Step 4. Test the flowchart:

X1	X2	X3	AV	Flowchart Output
4	9	2	5	5

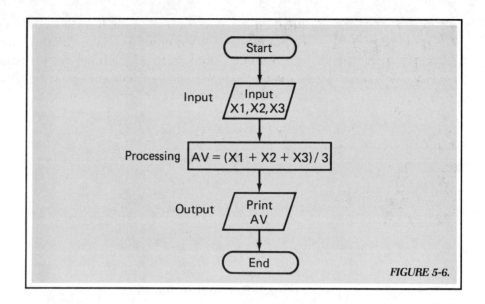

FIGURE 5-6.

EXAMPLE 2

SOLUTION

Modify the previous example so that if the average is greater than 90, the average and the message "GRADE = A" is printed; otherwise, simply print the average.

Step 1.   The revised algorithm is:

1. Input data.
2. Calculate AV.
3. Compare AV with 90. *If* AV $>$ 90, *then* print AV and the message; *else*, print only AV.
4. End.

Step 2.   Draw the flowchart. (See Figure 5-7.)
Step 3.   Test the flowchart using two data sets:

Data Set	X1	X2	X3	AV	Flowchart Output
1	90	80	70	80	80
2	90	95	91	92	92 GRADE = A

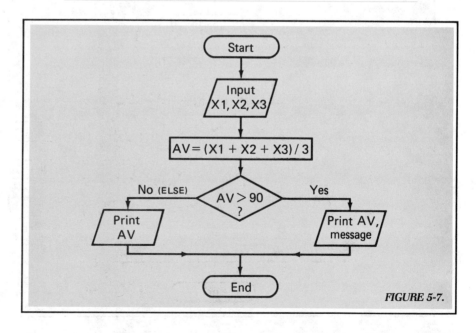

FIGURE 5-7.

EXAMPLE 3

SOLUTION

Read an employee's last name, hourly wage rate, and the number of hours worked. An employee is entitled to overtime pay at a rate of 1.5 times ("time and a half") his or her regular hourly wage rate for each hour worked in excess of 40 hours. Print the employee's name, gross pay, and overtime pay, if any.

Step 1. Assign variable names:

N$ = employee last name

W = hourly wage rate

H = number of hours worked

OP = overtime pay

G = gross pay

Step 2. Devise the algorithm:

1. Read an employee record.
2. Compare H with 40. *If* H > 40, *then* calculate overtime pay (OP) and gross pay (G) and print both; *else*, calculate simple gross pay as G = H * W and print G.
3. End.

Step 3. Draw the flowchart. (See Figure 5-8.)

Step 4. Test the flowchart using two data sets: one without overtime (H = 40) and one with overtime (H > 40):

Data Set	N$	W	H	OP	G	Flowchart Output		
1	Smith	6.00	40	0	240	Smith	240	
2	Smith	6.00	50	90	330	Smith	330	90

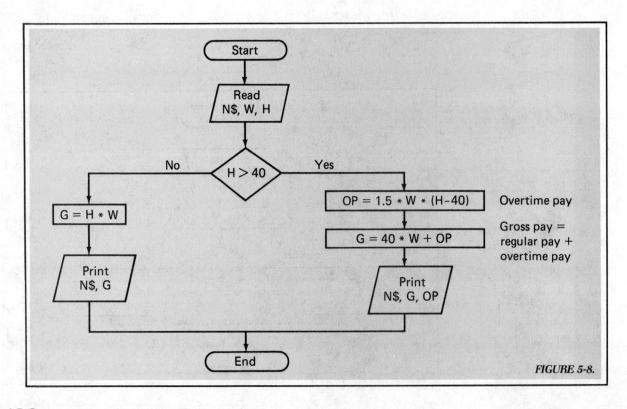

FIGURE 5-8.

The preceding example suffers from the fact that it is designed to process a *single* employee record. After the payroll calculations are completed and the results are printed for the single employee record, the program terminates. In order to process multiple employee records, all that is required is that after the processing of one record is completed, the flowchart loop back to the input symbol in order to process the next employee record. Suppose that there are 100 employee payroll records. After reading and processing the 99th record, the flowchart will loop back and read and process the 100th record; and after reading and processing the 100th record, the flowchart will loop back and ... a problem arises! We must make certain that when the program loops back there is always a record present to read. The program ends after the last employee record is read and processed. Since the programmer does not usually know the name of the last employee in the payroll file, a dummy or trailer record is inserted at the end of the file of records that is being read; it serves to alert the computer that the last record of the file has been read. The record that signals the end of a file is referred to by a variety of names, including *trailer record, program flag, sentinel record,* and *end-of-file* (EOF) record.

To create an end-of-file record, we may simply enter the characters EOF into an alphabetic field. In Figure 5-9, a trailer value has been inserted in the name field. A numeric trailer value, entered in a numeric field, may also be used. A commonly used numeric trailer value consists of a sequence of nines. Other trailer values may, of course, be selected, provided they are chosen in advance by the programmer and cannot represent actual data values; otherwise, the processing might prematurely terminate if an actual data record is encountered which contains this value in the specified field.

In processing an employee file, for example, each employee record is read, and *before* it is processed, the contents of the name field is compared with EOF. If they are the same THEN the last record of the file has been read; ELSE, the record

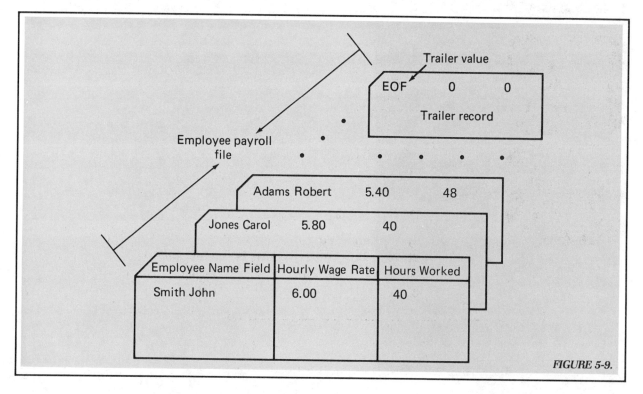

FIGURE 5-9.

represents an actual employee data record and is processed. In some programs there may be some additional processing that may be required *after* the EOF record is encountered. For example, summary totals may be printed only *after* the last record has been processed. (See Figure 5-10.)

Sometimes a numeric field will hold a value which will flag that the last data record of the file has been read. A value such as −9999 is commonly used to signal a trailer record since it would be extremely unlikely for this to be an actual data value. For example, suppose that in the previous example, an employee was identified by Social Security number rather than last name. The trailer record might then contain −9999 in the social-security-number field. The corresponding segment of the flowchart would be as shown in Figure 5-11 (SS = Social Security number).

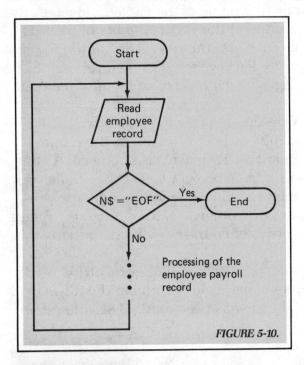

FIGURE 5-10.

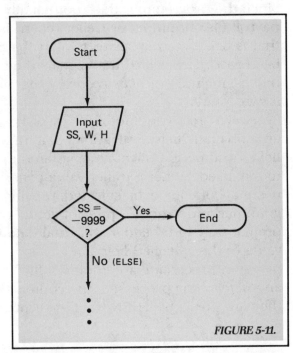

FIGURE 5-11.

Read in a series of credit account numbers and balances. Print the credit account numbers of only those accounts that are overdrawn (have a negative balance) with the message "OVERDRAWN."

Step 1. Assign variable names:

N = account number
B = account balance

Step 2. Device the algorithm:

1. Read a credit account record.
2. Check whether record is the last record. *If* N = −9999, *then* end; *else*, process the record.
3. Compare balance with 0. *If* balance is less than 0, *then* print account number and message; *else*, no action is required.
4. Go to step 1 to read next record.

Step 3. Draw the flowchart. (See Figure 5-12.)

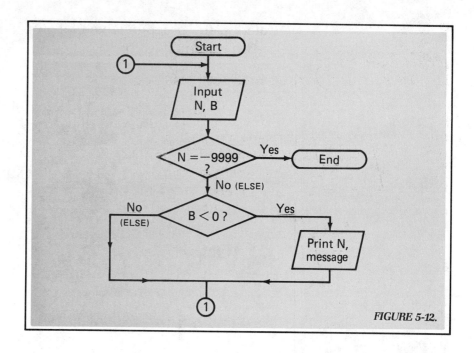

FIGURE 5-12.

Step 4. Test the flowchart by choosing representative sample test data that will test the conditions of the decision symbols. In the present example, data are chosen which include a positive and a negative value for the balance.

Record	N	B	Flowchart Output	
1	9103	315.25		
2	1562	−1.50	1562	OVERDRAWN
3	−9999	0		

HOW TO TERMINATE AN INTERACTIVE BASIC PROGRAM

In the following BASIC program the computer cues the user to enter two numbers, patiently waits for the two numbers to be entered, prints their product, and then loops back to ask the user for another pair of numbers.

```
10  PRINT "PLEASE ENTER TWO NUMBERS"
20  INPUT A, B
30  LET P = A * B
40  PRINT "PRODUCT =";P
50  GO TO 10
```

This process continues indefinitely, creating an "infinite" loop. How can the programmer provide for an appropriate exit mechanism?

In interactive programs of this type, it is common to ask "politely" the user whether he or she wishes to continue. In our example, an appropriate question would be, "do you wish to find another product?" We must also inform the user of the acceptable types of responses, say, "enter yes or no." We then compare the user's response with "YES;" if both are the same, then the program branches back to line 10; else, the program terminates. This commonly used technique is illustrated in the program which follows. (See Figure 5-13 for the corresponding flowchart.)

Corresponding BASIC Program

```
10  PRINT "PLEASE ENTER TWO NUMBERS"
20  INPUT A, B
30  LET P = A * B
40  PRINT "PRODUCT ="; P
50  PRINT "DO YOU WISH TO FIND ANOTHER PRODUCT?"
60  PRINT "ENTER YES OR NO"
70  INPUT R$
80  IF R$ = "YES" THEN 10
90  END
```

Sample Output

```
PLEASE ENTER TWO NUMBERS
? 5, 8
PRODUCT = 40
DO YOU WISH TO FIND ANOTHER PRODUCT?
ENTER YES OR NO
? NO
READY.
```

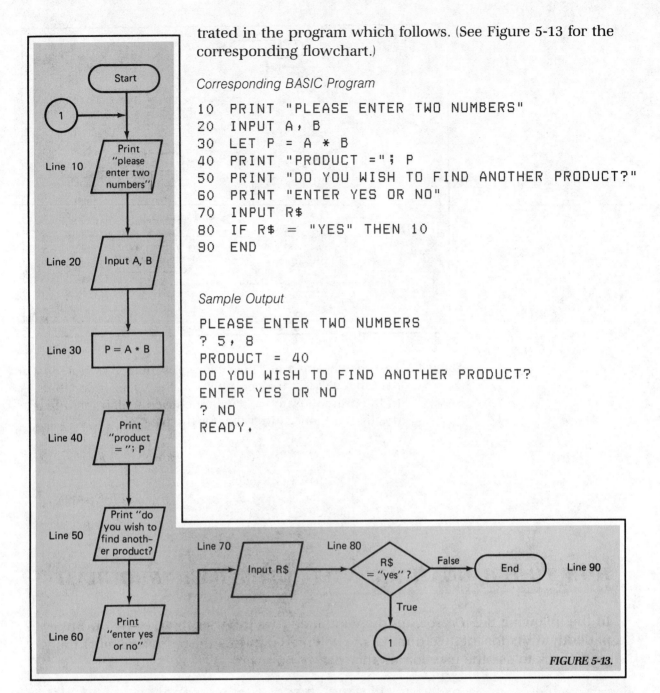

FIGURE 5-13.

Exercises

Draw a flowchart solution for each of the following problems assuming that more than a single set of data is to be processed. Include a definition of the variables used. In order to verify the correctness of the solution, make up your own sample test data and have them "processed" by your flowchart.

3. Read in two numbers. If the second number is not zero, then print their quotient; else, print the message "division by zero is not allowed."

4. Read in any nonzero number. Classify the number as negative or positive. Use zero as the trailer value.

5. Read in three unequal numbers. Print the smallest of the three numbers.

6. Read in four test scores and find the average. If the average is less than 65, then print the average and the message "FAIL"; else, print the average and the message "PASS."

7. A salesperson's gross salary consists of a base salary and a commission. The amount of the commission is based on the number of items sold and is computed as follows:

Number of Items Sold	Commission Schedule
Less than 100	$1.50 × number of items sold
Between 100 and 200	$150 + $0.75 × number of items sold
Greater than 200	$225 + $0.50 × number of items sold

Read in the salesperson's name, base salary, and the number of items sold. Print the salesperson's name, base salary, commission, and gross salary.

COUNTING AND SUMMATION LOOPS

In several examples of the preceding section, the processing was terminated by using a trailer record, with no provision for indicating the number of records that were actually processed. It is often useful to be able to ascertain and print this information. In order to accomplish this, a counting mechanism must be introduced.

AN EXAMPLE OF A COUNTING LOOP

Consider how the flowchart in Figure 5-14 would process the data 8, 5, 20, and −9999. In order to help analyze how the flowchart structures are manipulating the sample data we may use the following table:

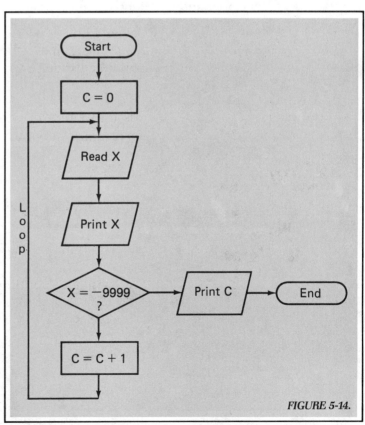

FIGURE 5-14.

Loop Repetition Number	X	C	Output	
		0		
1	8	1	8	
2	5	2	5	
3	20	3	20	
	−9999		3	The current value of C.

Notice that the effect of the program is merely to "echo" print whatever data value is read in *and* to keep count of the number of data values processed (excluding the trailer value). At the end of the processing cycle, as signaled by the trailer value −9999 being read, a count of the number of data values processed is printed. The statement C = C + 1 serves as a counter, increasing the current value of C by the constant value 1 each time the statement is executed. The new count is then stored back into memory cell C. In general, any statement of the form

$$C = C + \Box$$

may serve as a counter, where the box represents the number we wish to count by. If we wanted to count by 2, the required statement would be C = C + 2. The choice of the variable name C is immaterial, provided the same variable name appears on either side of the equal (=) sign.

Notice also that a counting loop contains three essential components:

- An *initialization* statement, which establishes the starting value of the counter. In our example, C was initialized at 0.

- An *incrementation* statement, which specifies the amount we wish to count by. In our example, C = C + 1 served as the incrementation step, with the value of C incremented (increased) by 1 each time the statement was executed.

- A *test*, which determines whether the control of the program should transfer out of the counting loop. In our example, the test X = −9999? provided the means by which the loop could be exited; if X = −9999, then the loop was terminated.

The following examples illustrate that a test of the current value of the counter may serve as a means for exiting the counting loop. This technique may be used when the exact number of data values to be read in is specified.

EXAMPLE 1 SOLUTION

Read in *exactly* five numbers and print each number.

Step 1. Assign variable names:

    X = data value

    C = counter value

Step 2/3. Devise an algorithm and draw the flowchart. (See Figure 5-15.)

Step 4. Test flowchart:

X	C	Output
	0	
5	1	5
19	2	19
11	3	11
8	4	8
7	5	7

Program terminates since C = 5.

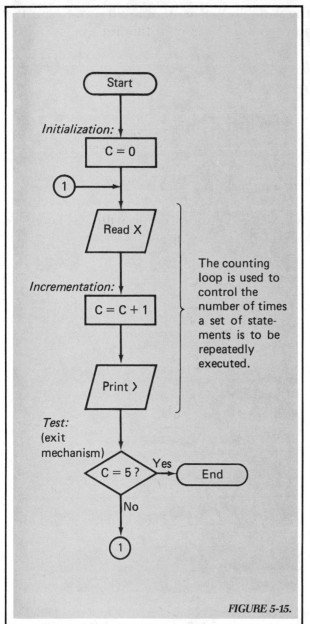

FIGURE 5-15.

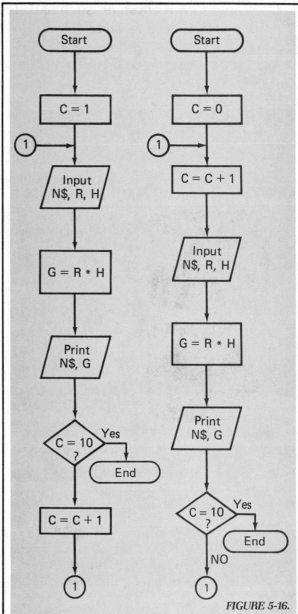

FIGURE 5-16.

EXAMPLE 2

SOLUTION

Revise the flowchart of example 3 in the preceding section so that exactly 10 employee records are processed.

Figure 5-16 illustrates two alternative solutions.

SUMMATION LOOPS

To accumulate the sum of a set of data values, it is necessary to construct a summation loop that includes a statement that will maintain a running total. The statement that accumulates the sum is similar in form to a counter, except that a counter adds a *constant* (such as 1) to the variable that is maintaining the count; a "summer" adds a *variable* amount to the variable that is maintaining the running total:

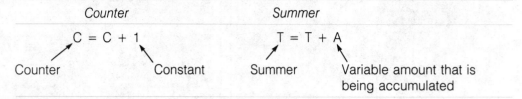

Counter	Summer
C = C + 1	T = T + A
Counter ↗ ↖ Constant	Summer ↗ ↖ Variable amount that is being accumulated

The following problem requires both a counter and a summer.

EXAMPLE 3

Read in a series of sales figures that terminates with a trailer value of −9999. Print the sum of the figures and the number of sales figures processed.

SOLUTION

Step 1. Assign variable names:

C = counter

T = sales total

S = individual sales figure

Step 2/3. Devise the algorithm and draw the flowchart. (See Figure 5-17.)

Step 4. Test the flowchart:

S	C	T	Flowchart Output
	0	0	
7	1	7	
15	2	22	
4	3	26	
−9999			3 26

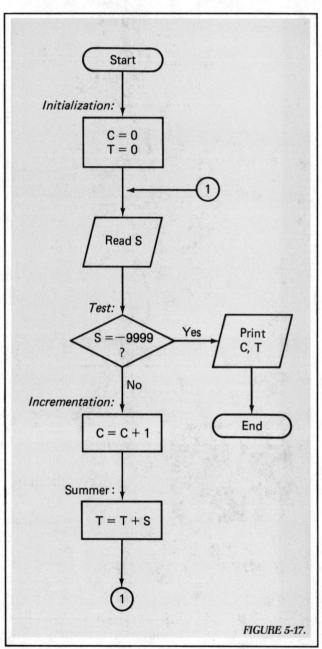

FIGURE 5-17.

136 *Flowcharts and Problem Solving*

EXAMPLE 4

SOLUTION

Read in a series of savings account transactions using a single variable name to represent either a deposit or a withdrawal. Deposits are entered as positive numbers while withdrawals are entered as negative numbers. Determine and print the sum of the deposits, the sum of the withdrawals, and the total number of transactions processed. (Use a trailer value of −9999 to terminate processing.)

Step 1. Assign variable names:

A = savings account transaction amount
C = counter
S = sum of deposits
W = sum of withdrawals

Step 2. Devise the algorithm:
If A is greater than 0, *then* S = S + A; *else* (A is less than 0), W = W + A.

Step 3. Draw the flowchart. (See Figure 5-18.)

Step 4. Test the flowchart.

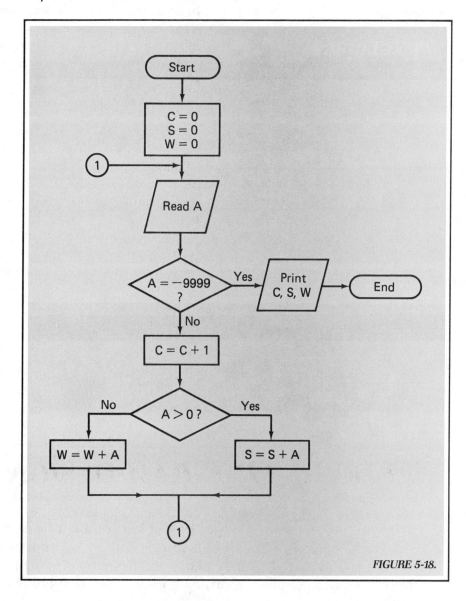

FIGURE 5-18.

A	C	S	W		Output	
	0	0	0			
100	1	100	0			
45	2	145	0			
−80	3	145	−80			
55	4	200	−80			
−70	5	200	−150			
−9999	5	200	−150	5	200	−150

A manual check shows that these are indeed the correct results.

Exercises

Draw a flowchart solution for each of the following problems. Check the logic of your solution by choosing appropriate test data and "walking them through" the flowchart.

8. Read in ten numbers and print their average.
9. Read in a series of nonzero numbers, using zero as the trailer value. Print:
   a. The *number* of negative numbers
   b. The *sum* of the positive numbers
10. A program is to be designed to read in a salesperson's ID number (4 digits), the quantity sold of an item, and its unit price. The program is to print:
    a. The salesperson's number, the quantity sold, and the value of the items sold
    b. An asterisk next to the salesperson's number if the salesperson has sold more than 100 items
    c. Summary totals of the quantity sold and the value of all items sold
11. A program is to be designed to process checking account transaction records. Each transaction record contains:
    a. the customer account number
    b. the current balance
    c. a single transaction amount
    d. a transaction code: 1 = deposit, 2 = debit, 0 = trailer record
    Determine and print:
    (1) the customer account number and the updated balance
    (2) the sum of all customer deposits
    (3) the sum of all customer debits
    (4) the total number of customer records processed

TOP-DOWN PROGRAM DESIGN

When confronted with a large complicated problem, it is often helpful to try to divide the original problem into several smaller, more manageable problems. A housewife, for example, may plan a busy day by organizing her chores for the day into three smaller tasks: morning chores, afternoon chores, and evening chores.

Under each category, she might list the corresponding set of required tasks. Her morning tasks might consist of preparing her children for school and cleaning the house. In readying her children for school, she must remember to lay out their clothes and prepare their box lunches. In cleaning the house, she must remember to clean the living room. Cleaning the living room involves vacuuming the carpet and dusting the furniture. Notice that each task may be broken down into one or more component tasks until the original task is reduced to a set of basic tasks which completely defines the solution to the original problem.

What does this have to do with programming? It is not unusual for a programming-related problem to assume such large proportions that the algorithm necessary to accomplish the desired processing task becomes obscured by the complexity of the problem. The programmer is then faced with the problem of where to begin. A flowchart may not be appropriate, since a standard flowchart analysis assumes that a significant part of the solution algorithm, if not all of it, is known at the outset. An alternative diagrammatic approach is required in which the algorithm is not necessarily known at the initial stages of problem analysis. The approach used is similar to the one taken by our housewife and is based on systematically identifying *what* tasks are to be performed rather than *how* they are to be accomplished.

The analysis proceeds by taking the original problem and, by working backwards, identifying the set of tasks that must immediately precede it, using a "tree" type of diagram. Each of these tasks is then resolved into its component tasks, and so on until the lowest-level task related to the accomplishment of the original global task is identified. A self-contained component task is referred to as a program *module*. In our housewife example, the global task would be organizing the chores for the day. The first set of modules would be the morning chores, afternoon chores, and evening chores. Under each of these modules would be another set of program modules, which would describe the particular chores required under each of these categories. (See Figure 5-19.)

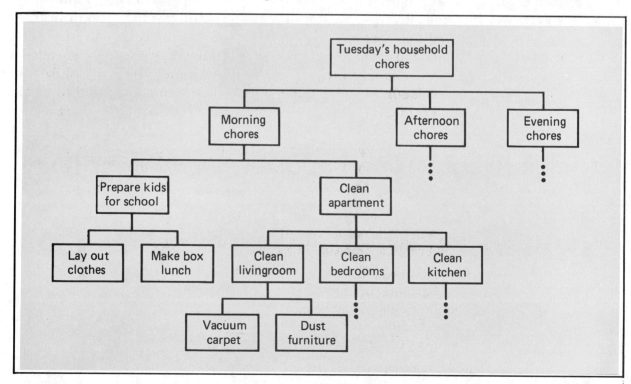

In a programming context, the global task would represent the end result or purpose of the processing. The first level of program modules would include an *input* module, a *processing* module, and an *output* module. Under each of these modules, the required tasks would be identified in a hierarchical fashion.

The pattern of program modules that unfolds as a result of this type of diagrammatic analysis is called a *structure chart* and serves to define the algorithm necessary to solve the original problem (global task). Since the solution is read from the top module to the lowest level of modules, this method of breaking down a problem into smaller, more manageable component problems is referred to as a *top-down modular design* approach. Figure 5-20 shows the general form of a struc-

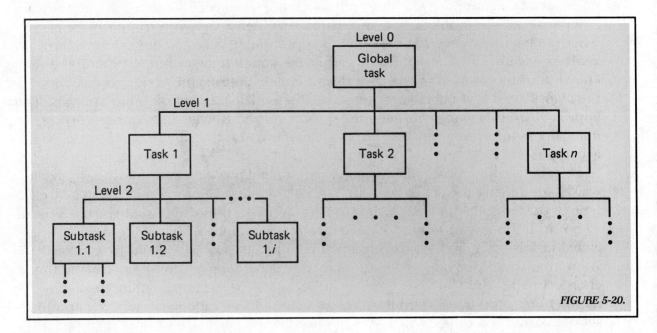

FIGURE 5-20.

ture chart. As we move from top to bottom, the levels define tasks of increasing specificity. Theoretically, we progress step by step from level to level until the problem is resolved into modules of sufficient detail so that the pattern of modules developed can be coded directly into a programming language. (This is called *stepwise refinement.*) The ability to produce and directly code from a structure chart, as well as an appreciation of its usefulness, tend to be directly related to the facility one has in the programming language into which the structure chart will be translated.

In order to aid in program planning, the structure chart shown in Figure 5-21 may be translated into an English-like *pseudocode* outline solution. Each of the modules can be further resolved into lower level component tasks.

1. Read customer data
   1.1 Read customer master record
   1.2 Read customer transaction record

2. Perform computations
   2.1 Compute sum of purchases
   2.2 Compute sum of payments
   2.3 Compute interest
   2.4 Compute updated balance

3. Write updated master record

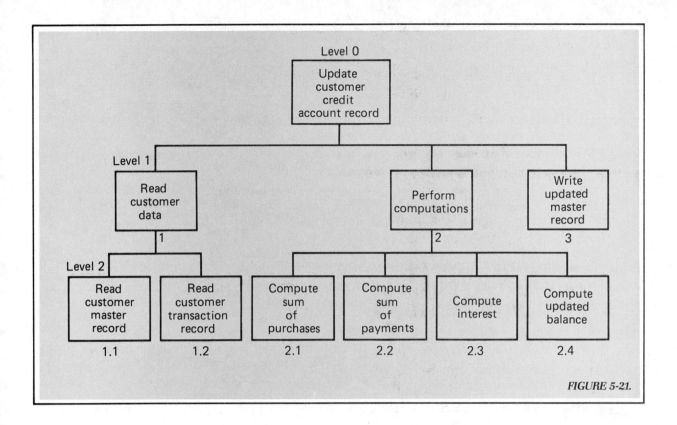

FIGURE 5-21.

There are several important advantages associated with the top-down design approach:

■ It is not necessary to specify the required algorithms in advance of the development of the structure chart which defines the program solution. Implicit in the top-down structure that evolves from this analysis are the needed algorithms.

■ The top-down design naturally divides the program into a set of individual program modules which can be independently tested and debugged. This tends to increase program reliability while decreasing the amount of time necessary to debug a program.

■ A modular design approach:

1. Allows more than one programmer to work on the development of the same programming project, thereby decreasing the time necessary to complete the project.

2. Facilitates *program maintenance*, which refers to the need to modify an existing program after it is in use, based on the changing needs of the organization which the program services.

3. Tends to minimize duplication of programming efforts. Different programs often include several of the same modules (e.g., a sort or print module). Frequently these same program modules may be readily adapted for use in a variety of programs.

■ A flowchart may have so many loops and program branches that it is decipherable only by the original programmer. Furthermore, such complicated "spaghetti-like" flowcharts are difficult to code and are a major source of error. A structure chart that results from a top-down design approach is easier to read and tends to produce fewer errors in the coding process.

There are, however, one or two minor disadvantages associated with the top-down design approach:

■ The program modules may not be truly independent as they may involve the same program variables.

■ The algorithm needed to accomplish a task given within a module may still not be obvious, and a flowchart type of analysis of that small segment of the structure chart may still prove useful. (Chapter 6 discusses the related topic of structured programming and flowcharts.)

It is generally recognized that the advantages of the top-down design approach far outweigh any disadvantages one may cite. Consequently, a structure chart analysis is used extensively in a variety of data processing applications.

PROBLEM ANALYSIS: FLOWCHARTS VERSUS STRUCTURE CHARTS

Although both flowcharts and structure charts are widely used in data processing, it has become somewhat fashionable to emphasize the disadvantages of a flowchart analysis compared to a structure chart or a pseudocode approach. However, it must be stressed that these methods share and accomplish the same two goals:

■ to provide an established and proven method for *planning before coding*

■ to supplement the resulting computer program with a language independent document that describes the logic used in the language coded program

In planning a solution to a problem, either technique can function as an extremely powerful problem solving tool. Like any tool, however, each must be correctly applied in the appropriate circumstance.

The reader at this point may be wondering which is the preferred method. Since advantages and disadvantages can be cited for each approach, the decision on which one to use is often a matter of personal preference or, in a professional setting, may be determined by the policy established by the chief programmer. Often the nature of the problem will suggest one method over another. Problems that center on the application of a computational algorithm tend to lend themselves to a flowchart analysis. Complex problems in which the algorithm is not immediately obvious can be best tackled by using a structure chart analysis in order to help identify the key component tasks and to establish their hierarchical relationships. Often a flowchart may be used to advantage in detailing how a particular module task is to be accomplished.

In order to illustrate further the differences in approach required by the two methods, the following example will be solved by offering both a flowchart and a structure chart analysis.

EXAMPLE

A certain department store uses the following coding system to indicate the method of customer payment:

1 = payment by cash or check

2 = payment by credit card

Assume for simplicity that a customer transaction record only includes the following items: customer name, amount of purchase, and the payment code. Design (1) a flowchart and (2) a structure chart which determines and prints:

a. The number of transaction records processed
b. The sum of the payments made by cash or check and by credit card
c. The total amount of customer payments

In addition, print the name and purchase amount for any amount that exceeds $500.

Assume that the trailer record has a payment code of 3, which signals the end of processing.

SOLUTION

1. Flowchart solution.
   (See Figure 5-22.)
   Definition of program variables:

P = payment code

A = purchase amount

N$ = customer name

C = count of customer transaction records

S1 = sum of payments made by cash or checks

S2 = sum of payments made by credit cards

T = total of customer payments

2. Structure chart solution.
   (See Figure 5-23.)

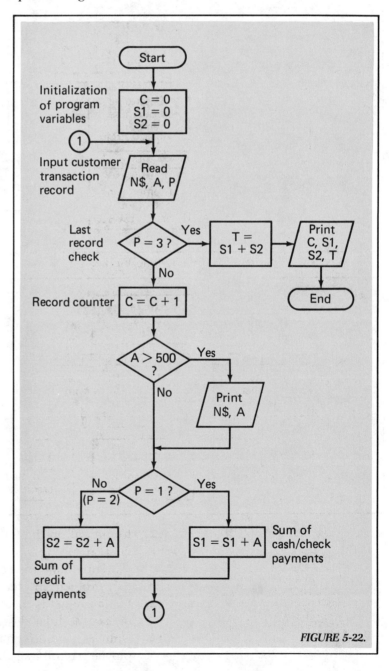

FIGURE 5-22.

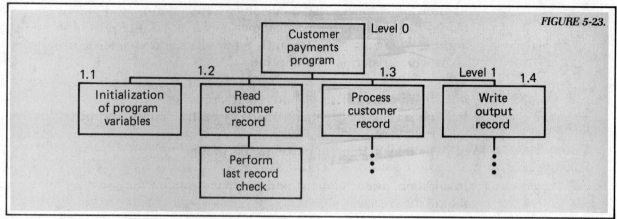

FIGURE 5-23.

We now expand module 1.3. (See Figure 5-24.)

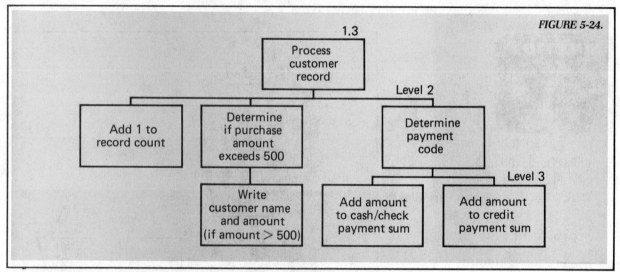

FIGURE 5-24.

We now expand module 1.4. (See Figure 5-25.)

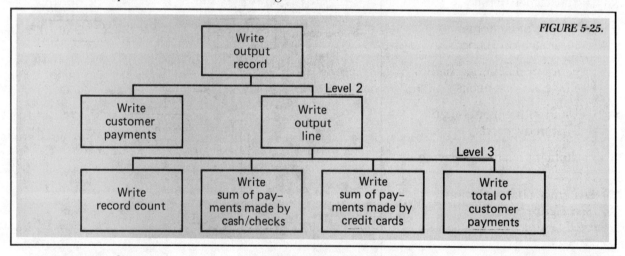

FIGURE 5-25.

Exercises

12. Comment on the following: A flowchart and a structure chart resulting from a top-down design approach are fundamentally the same since both display the solution to a problem in pictorial form.

13. Explain what is meant by *program maintenance*. How does a modular design facilitate program maintenance?

14. Draw a structure chart for producing an updated employee payroll master record. Use Figure 5-20 as a model.

MODULAR PROGRAMMING WITH BASIC

The top-down design approach is implemented in BASIC through the GOSUB ... RETURN program structure, which provides the programmer with the ability to leave the main program in order to perform a subtask and then (when the RETURN statement is encountered) to return to the point of departure in the main program. For example, the main program may require that data be first sorted before they can be processed. The set of statements designed to accomplish the sort may be written as a subprogram—a program within a program—which would be "called" by the GOSUB statement. The GOSUB control structure is illustrated in Figure 5-26.

The program illustrated in Figure 5-26 begins, as all BASIC programs do, by executing statements in line number order. When statement 100 is executed, pro-

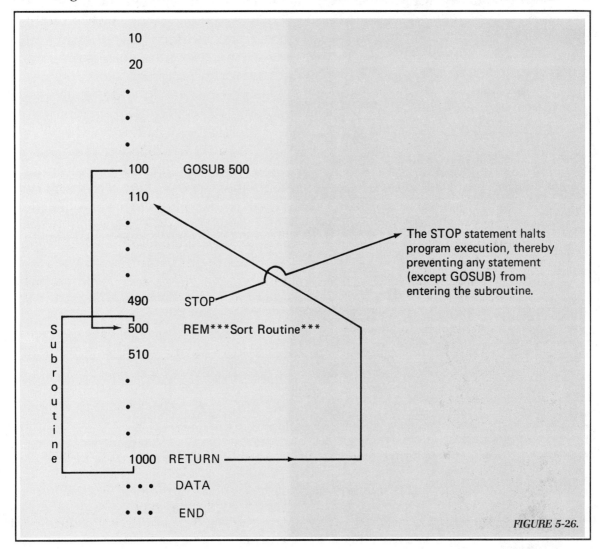

FIGURE 5-26.

Note: In Figure 5-26, the REMark statement in line 500 is added by the programmer to increase the program's readability; it is *not* executed by the computer. In this program it is used to caption the beginning of the SORT routine. In general, the REMark statement takes the form:

line no.   REM . . . .
_____
descriptive phrase or comment

gram control is automatically transferred to line 500. Line 500 is a nonexecutable statement, which merely identifies (for the benefit of the *programmer*) the purpose of the set of statements that follows. In general, the REMark statement may be freely inserted into programs in order to annotate or explain key parts of the program. This allows the program to be read easily by another programmer or by the same programmer who may, at some future date, have to refer back to the program. Frequently the REMark statement is used at the beginning of a program to identify the programmer and to define what the BASIC variables used in the program represent.

In Figure 5-26 the set of statements between 510 and 1000 is referred to as a *subroutine.* In general, a subroutine is a self-contained block of program instructions that is referenced or "called" by another statement in the program for the purpose of performing some essential component task that is required in the accomplishment of the main processing task. When line 1000 is executed, program control is automatically transferred back to the program statement whose line number immediately succeeds in value the line number of the corresponding GOSUB statement—in this case, line 110. The program then continues to execute statements in line number sequence. In order to prevent the normal program flow from entering the subroutine, a STOP statement is used in line 490.

A program may include more than one subroutine. In addition, the same subroutine may be called more than once in the execution of a program. Thus when the same set of program instructions must be repeated several times in the program, it may be written as a subroutine. Furthermore, different programs may have need for the same or similar subroutines. For example, a sort subroutine may be used in a variety of program application areas. Once written, a sort subroutine may be saved and then "plugged" into a program with little or no modification, thus saving the programmer much time and effort. To give a concrete illustration of a top-down BASIC programming solution to a problem, the following example is presented. It should be noted that the use of a subroutine in this problem is *not* essential; it merely demonstrates a programming approach and style that may prove productive in more complicated problems.

Read in a series of nonzero numbers, using zero as the trailer value. Print: 1. The number of negative numbers
2. The sum of the positive numbers.
(See Exercise 9, page 157.)

The reader should consult the flowchart drawn for Exercise 9. The actual coded solution is given in Figure 5-27. The reader will notice at once that the solution given is not of the "bare bones" type. Considerable emphasis has been placed on format, with the REMark statement being used liberally in order to give the program a self-documenting quality. This feature is essential for programs that are prepared for use in a commercial environment.

The reader should trace the program listing using the sample data supplied and verify that the output will be as follows:

```
NUMBER OF NEGATIVE NOS. = 2
SUM OF POSITIVE NOS. = 16
```

Needless to say, the program could have been written without the use of a subroutine structure and without any REMark statements. The advantages of using the REMark statement in terms of enhancing program clarity should be obvious. The value of subroutines becomes increasingly apparent as the complexity of the program increases.

```
10   REM***PROGRAM FINDS THE NUMBER OF NEGATIVE NUMBERS *******
20   REM*   AND THE SUM OF POSITIVE NUMBERS IN A GIVEN LIST ****
25   REM*                                                      *
30   REM*   PROGRAMMER: L. LEFF                                *
35   REM*                                                      *
40   REM*   VARIABLE NAMES:                                    *
45   REM*                  X = DATA VALUE                      *
50   REM*                  C = COUNTER VALUE                   *
55   REM*                  S = SUMMER VALUE                    *
60   REM*                                                      *
65   REM***INITIALIZATION OF PROGRAM VARIABLES ****************
70   LET C = 0
80   LET S = 0
85   REM***INPUT/OUTPUT OPERATIONS***
90   READ X
100  IF X = 0 THEN 130
110  GOSUB 500
120  GO TO 90
130  PRINT "NUMBER OF NEGATIVE NOS. ="; C
140  PRINT "SUM OF POSITIVE NOS. ="; S
150  STOP
155  REM
500  REM***SUBROUTINE FOR PROCESSING***
505  REM
510  IF X > 0 THEN 540
520  LET C = C + 1
530  GO TO 550
540  LET S = S + X
550  RETURN
555  REM
600  DATA 5,-2, -8, 10, 1, 0
700  END
```

FIGURE 5-27.

SUBROUTINE IN COBOL

In COBOL a subroutine is implemented through the PERFORM ... UNTIL structure:

```
     PERFORM PROCESSING-SUBROUTINE UNTIL PROGRAM-FLAG = 999.
        . . . . . .
        . . . . . .
        . . . . . .
     PROCESSING-SUBROUTINE.
```

. . . . . . } A *subroutine* is a program module consisting of a set of statements
. . . . . . } that is repeatedly executed provided the variable PROGRAM-FLAG
. . . . . . } is NOT equal to 999.

The PERFORM statement is analogous to the GOSUB statement in BASIC. The name PROCESSING-SUBROUTINE is a user-defined COBOL paragraph name (label), which corresponds to the line number that follows the BASIC GOSUB statement. When the PERFORM ... UNTIL statement is encountered, the computer will test whether the value of PROGRAM-FLAG is equal to 999. If PROGRAM-FLAG is *not* equal to 999, then program control is passed to the set of statements that make up the paragraph that has the name PROCESSING-SUBROUTINE (the paragraph name that is sandwiched between the keywords PERFORM and UNTIL). This procedure continues until PROGRAM-FLAG = 999, at which time the statement that immediately follows the PERFORM statement is executed.

In a COBOL program, all processing functions such as calculations, comparisons, and input and output operations are contained in a self-contained section of the program called the *procedure division*. The segment of a COBOL program illustrated in Figure 5-28:

■ reads SOCial-SECurity number, HOURS, and wage RATE from a CARD-IN-FILE of employee payroll records

■ multiplies HOURS by RATE, giving SALARY

■ moves SOC-SEC number and SALARY to temporary internal storage areas, called SOC-SEC-OUT and SALARY-OUT, where they await an output operation

■ writes (prints) CALCULATION-LINE-RECORD, which includes SOC-SEC-OUT and SALARY-OUT.

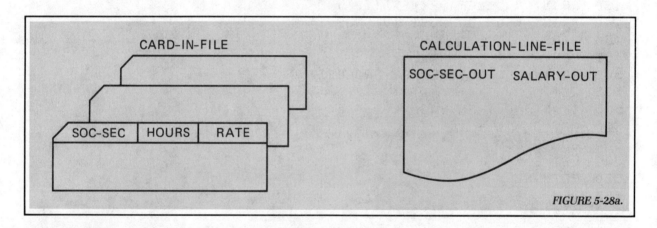

FIGURE 5-28a.

PROGRAM COMMENTARY

The procedure division begins by opening input and output files. The MOVE operation then initializes the value of PROGRAM-FLAG at 0. An employee record is then read from CARD-IN-FILE. If no card is present, the value of 999 is automatically moved to (stored in) PROGRAM-FLAG. If there is a card present, the PERFORM statement is encountered and PROCESSING-SUBROUTINE is executed.

Spaces are moved to CALCULATION-LINE-RECORD in order to blank out any characters present from a previous output operation. After salary is computed, SOC-SEC and SALARY are moved into reserved memory locations, SOC-SEC-OUT and SALARY-OUT. The CALCULATION-LINE-RECORD, which includes the fields SOC-SEC-OUT and SALARY-OUT, is then printed. The next employee record is read, and the process is repeated. If no record is present, program control is transferred to the statement which immediately follows the PERFORM statement. In our example, this statement causes input and output files to be closed. The next statement stops program execution.

The COBOL *data division* immediately precedes the procedure division and would include a definition of the record formats for CARD-IN-FILE and CALCULATION-LINE-FILE.

COBOL PROGRAM SHEET

System IBM 3083			Punching Instructions					Sheet 2 of 2
Program PAYROLL		Graphic	Ø			Card Form #		Identification
Programmer LAWRENCE S. LEFF Date 10-27-83	Punch	ZERO						73] [80

```
PROCEDURE DIVISION.
PROGRAM SEGMENT.
    OPEN INPUT CARD-IN-FILE, OUTPUT CALCULATION-LINE-FILE.
    MOVE Ø TO PROGRAM-FLAG.
    READ CARD-IN-FILE
        AT END MOVE 999 TO PROGRAM-FLAG.
    PERFORM PROCESSING-SUBROUTINE UNTIL PROGRAM-FLAG = 999.
    CLOSE CARD-IN-FILE, CALCULATION-LINE-FILE.
    STOP RUN.

PROCESSING-SUBROUTINE.
    MOVE SPACES TO CALCULATION-LINE RECORD.
    MULTIPLY HOURS BY RATE GIVING SALARY.
    MOVE SOC-SEC TO SOC-SEC-OUT.
    MOVE SALARY TO SALARY-OUT.
    WRITE CALCULATION-LINE-RECORD.
    READ CARD-IN-FILE
        AT END MOVE 999 TO PROGRAM-FLAG.
```

FIGURE 5-28b.

THE PROBLEM-SOLVING PROCESS

Generally speaking, it is *people* who solve problems, not computers. The burden of designing a computer solution to a problem rests with the computer programmer. Once the problem is solved, a coded set of program instructions can be prepared which will direct the computer to perform a sequence of steps that will lead to a computer "solution" to the problem. The complexity of many problems requires that the programmer approach problems in a systematic fashion. Flowcharting and/or preparing structure charts are a significant but small part of the overall problem-solving process. There are distinct stages in the design of a computer solution to a problem, which may be categorized as follows:

■ *Stage 1: Problem definition.*   Programmers are not always faced with a clear statement of the problem. Requests for programs are often initiated by nontechnical management personnel or field customers who describe their needs in general terms.

In this stage, the programmer seeks answers to such questions as: Do I really understand the problem or is further clarification necessary? What is given (input)? What is to be accomplished (output)? Is the problem suitable for computer solution? Is there sufficient information available to accomplish the task?

This stage seeks an unambiguous statement of the problem, flushing out any hidden assumptions or facts, while articulating its input and output requirements.

Often this part of the problem-solving process is performed by the *systems analyst*. The systems analyst may also be concerned with additional factors that may affect the nature of the solution:

1. What related hardware and software will be used?

2. Is there a strict budget that must be adhered to? Is a computer solution economically practical? (Some tasks are better handled manually.)

3. What is the time frame in which the program is to be developed? Is there an absolute deadline date?

4. Who will be using the program—a technical staff or nontechnical personnel?

Stage 2: Problem analysis and organization. The first stage focused on defining *what* the problem is. This stage is devoted to determining *how* the problem can be solved. The required algorithm is developed and specified with the help of such tools as flowcharts and structure charts.

The data structure and the format that the output is to take are also planned. The appropriate computer language to be used must also be decided upon. During this stage the systems analyst may also play an active role. (There is some overlap between the first two stages.)

Stage 3: Program coding. In this stage, the program logic developed in the previous stage is translated into a set of computer program instructions coded in a specified programming language. In order to facilitate this process, special program coding forms are available for many of the programming languages.

Stage 4: Program testing. Having a coded set of program instructions does not imply that the task has been accomplished successfully. A series of "dry runs" must be performed in order to verify that the program does indeed work as intended. During this phase, errors in program language syntax and logic show up and must be corrected.

The larger the program the more difficult it is to identify that part of the program that is producing the error. Much time can be saved if the program's structure conforms to a top-down, modular design so that as each program module is developed it can be independently tested. When an error in program logic is detected, the programmer returns to stage 2, making the appropriate modifications in the flowchart or structure chart. STAGES 2, 3, and 4 are repeated until all errors have been eliminated.

Stage 5: Program documentation. The finished product must be suitably packaged so that a person who was not involved in the problem-solving process can fully understand the nature and logic of the program. Program documentation typically includes:

1. An overview of the program consisting of a general description of the purpose of the program, the programming language used, the hardware it is designed to be run on, and any special features of the program

2. A user's manual, detailing practical aspects related to how the program is to be used, including the required data types and input formats, options in output formats, and any special limitations imposed by the program

3. A thorough explanation of the logic used in the design of the program, supported by flowcharts, structure charts, program listings, and sample test runs

A properly documented program attests to its reliability and is essential for effecting subsequent program maintenance. Although program documentation has been listed last, it should be emphasized that program documentation is an ongoing process, requiring attention at every stage of program analysis, development, and implementation.

SOME ADDITIONAL PROBLEM-SOLVING TOOLS

In conjunction with the structure charts discussed earlier in this chapter, another document, referred to as an *input–process–output* (IPO) chart, is commonly used. The structure chart is particularly useful in outlining the program solution. The IPO chart, on the other hand, focuses on the processing details associated with each program module. An IPO chart:

▪ Provides an additional and more detailed form of program documentation

▪ Facilitates the detailing of the processing needed for each program module by identifying the required input and processing as well as the resulting output

Figure 5-29 illustrates a typical IPO chart, which documents the READ CUSTOMER DATA module that appears in level 1 of the structure chart given in Figure 5-21. A set of documents that includes a structure chart and the related IPO charts is often referred to as a HIPO package (hierarchy–input–output–processing).

I P O Chart		
Programmer: L. LEFF	Program: UPDATING CREDIT ACCOUNT	Date: May 5, 1983
Level: I	Module: READ CUSTOMER DATA	Page 3 of 10
Input	Processing	Output

1. Master customer record.	1. Read master record and assign variable names to
	  a. customer account no.
	  b. previous account balance
		1. Variable amounts for purchases, payments, and previous balance

2. Customer transaction record.	2. Read transaction record and assign variable names to:
	  a. customer account no.
	  b. customer payments.
	  c. customer purchases.
	
	3. Verify master and transaction records match. If not, print an error message.
		2. An error listing

FIGURE 5-29.

DECISION TABLES

Most programs involve one or more decisions. When the pattern of logical comparisons becomes complex and the resulting outcomes are difficult to identify, a *decision table* is often used *in addition to* flowcharts and/or structure charts. A decision table organizes the comparison conditions (IF . . .) and the resulting actions (THEN . . .) of a series of decisions using a compact table format. Within the borders of a rectangular box, a decision table vertically lists the set of conditions to be tested followed by the corresponding set of actions. The conditions may all be true, each may be false, or some may be true while others are false. All possible combinations of true conditions, called *rules*, are indicated in an adjacent set of vertical columns. (See Table 5-2.)

Notice that in Table 5-2 a Y is entered if an indicated condition is true; the associated action is then indicated by an entry of the letter X. An N is usually entered if the condition is *not* true, in which case no entry is made in the action that corresponds to that condition. The corner of the table that consists of the comparison conditions is called the *condition stub*; the area of the table that includes the corresponding set of actions is the *action stub*. The table section that is reserved for the Y/N entries, which indicate whether a condition is true or not true, is referred to as the *condition entry*; the region of the table in which the actions to be taken are denoted by an X is called the *action entry*. A vertical column of Y/N entries in the condition entry section is referred to as a rule. In order to identify a particular rule, rules are sequentially numbered beginning with the number 1.

TABLE 5-2

		Rules				
	Table Description	1	2	3	4	. . .
Condition stub	Condition a	Y	N	Y		
	Condition b	N	Y	Y		
	. . . . . .					
Action stub	Action a	X				
	Action b		X			
	Action c			X		
	. . . . . .					

Condition entry (condition a, condition b rows) — Action entry (action a, b, c rows)

Note   The table indicates that if condition a is true, then action a is to be taken; if condition b is true, then action b is taken. If condition a and condition b are true, then action c is taken.

Table 5-3 illustrates a decision table designed to analyze the necessary decisions and actions required in comparing two data values, A and B.

TABLE 5-3

Decision Table for Comparing Data Value A with Data Value B	Rules		
	1	2	3
A > B?	Y	N	N
A < B?	N	Y	N
Print A greater than B	X		
Print A less than B		X	
Print A equals B			X

EXAMPLE

Construct a decision table that defines the decisions and actions required in the following situation: A person's account number, unpaid credit card account balance, and credit limit are inputted. The interest charges are calculated as follows:

Balance	Interest Charges
500 or less	1.5% of balance
Greater than 500	$7.50 + 1% of balance in excess of 500.

In addition, if the unpaid balance exceeds the person's credit limit, a warning message is printed. (Each person's credit limit exceeds $500.)

SOLUTION

If the balance is less than or equal to $500, *then* the interest is equal to 0.015 * balance; *else*, the interest is equal to $7.50 + 0.01 × (balance * 500).

Decision Table for Credit Account	Rules		
	1	2	3
Balance 500 or less?	Y	N	N
Balance greater than 500?	N	Y	Y
Balance greater than credit limit?	N	N	Y
I = 0.015 * balance	X		
I = 7.5 + 0.01 * (balance − 500)		X	X
Print warning message			X

When used in conjunction with flowcharts, decision tables can greatly assist the programmer in anticipating the necessary program decision structures. There are, however, certain disadvantages associated with decision tables:

■ Unlike with flowcharts, a direct translation from the decision table to the corresponding coded set of program instructions cannot be made.

■ As the number of decisions to be made increases, the table becomes increasingly unwieldy, with the number of rules (Y/N columns) increasing exponentially (generally, 2 raised to the power that represents the number of decision conditions). Often, however, this disadvantage may be minimized by a careful examination of the validity of each rule. It may happen, for example, that rules may be redundant, or the Y/N entries in a rule may establish contradictory conditions so that the rule is invalid and need not be included in the decision table. In fact, the decision table used for the preceding credit account problem was "collapsed" from a table having potentially eight rules to the table used, which has three rules. The five rules that were omitted each represented a contradictory condition:

Decision Table for Credit Account Example	Rules							
	1	2	3	4	5	6	7	8
Balance 500 or less?	Y	N	N	Y	N	Y	Y	N
Balance greater than 500?	N	Y	Y	Y	N	N	Y	N
Balance greater than credit limit?	N	N	Y	N	Y	Y	Y	N
. . . .								
. . . .								

Note that in rule 4 there is a logical contradiction—the balance cannot be greater than 500 and 500 or less at the same time. This rule can be omitted from the table. The remaining entries for rules 5, 6, 7, and 8 also lead to contradictory conditions.

SYSTEM FLOWCHARTS

In order to facilitate the analysis or modification of an existing system, or to aid in the design of a new system, it is often helpful to be able to diagram the flow of information through a system. The person in a business organization generally responsible for undertaking this type of analysis is the systems analyst. In addition to designing a system, the systems analyst often serves as an interface between management personnel and the programming team responsible for implementing the electronic data processing requirements of the system.

Although program and system flowcharts both define a process using an ordered sequence of geometric shapes, they are fundamentally different in concept and purpose. A program flowchart focuses on the logic necessary to accomplish a processing task, reducing each task to its elemental steps, which can then be translated into a computer solution. Each program flowchart symbol corresponds to a *single* logical operation. System flowcharts trace the movement of information through an organization, concentrating on identifying which data processing operations are required rather than on how they are to be performed. In contrast, a program flowchart details how a specific processing task is to be accomplished. Although a sorting operation, for example, encompasses a number of individual logical operations, a sorting task is represented by a *single* system flowchart symbol. Figure 5-30 displays some commonly used system flowchart symbols.

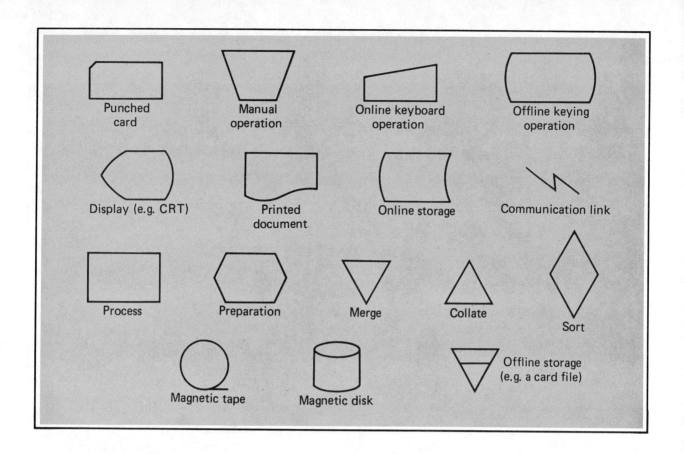

Punched card
Manual operation
Online keyboard operation
Offline keying operation

Display (e.g. CRT)
Printed document
Online storage
Communication link

Process
Preparation
Merge
Collate
Sort

Magnetic tape
Magnetic disk
Offline storage (e.g. a card file)

EXAMPLE 1

In a certain business organization all employees are required to punch a time card. At the end of each work week, a payroll secretary collects the time cards, and then keypunches and verifies the relevant data. The punch cards are then brought to the data processing department which sorts the cards and then processes the payroll job, thus producing payroll checks and an updated employee payroll master tape file. Draw a system flowchart which summarizes the major aspects of this process.

SOLUTION

See Figure 5-31.

EXAMPLE 2

When a person makes a credit card purchase in a store, the sales clerk is required to phone the credit card service bureau in order to get an authorization. Before it gives the authorization, the credit card service bureau must first verify that the account's balance has not exceeded its maximum value. Draw a system flowchart that describes the major aspects of this process.

SOLUTION

See Figure 5-32.

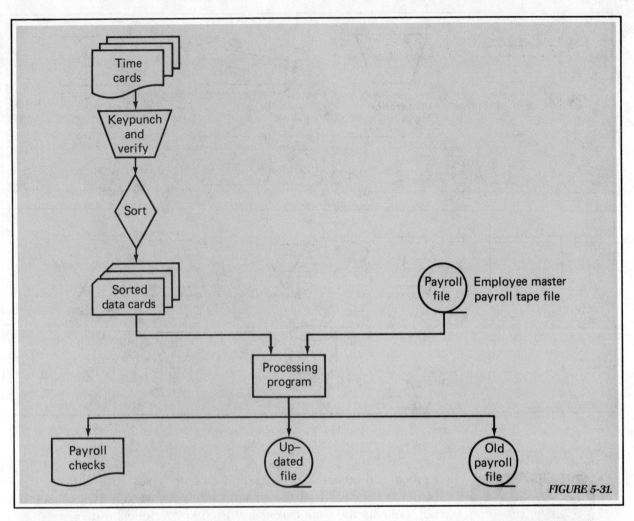

FIGURE 5-31.

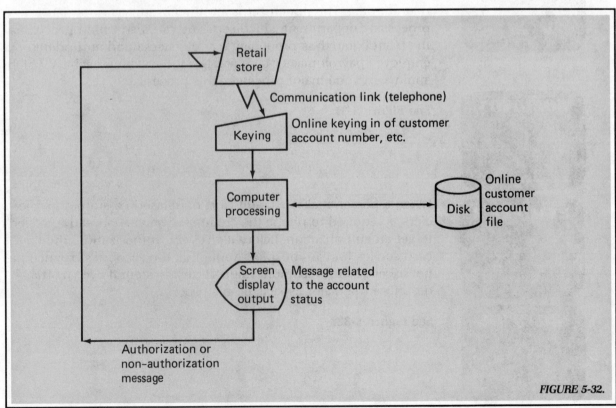

FIGURE 5-32.

REVIEW EXERCISES

True or False?

1. A flowchart is intended for use only by the programmer.
2. An IPO chart is a form of program documentation.
3. Input and output operations are indicated using the same flowchart symbol.
4. A counter would be inserted in a diamond-shaped flowchart symbol.
5. A weakness of decision tables is that they cannot be translated directly into a corresponding set of program statements.
6. If the test for a trailer value yields a "false" result, then the current record is processed.
7. Program maintenance refers to providing a safe location for programs.
8. Program flowcharts and system flowcharts both describe data processing functions in terms of geometric shapes.
9. In a structure chart, as the level number increases, the complexity of the task increases.
10. A flowchart analysis is sometimes used to supplement a structure chart.
11. A structure chart type of problem analysis may be loosely described as a "divide and conquer" approach.
12. Flowcharts tend to be geared to a specific programming language.
13. Structure charts feature different geometric shapes in order to represent specific data processing functions.
14. The preparation of program documentation is the final step in the computer problem-solving process.
15. Flowcharts define which tasks are to be performed while structure charts describe how the tasks are to be performed.
16. The major purpose of a system flowchart is to identify the personnel responsible for performing a specific data processing task.
17. In general, the more complete the documentation of a program, the greater the reliability of the program.
18. A processing operation represented by a single system flowchart symbol would usually be represented by several program flowchart symbols.
19. In general, a system flowchart would be more useful to management personnel than a program flowchart.
20. The assignment statement N = 2 * N has the effect of counting by 2.

Multiple Choice

21. Which of the following accumulates the sum of RECEIPTS and designates the running total as TOTAL?
    a. RECEIPTS = TOTAL + RECEIPTS
    b. TOTAL = TOTAL + RECEIPTS
    c. RECEIPTS = RECEIPTS + 1
    d. TOTAL = TOTAL + 1

22. Which of the following is generally associated with top-down design?
   a. flowchart   **c.** program documentation
   b. structure chart   **d.** computer circuit
23. Which is not an advantage of structure charts?
   a. modular design
   b. language independence
   c. its identification of which functions are to be performed
   d. its development of how the tasks are to be performed
24. Which is not considered part of problem definition?
   a. clarifying the requirements of the problem
   b. determining whether the problem is suitable for computer solution
   c. determining the programming language to be used
   d. determining whether a computer solution is economically feasible
25. Which of the following lists the correct sequence of events in the problem-solving process?
   a. program documentation; problem definition and analysis; program coding; program testing
   b. problem definition and analysis; program coding; program testing; program documentation
   c. problem definition and analysis; program documentation; program coding; program testing
   d. none of these

Draw a flowchart solution to each of the following problems. Check the logic of your solution by "walking through" appropriate test data.

26. Find the difference between the largest and smallest data values in a set of data values having -9999 as a trailer value.
27. Find the sum of all integers between 1 and 100, inclusive.
28. A data list contains only zeros and ones, except for a trailer value of -9999. Determine the number of ones and the number of zeros in the list.
29. The formula to convert degrees Celsius (C) into degrees Fahrenheit (F) is given by the formula: $F = 1.8C + 32$. Read in exactly five Celsius temperatures. Print the equivalent Fahrenheit temperatures and the messages "BELOW FREEZING" if F is less than 32; "FREEZING" if $F = 32$; and "ABOVE FREEZING" if F is greater than 32.
30. Find the sum of all *odd* integers between 15 and 99, inclusive.
31. Read in a series of student records containing each student's last name and three test scores. Print:
   1. Each student's name and test average
   2. The name of the student who has the highest average
32. Find the smallest integer value of N such that the sum of the terms in the series:

$$1 + \frac{1}{2} + \frac{1}{3} + \frac{1}{4} + \ldots + \frac{1}{N}$$

exceeds 4.

33. Alphanumeric data may be compared as follows: An A is considered to be less than a B; a B is considered to be less than a C; and so on. Names may be compared in like fashion:

"ALLAN" < "BARRY"   since A < B.

"MARK" < "MARY"   since the first three letters are identical, the fourth letters are compared, and K < Y.

"JOHN" < "JOHNSON"   since a blank following N in JOHN is considered to be less than any letter.

Read in three last names and print the name that would come first if the names were to be arranged in alphabetical order.

34. Read in three unequal numbers. Print the numbers in ascending order, from the smallest to the largest value.

35. Construct a decision table that describes the decisions necessary to determine the largest of three unequal numbers.

36. Construct an IPO chart for the *perform computations* module that appears in level 1 of the structure chart presented in Figure 5-21.

37. A savings bank maintains three on-line key entry devices for tellers to use in posting customer savings account transactions. Each customer transaction generates two outputs: a passbook entry and an updated customer savings account record that is maintained on disk. Draw a system flowchart that describes what actions are taken when a customer presents a teller with a savings account transaction.

 # EXCURSION INTO BASIC

PROBLEM-SOLVING USING THE BASIC PROGRAMMING LANGUAGE

In this section, we illustrate through a series of examples how to design a computer solution to a problem using the BASIC programming language.

EXAMPLE 1 One inch is equivalent to 2.54 centimeters. Given any number of inches, determine the equivalent number of centimeters.

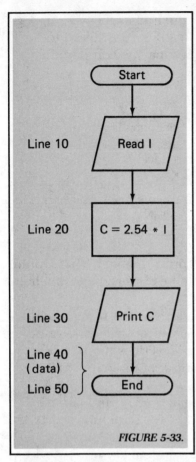

Line 10 — Read I

Line 20 — C = 2.54 * I

Line 30 — Print C

Line 40 (data)
Line 50 — End

FIGURE 5-33.

Step 1. Analyze.

Input:	I = number of inches
Output:	C = number of centimeters
Processing:	C = 2.54 * I

Step 2. Draw a flowchart. (See Figure 5-33.)
Step 3. Code the BASIC solution:

```
10   READ I
20   LET C = 2.54 * I
30   PRINT C
40   DATA 10
50   END
```

Step 4. Walk sample test data through program.

I	C	Output
10	25.4	25.4 ✓

Step 5. Run and debug program, if necessary. (Compare with expected output obtained in step 4.)

Refine the previous program so that a *series* of measurements expressed in inches is converted into centimeters.

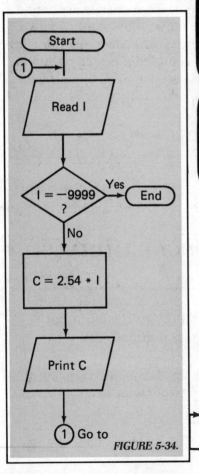

FIGURE 5-34.

Step 1. Analyze. A trailer value must be used, say, −9999.
Step 2. Draw a flowchart. (See Figure 5-34.)
Step 3. Code the BASIC solution. Translate the flowchart symbols, moving down vertically. When the decision symbol is encountered, follow the *No* branch.

```
10   READ I
20   IF I = -9999 THEN . . .
30   LET C = 2.54 * I
40   PRINT C
50   GO TO 10
60   DATA 10, 50, -9999
70   END
```

Fill in line number after all the program statements have been coded.

Now return to line 20, and enter line 70 following the THEN clause.

Step 4. Walk sample test data through the program.

I	C	Output
10	25.4	25.4
50	127	127
−9999	↓	Program ends

Step 5. Run and debug program, if necessary. (Compare with expected output obtained in step 4.)

Modify the previous program so that if the number of inches is greater than 100, the measurement is converted into *meters*, rather than centimeters. (1 inch = 0.0254 meter.)

Step 1. Analyze. *If* I > 100, *then* meters = 0.0254 * I; *else*, centimeters = 2.54 * I.

Step 2. Draw a flowchart. (See Figure 5-35.)

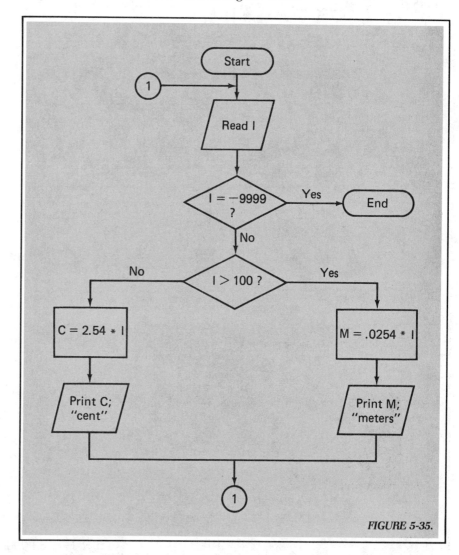

FIGURE 5-35.

Step 3. Code the BASIC solution. We follow the flowchart vertically down, following the NO branches and then returning to provide for the YES branches.

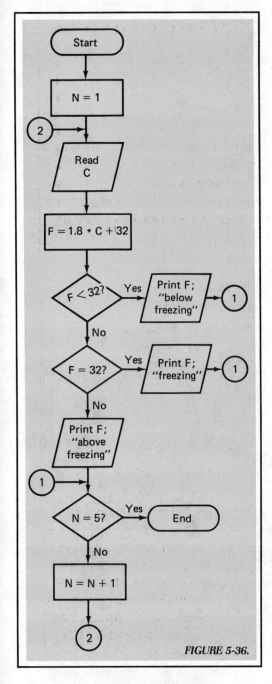

FIGURE 5-36.

```
                    10    READ I                     ┌─►110
                    20    IF I = -9999 THEN ...
                    30    IF I > 100 THEN ...
              ┌─ 40    LET C = 2.54 * I    └──►70
    Code    ─┤  50    PRINT C; "CENTIMETERS"
 NO branch    └─ 60    GO TO 10

              ┌─ 70    LET M = 0.0254 * I
    Code    ─┤  80    PRINT M; "METERS"
 YES branch   └─ 90    GO TO 10

              ┌─ 100   DATA 10, 100, 500, -9999
              └─ 110   END
```

Now return to lines 20 and 30 to fill in the line numbers following the THEN clause (lines 110 and 70, respectively).

Step 4. Test program by walking data through the program.

I	C	M	Output
10	25.4		25.4 CENTIMETERS
100	254		254 CENTIMETERS
500	↓	12.7	12.7 METERS
-9999	↓	↓	Program ends

Step 5. Run and debug program, if necessary. (Compare with expected output obtained in step 4.)

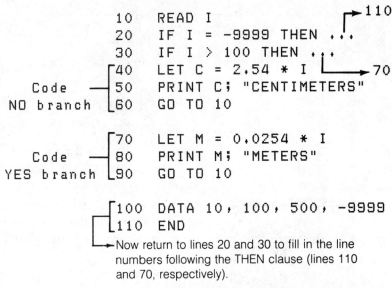

The formula for convert degrees Celsius (C) into degrees Fahrenheit (F) is given by the formula: F = 1.8C + 32. Read in exactly five Celsius temperatures. Print the equivalent Fahrenheit temperature *and* the message: "BELOW FREEZING" if F is less than 32; "FREEZING" if F = 32; "ABOVE FREEZING" if F is greater than 32. (This is Exercise 29 of the Review Exercises, page 158.)

Step 1.
Input	C = Celsius temperature
Output	F = Fahrenheit temperature
Processing	1. Construct a counting loop to read in the five Celsius temperatures.

2. Calculate the corresponding Fahrenheit temperatures using:

$$F = 1.8 * C + 32$$

3. Compare F with 32:
   a. *If* F < 32, *then* print "BELOW FREEZING"
   b. *If* F = 32, *then* print "FREEZING"
   c. *Else,* print "ABOVE FREEZING"

Step 2. Draw a flowchart. (See Figure 5-36.)

Step 3. Code the BASIC solution.

```
10    REM***CENTIGRADE TO FAHRENHEIT CONVERSION ****************
20    REM                                                       *
30    REM          PROGRAMMER:  L. LEFF    DATE:  04-18-83       *
40    REM                                                       *
50    REM          COMPUTER:  COMMODORE PET 4032N                *
60    REM                                                       *
70    REM          VARIABLE NAMES:                               *
80    REM                                                       *
90    REM                    C = CENTIGRADE TEMPERATURE          *
100   REM                    F = FAHRENHEIT TEMPERATURE          *
110   REM                    N = COUNTER                         *
120   REM ****************************************************
125   REM
130   LET N = 1
140   READ C
150   LET F = 1.8 * C + 32
160   IF F < 32  THEN . . .
170   IF F = 32  THEN . . .
180   PRINT F; "ABOVE FREEZING"
190   REM***LAST RECORD TEST FOLLOWS***
200   IF N = 5 THEN . . .
210   LET N = N + 1
220   GO TO 140
230   PRINT F; "BELOW FREEZING"
240   GO TO 190
250   PRINT F; "FREEZING"
260   GO TO 190
270   DATA 100, -15, 40, 0, -35
280   END
```

Notice that the line numbers following the THEN clause in program statements 160, 170, and 200 have been intentionally omitted. This parallels the procedure actually followed in translating the flowchart into coded program statements: the statements are generally coded from flowchart symbols progressing from one flowchart symbol to the next in linear fashion. Program branch line numbers are temporarily omitted until the corresponding task has been coded and assigned a line number. Lines 160, 170, and 200 should read as follows:

```
160   IF F < 32   THEN 230
170   IF F = 32   THEN 250
200   IF N = 5    THEN 280
```

Step 4. Test the program using sample test data. Notice that values have been included in the DATA statement which test each of the program branches:

N	C	F	Output
1	100	212	212 ABOVE FREEZING
2	−15	5	5 BELOW FREEZING
3	40	104	104 ABOVE FREEZING
4	0	32	32 FREEZING
5	−35	−31	−31 BELOW FREEZING
			Program terminates

Step 5. Run and debug program, if necessary. (Compare with expected output obtained in step 4.)

BASIC
Exercises

In Exercises 1 and 2, code the solutions to each of the following exercises, which appeared as Review Exercises, page 158.

1. Exercise 26
2. Exercise 32

The INTeger function always takes a number and rounds down to the largest integer less than or equal to the number inside the parentheses (called the argument of the function):

INT(3)	= 3
INT(2.99)	= 2
INT(0.75)	= 0
INT(12/3)	= INT(4) = 4
INT(14/5)	= INT(2.8) = 2

The INTeger function may be used to determine whether one number is divisible by another number:

$$\left. \begin{array}{l} \text{INT(15/3)} = \text{INT(5)} = 5 \\ \underline{} \text{equal} \underline{} \end{array} \right\} \text{15 is divisible by 3.}$$

On the other hand,

$$\left. \begin{array}{l} \text{INT(3/2)} = \text{INT(1.5)} = 1 \\ \underline{} \text{unequal} \underline{} \end{array} \right\} \text{3 is } not \text{ divisible by 2.}$$

In general, *If* INT(N/I) = N/I, *then* number N is divisible by number I.

3. Read in a series of whole numbers that terminates in a trailer value of −9999. Determine the number of even numbers in the list and the number of odd numbers in the list. In addition, print the total number of data values read.
4. Read exactly five pairs of whole numbers. For each pair of numbers, print whether the second number is divisible by the first number.
5. Input a decimal number and print the number rounded off to the nearest whole number.

D SOFTWARE SYSTEM

PROGRAMMING LANGL

AGES AND SOFTWARE

SYSTEMS PROGRAMMI

LANGUAGES AND SOFT

CHAPTER

6

PROGRAMMING LANGUAGES AND
SOFTWARE SYSTEMS

PROGRAMMING LANGU

D SOFTWARE SYSTEMS

STRUCTURED PROGRAMMING

As we entered the third computer generation, a somewhat alarming trend began to emerge. Progress in software development began to lag noticeably behind the technological advances realized in hardware development. This was reflected by a proportionately larger share of the economic budget of a computer installation being devoted to the development and maintenance of software. Experts in the field attributed this, in large part, to the unscientific manner in which programmers approached the programming process. Studies revealed that programmers tended to begin the coding process before having adequately analyzed and planned the solution. This resulted in program testing and debugging occupying a disproportionate amount of a programmer's workday. Poor programming habits had developed as a result of the lack of industry-wide standards in programming methods and approaches. It was not surprising to find that the programs being produced in this environment were unreliable, difficult to debug, and written in an individualized programming style, which tended to decrease program clarity. Differences in programming style created major problems in the area of program maintenance, since the programmers assigned to modify an existing program were often not the authors of the original program.

In direct response to these problems, the concept of *structured programming* evolved. The overall goal of structured programming is to maximize the productivity of a programmer by placing increased emphasis on program planning and documentation. This is accomplished by imposing a set of strict guidelines on the structure of a program. The use of clever or "cute" programming tricks, for example, is *not* encouraged. Instead, a major objective of structured programming is to have programs written by different programmers in a given language to look the same. This attempt to standardize programming style is sometimes referred to as "egoless" programming. To accomplish this, structured programming seeks to restrict the programmer to the planned application of only three types of program statement sequences. All data processing tasks, regardless of how complex, must be reduced to combinations of the following three fundamental types of program sequences:

1. A *simple sequence* of statements to be executed as a block, one statement following the other in consecutive fashion.

2. A *selection sequence* in which a logical comparison is made and one of two possible program paths is selected based upon the results of the comparison. This is sometimes referred to as the IF/THEN/ELSE structure.

3. A *repetition sequence* in which the same set of statements is repeatedly executed within a looping structure, provided a test condition is satisfied. This pattern is sometimes referred to as a DO WHILE structure.

Figure 6-1 illustrates the three fundamental control sequences. Computer scientists C. Bohm and G. Jacopini established that any program solution can be defined using only these three control structures. A simple sequence consists of one or more statements that are executed in the order in which they are written. (See Figure

6-1a.) A selection sequence is expressed in the form: *If* condition *p* is true, *then* take action *q*; otherwise (*else*) take action *r*:

IF p   THEN q   ELSE r

(See Figure 6-1*b*.) In a repetition sequence *do* a process *while* condition *p* is true; if condition *p* is not true, then exit from the loop. (See Figure 6-1*c*.)

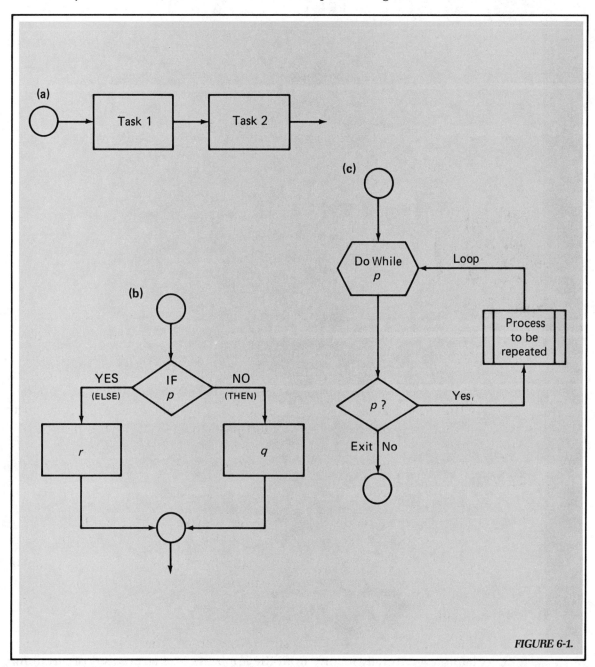

FIGURE 6-1.

    An important feature of structured programming is that there must be exactly one entry point and one exit point for each of the three program sequences; branching to a statement within a sequence is not permitted. This implies that the program can be read easily from top to bottom, making the logic of the program readily apparent to both the original programmer and any programmer who may at some later date be asked to modify the program.

Classify each of the following sequences of BASIC program instructions as a simple sequence, a selection sequence, or a repetition sequence.

```
1.  40  IF A < B THEN 70
    50  LET C = A
    60  GO TO 80
    70  LET C = B
    80  . . .

2.  30  LET R = 2 * L
    40  PRINT R
    50  LET D = P / 3

3.  40  LET N = 0
    50  IF N > 5 THEN 90
    60  LET S = S + N
    70  LET N = N + 1
    80  GO TO 50
    90  . . .
```

SOLUTIONS

1. a selection sequence
2. a simple sequence
3. a repetition sequence

The undisciplined use of the GO TO statement is considered harmful, since it tends to encourage carelessly planned programs in which the GO TO statement is used to patch up programs by joining statements to the body of the program which have been added as an afterthought. Furthermore, program clarity is compromised by the liberal application of the GO TO statement since such programs are generally characterized by a complicated pattern of overlapping program branches.

The following advantages usually result from a structured design approach to program development:

- A standard format and style, which tend to make the program logic more readily transparent, thus simplifying program debugging and maintenance.

- Increased attention to program planning and documentation, which results in fewer logic errors appearing during the testing phase of program development; debugging is therefore less time consuming while program reliability is increased.

- A modular, top-down program structure, with its inherent advantages (see Chapter 5) naturally follows from the application of structured programming principles.

It should be emphasized that not all programming languages are equally well suited to implementing a structured programming design approach. Most of the popular versions of BASIC, for example, do not support the IF/THEN/ELSE or the DO WHILE structures. On the other hand, features have been added to the original versions of FORTRAN and COBOL in order to make them more compatible with structured programming methods. PASCAL, on the other hand, is a language specifically designed to include features that make it ideally suited to the application of structured programming methods. Regardless of the extent to which the features of a particular programming language support the application of the three fundamental program structures, thorough problem analysis and program planning, with an eye cast toward program clarity, will generally lead to well structured programs.

THE FOR/NEXT LOOP

A repetition sequence may be conveniently expressed in BASIC by using the FOR/NEXT structure, which controls the number of times the set of statements enclosed between the FOR statement and the NEXT statement is executed. Let us analyze the following program, which uses a FOR/NEXT loop to print all integer values of N from 1 to 5:

```
10  FOR N = 1 TO 5  STEP 1
20  PRINT N
30  NEXT N
40  END
```

The FOR statement in line 10 declares the range of values that the *index variable* N may assume: the initial value is 1 and the final value is 5. The value of N is to be incremented in steps of 1. (Actually, if the step part of the FOR statement is omitted, then the increment value is automatically assumed to be 1.) During the first execution of line 10, N is set equal to 1, and then the statements that follow are executed; line 20 outputs the current value of N and line 30 automatically transfers control of the program back to line 10. At this time, two things happen:

▨ The value of the index variable is incremented by the step value, in this case by 1.

▨ The resulting value of the index variable is compared with the final value, 5. If the value of N does not exceed 5, then the set of statements between the FOR and the NEXT statements are again executed, thus forming a loop. In other words, line 20 is executed repeatedly until N exceeds 5. When N does exceed 5, the program exits from the FOR/NEXT loop, with program control being transferred to the next highest line number following the NEXT statement. In this example, the program will end.

The general form of the FOR/NEXT loop is as follows:

```
┌►FOR V = A TO B STEP C
│   ·┐
│   · ├ Loop body
│   · │
│   ·┘
└─NEXT V
```

where

    V = index variable
    A = initial value
    B = final (test) value
    C = step (increment) value

The statements within the loop body are executed repeatedly until the value of the index variable V exceeds the final value B.

Determine the output for each of the following programs.

1.
```
5  LET S = 0
10 FOR N = 1 TO 4
20 LET S = S + N
30 NEXT N
40 PRINT S
50 END
```

2.
```
10 FOR K = 3 TO 11 STEP 2
20 PRINT K
30 NEXT K
40 END
```

1.

N	S	Output
1	1	
2	3	
3	6	
4	10	
Exit value		10

2.

K	Output
3	3
5	5
7	7
9	9
11	11
Exit value	

As a matter of programming style, the set of statements bounded by the FOR and NEXT statements may be indented. This practice tends to increase the clarity of the program by highlighting those statements that form the body of the loop and which are executed repeatedly. For example, the following program uses a FOR/NEXT loop to read in exactly ten pairs of data values, calculating and printing their sums:

```
10  FOR N = 1 TO 10
20    READ A, B
30    LET S = A + B    ⎤
40    PRINT A, B, S    ⎦─Body of FOR/NEXT loop
50  NEXT N
60  DATA . . .
70  END
```

The FOR/NEXT loop is an extremely useful and powerful BASIC programming structure, which will be discussed at greater length in the Excursion Into BASIC at the end of this chapter.

PSEUDOCODES

In order to produce structured programs, a certain discipline of mind and habit is required. In planning a computer solution to a problem using a structured design methodology, programmers think exclusively in terms of the three control structures: a simple sequence, an IF/THEN/ELSE decision sequence, and a DO WHILE repetition sequence. In fact, programmers will often frame a tentative solution to the problem using an English-like paragraph-form description that depends heavily on the phrases IF/THEN/ELSE and DO WHILE. This type of solution is called a *pseudocode*, since it is not an actual programming language. Since a pseudocode *resembles* a programming language, it can easily be coded into a computer program.

Read in a series of customer checking account transactions. A code number of 1 is used to indicate a deposit. If the code is 1, then the transaction amount should be added to the account balance; otherwise, it should be subtracted from the account balance. Print the updated customer checking account record. Assume that a trailer record with an EOF entry will terminate the processing. Develop a flowchart and a pseudocode solution to indicate the nature of the processing that is required.

The flowchart is displayed in Figure 6-2. The pseudocode is as follows:

```
Start
READ first record
DO WHILE not EOF
     IF code = 1 THEN
          Add transaction
          amount to balance
     ELSE
          Subtract transaction
          amount from balance
     END of IF sequence
     PRINT customer checking
          account record
     READ next record
END of DO WHILE loop
Stop
```

Note that paragraph indentation is used to improve the clarity of the pseudocode solution.

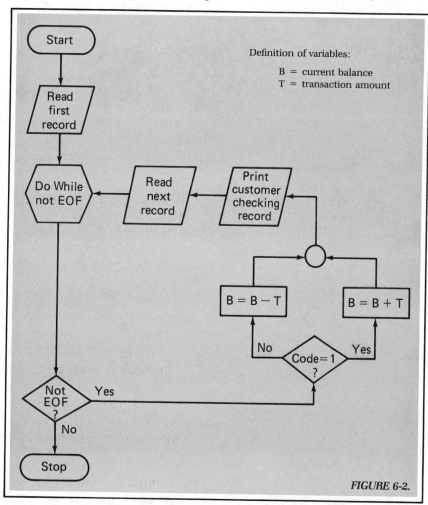

FIGURE 6-2.

In the next example we dispense with a flowchart and indicate how a pseudocode solution may be developed using the method of stepwise refinement.

Read in a series of customer credit account records, which includes the month's payments and purchases and the previous month's balance. If the unpaid balance is $500 or less, interest is computed at the rate of 1.5%. If the unpaid balance is more than $500, then the interest is $7.50 plus 1% of the amount in excess of $500. Print the updated balance for each customer and the sum of the interest computed for each customer.

Step 1. Give a general description of the processing required:

Start
Read customer record
Process customer record
Print sum of interest
Stop

Step 2. Begin to refine solution in a stepwise fashion. The program must be designed to process more than a single customer record. A repetition sequence is needed which reads and processes records until the EOF record is read.

Start
Read first customer record
DO WHILE not EOF
    Process customer record
    Read next record
End
Print sum of interest
Stop

Step 3. Continue stepwise refinement by elaborating on the processing that is required. Note that the paragraph indentation offers increased clarity.

Start
READ first customer record
DO WHILE not EOF
    Calculate unpaid balances
    IF unpaid balance is less than 500 THEN
        Calculate interest at 1.5% of unpaid balance
    ELSE
        Calculate interest at 7.50 plus 1% of the difference
        between the unpaid balance and 500
    END of IF sequence
    Accumulate interest totals
    Calculate updated balance
    PRINT customer account record
    READ next customer record
END of DO WHILE loop
PRINT sum of customer interest
Stop

After an appropriate number of stepwise refinements, this solution can be coded easily into the actual programming language.

PROGRAMMING LANGUAGES

Generally speaking, there are three levels of programming languages: machine, assembly-level, and high-level. *Machine language* is characterized by its all-numeric binary-based structure and its concern with how the particular computer to be used has been designed to store and manipulate data. In the early days of computing, machine language programming was the only available means for expressing program instructions. Recognizing that machine language is cumbersome, time-consuming, error-prone, and dependent on the particular machine being used, *high-level* program languages were developed. BASIC, COBOL, FORTRAN, and PL/1, to name just a few, are examples of high-level languages. High-level programming languages feature an English-like or an algebraic-like structure and do not require any special knowledge of the internal operation of the computer. Since the only language a computer can "understand" is machine language, each high-level language program must be interpreted for the computer by its own special language translator program. In order to conserve space in main memory, language translators are typically stored on disk (or diskette) and called into memory from the disk drive only when needed. Most personal computers, however, have a BASIC language interpreter permanently in residence on a ROM memory chip.

An *assembly* language is very similar to machine language, except that it uses mnemonics (memory-aiding alphabetic abbreviations) to refer to computer operations instead of a sequence of binary numbers. Assembly language is a low-level language since it is close to machine language and requires greater attention to the manner in which a computer operates internally than a high-level language. Let's take a closer look at each of the three levels of programming languages.

MACHINE AND ASSEMBLY LANGUAGES

A typical machine language instruction takes the following form:

Machine language instruction		
Op code	Operand 1	Operand 2

The op code defines the type of operation, while the operands identify the addresses of the quantities to be operated on. When programming in machine language, the task of assigning and keeping track of the numeric addresses of the storage locations (expressed in binary form) rests with the programmer. Each available machine operation is defined by a numeric op code. For example, the op codes which define arithmetic operations involving the contents of registers in the IBM System/370 are given below:

Operation	Op Code
Add register to register	00011010
Subtract register from register	00011011
Multiply register by register	00011100
Divide register by register	00011101

An instruction which adds the contents of memory register 6 to the contents of register 5 would be:

00011010	0101	0110
op code	register 5	register 6

Although this instruction is 16 bits in length, other instructions may be 32 bits in length.

As a machine language program manipulates data, each aspect of the machine's internal electronic operation, no matter how minute in detail, must be accounted for by an individual machine language instruction. For example, in order to find the sum of two data values in main memory, say, A and B, and then to store the result in main memory, location C, a machine language programmer would typically write a set of machine language instructions that would:

1. load the contents of A into a work register

2. load the contents of B into another work register

3. add the contents of the registers

4. store the sum back in main memory in location C

The same operation could be performed by a BASIC programmer using the single statement LET C = A + B. (The BASIC language translator would then translate the statement into the four machine language instructions.) Needless to say, programming in machine language is extremely difficult, tedious, time-consuming, and subject to error.

In order to simplify the programming process, symbols were introduced to replace the binary structure of a machine language instruction. Assembly language retains the detail of machine language, but is based on mnemonic op codes. The op codes for the four arithmetic operations listed above are AR (add), SR (subtract), MR (multiply), and DR (divide). The assembly language instruction which adds the contents of register 6 to the contents of register 5 would be AR 5, 6.

Assembly language is a machine-oriented language, with each assembly language instruction typically being translated into a single machine language instruction. This implies that the assembly language programmer must be concerned with both the development of the algorithm necessary to solve the problem at hand and the details of how the machine is to implement the coded algorithmic solution.

The program that translates an assembly language program into an equivalent set of machine language instructions is called an *assembler*. Figure 6-3 illustrates the translation of an assembly language instruction. There are three programs involved in this process:

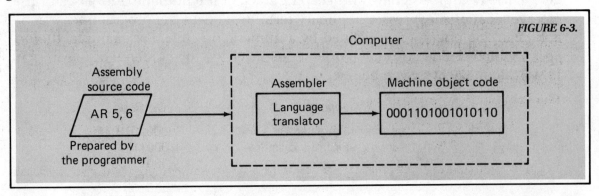

FIGURE 6-3.

1. The *source* program, which in this case is the assembly language program prepared by the programmer.

2. The *assembler* or language translator program, which converts each assembly language instruction into the corresponding machine language instruction.

3. The *object* program, which is the translated machine language version of the source program.

Typically, each computer has its own assembler language, with the assembler program being supplied by the computer manufacturer. An assembly language program is said to be machine dependent, that is, a program written for brand X computer will usually not run on brand Y computer.

HIGH-LEVEL LANGUAGES

Input and output operations are particularly awkward to code in assembly language. Moreover, the pattern of instructions needed to input or output data, regardless of the nature of the program, is basically the same. The computer manufacturer typically makes available to the programmer a set of input/output *macroinstructions.* Each macroinstruction generates a sequence of machine language instructions, thus simplifying the coding process.

High-level languages are based on the macroinstruction approach. Each language statement in a high-level language is translated into a series of machine language instructions. This characteristic of high-level languages leads to a number of significant advantages compared to assembly language:

- The programmer need not have any special knowledge of the internal operation of the machine in order to write a program. The programmer using a high-level language is able to focus on how to solve a problem rather than on how to orchestrate the internal movement of data in the machine.

- High-level language statements tend to be English or algebraic in appearance, making programs written in a high-level language easier to code, read, debug, and document.

- Many high-level languages have been standardized by organizations such as the American National Standards Institute (ANSI) and the International Standards Organization (ISO). This has permitted translator (*compiler*) programs to be written so that a program coded in a standardized version of a high-level language can be run on different computer systems. High-level languages are said to be *machine independent.*

A compiler program is analogous to an assembler program. Each translates the source code provided by the programmer into an equivalent machine language object code. The translation process for high-level languages is referred to as compiling or compilation; for assembly language translation the term is assembling. The compilation process usually proceeds as follows:

1. The appropriate compiler is loaded into main memory from a secondary storage device.

2. The source program is read as data by the compiler program and is translated into the corresponding object (machine language) program.

3. Diagnostic warning messages are generated if the compiler does not recognize a source language statement. That is, if a syntax error is encountered, the offending line that contains the error will be flagged. Programs that contain syntax errors cannot be executed.

4. Upon successful compilation the corresponding object program (also called *object module*) is produced and usually stored on an on-line secondary storage device (usually a disk), where it awaits execution. (See Figure 6.4.)

5. Following some established scheduling system, the object module is then loaded into main memory and executed. (This will be discussed in more detail later in this chapter.)

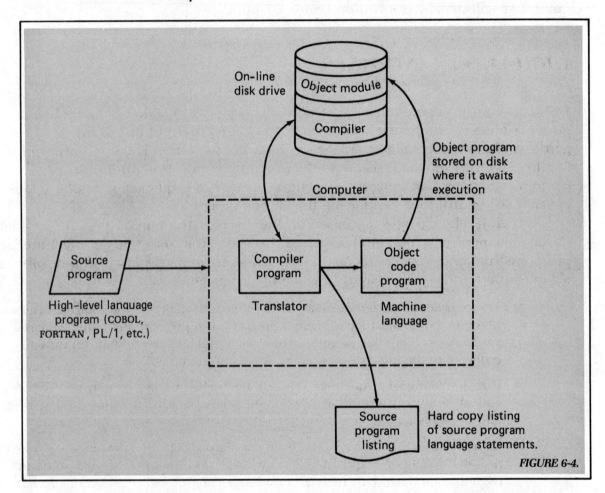

FIGURE 6-4.

All syntax errors must be eliminated before a program can be executed. The compiler, however, cannot detect errors in program logic. It is possible that a program may compile successfully, yet produce no output during execution because of an error in program logic. In fact, it is not uncommon for programs to be aborted (prematurely terminated) during the execution phase due to such an error. It should also be stressed that in a successful compilation there are two types of output: a source program listing and the object program.

High-level languages, sometimes referred to as compiler languages, fall into two general categories: *procedure-oriented* languages and *problem-oriented* languages. Procedure-oriented languages are general-purpose languages that can be used in a variety of application areas. BASIC, FORTRAN, COBOL, PL/1, APL (a programming *l*anguage), and Pascal are examples of procedure-oriented languages. AL-

GOL (*algorithmic language*) is another procedure-oriented language, which is used primarily in European countries. Some of these procedure-oriented languages will be discussed in greater detail in the next section. RPG, SNOBOL, LISP, SIMSCRIPT, and GPSS are examples of problem-oriented languages, with each being designed to handle a specific type of data manipulation or processing application. RPG (*report program generator*), for example, is used for producing management reports that require a minimum of computation. An RPG compiler is smaller than a COBOL compiler; it is therefore particularly well suited to minicomputers and small business computer systems where the amount of available main memory storage is small relative to larger computer systems. SNOBOL (*string-oriented symbolic language*) and LISP (*list processing*) are very specialized languages useful in manipulating and processing character rather than numeric data. Typical application areas include text editing, language translation, and artificial intelligence. SIMSCRIPT and GPSS are simulation languages used to formulate and test models that describe physical or economic systems. There is a multitude of programming languages available; only the most widely used and commonly known have been mentioned.

MICROCOMPUTERS AND PROGRAMMING LANGUAGES

The BASIC language translation that occurs within a microcomputer is typically performed by a language *interpreter*, which resides on a ROM memory chip. A language interpreter differs from a compiler in the following respect. After having translated each source language *statement*, a language interpreter immediately executes it and then moves on to the next source language program statement. A compiler, however, translates the entire source program into a machine language object program before executing any of the machine language program statements.

Microcomputers that support other languages in addition to BASIC have the appropriate language compilers stored on floppy disks. The appropriate compiler is then loaded into memory via a disk drive. Compiler programs are usually made available by the manufacturer of the computer or by special software vendors. Not all microcomputers, however, support additional high-level languages. It should also be noted that in almost all of the popular brand name microcomputers, the sophisticated programmer can use an appropriate set of system commands to access the internally supplied assembler and then program in assembly language.

HIGH-LEVEL VERSUS ASSEMBLY LANGUAGES

Considering the obvious advantages of high-level languages (including ease of program development and maintenance as well as machine independence), the question naturally arises, why use assembly language? Assembly language is more *efficient* than any of the high-level languages. It is translated into machine language faster and executes more rapidly than a comparable program coded in a high-level language. Furthermore, assembly language is more *powerful* than high-level languages. Since there is a direct correspondence between assembly and machine language, with each assembly language instruction typically generating one machine language instruction, the assembly language programmer has complete access to the full range of the computer's capabilities. With a high-level language, on the other hand, the programmer is confined to the features defined by the instruction set offered by the user-oriented compiler. As a result, high-level languages are generally applied to solving user problems (that is, developing *applications* programs), while assembly languages are used to control and help monitor machine operations (that is, developing *systems* software). Table 6-1 compares assembly and high-level languages.

TABLE 6-1

Feature	Assembly Language	High-Level Language
Language translator	Assembler.	Compiler.
Standardization	Machine dependent.	Many high-level languages have been standardized, including FORTRAN and COBOL. High-level languages are considered to be machine independent.
Efficiency	Highly efficient. Each assembly instruction typically generates a single machine language instruction.	Relatively inefficient. Each high-level language instruction typically generates a series of machine language instructions.
Program preparation	Relatively difficult and time consuming. Programmer must be concerned with machine-level detail. All of the special capabilities of the computer may be referenced.	Relatively easy due to its resemblance to English and the lack of concern with machine-level operations.
Application area	Primarily used to control computer system activities.	Used for problem solving, data manipulation, and processing related to report generation.

HIGH-LEVEL LANGUAGES

In this section some of the major features of the more popular of the procedure-oriented languages are presented and contrasted. Keep in mind that all high-level languages have the following features in common:

◾ *Lack of attention to machine-level detail.* Unlike with assembly languages, each program instruction in a high-level language is a macroinstruction translated by a compiler program into a number of machine-level instructions. Thus high-level languages do not require any special knowledge of the operation of the machine. Furthermore, high-level language statements resemble English- or algebra-like sentences.

■ *Program portability.* The publication of standardized versions of most high-level languages has led to the development of compiler programs which make high-level language programs relatively machine independent. High-level programs may be run with little or no modification on computer systems that support the standardized version of the given language. Assembly languages, on the other hand, are machine dependent.

BASIC (BEGINNER'S ALL-PURPOSE SYMBOLIC INSTRUCTION CODE)

Although BASIC has come to be associated with personal microcomputers, it was originally designed as a student-oriented problem-solving language that would allow users sitting at an on-line keyboard terminal to interact directly with a mainframe computer. After entering a BASIC program at a terminal, for example, the user types a command, such as RUN, in order to execute the program. If there are any syntax errors, the computer will immediately inform the user with error-diagnostic messages and give the user the opportunity to enter the correction. BASIC also has the capability (via the INPUT statement) of executing a program with the data being supplied by the user as they are needed while the program executes. For these reasons, BASIC is sometimes referred to as a *conversational* or *interactive* language.

BASIC was developed in the late 1960s at Dartmouth College by John G. Kemeny. It is simpler than other high-level languages and can be applied to designing computer solutions to problems after a relatively short time of study. The BASIC language is not particularly well suited to a structured design approach. Liberal insertion of REMark statements, combined with use of the GOSUB/RETURN structure to help create processing modules, can lead to "structured" BASIC programs; such efforts, however, may result in programs that are needlessly complicated, thus defeating one of the major advantages of BASIC—its simplicity. (See Chapter 5.)

At present, numerous versions of BASIC are being implemented. There are, however, several well-known versions of BASIC that are supported by some mainframes as well as by microcomputers, including Waterloo BASIC, ANSI Minimal BASIC, BASIC Plus, and Microsoft BASIC.

FORTRAN (FORMULA TRANSLATION)

FORTRAN has the distinction of being the oldest high-level language, with the first version developed by IBM in the mid 1950s. The concise, algebra-like nature of the language greatly resembles that of BASIC, although most versions of FORTRAN offer a greater number of built-in mathematical functions, which helps to account for its continued popularity in scientific, statistical, and engineering computing environments. While most versions of BASIC limit the length of a line of output (a maximum of 72 to 80 characters per line is typical), FORTRAN supports the standard

132-character output line length. Like BASIC, its major weaknesses lie in the area of processing string (nonnumeric) data and in manipulating large data files.

FORTRAN has been standardized since 1966, when FORTRAN IV was issued by the American National Standards Institute (ANSI). FORTRAN 77 was published by ANSI in 1978 and represents the most recent standardized version of FORTRAN. Expanded file processing features, the ability to declare data types explicitly (for example, integer versus decimal versus character data), and additional built-in functions which facilitate the manipulation of character data were introduced into FORTRAN 77. Features such as the IF/THEN/ELSE structure (commonly referred to as the block IF) were also added in order to encourage a structured design approach in the development of a FORTRAN program. In earlier versions of FORTRAN, each input and output statement required an accompanying FORMAT statement in which the record layout of the corresponding input/output record had to be specified, including a definition of the field widths to be reserved for each variable used in an input/output operation. FORTRAN 77 provides for both *format-directed* and *format-free* input/output statements. Format-free (also referred to as *list directed*) input/output statements resemble the input/output statements used in BASIC, and therefore increase FORTRAN 77's appeal to a programmer working in an interactive computing environment. (Not all computer systems offer an interactive version of FORTRAN.)

WATFIV (*Waterloo FORTRAN IV*) is a popular student-oriented version of FORTRAN developed at the University of Waterloo. It features a more comprehensive set of error diagnostics and warning messages. WATFIV-S is an enhanced version of WATFIV, offering structured program instructions such as the IF/THEN/DO/ELSE DO block and the WHILE DO loop structure.

COBOL (COMMON BUSINESS-ORIENTED LANGUAGE)

With the active support and involvement of the United States government, COBOL was introduced in the late 1950s with features designed to encourage its use in business data processing. Unlike FORTRAN, its program statements are English-like sentences and are well-suited to file processing operations. COBOL can process large volumes of data efficiently and easily produce corresponding volumes of formatted printed reports. Typically, COBOL programs input and output large volumes of data but do not subject the data to sophisticated or lengthy mathematical calculations. An ANSI COBOL version was published in 1968 and updated in 1974. COBOL remains the most widely used language in the area of business data processing.

The paragraph organization and the English-like sentence structure make a COBOL program relatively easy to read while giving it a self-documenting quality. Table 6-2 illustrates the organization of a COBOL program. All COBOL programs include four distinct *divisions*: an *identification* division, an *environment* division, a *data* division, and a *procedure* division. Each division includes one or more *paragraphs*. Paragraphs may contain one or more sentences, each ending with a period.

Figure 6-5 displays a COBOL program which determines the sum of two data values. It proceeds as follows:

1. It reads in a record named CARD-IN-RECORD from a file named CARD-IN-FILE.

TABLE 6-2

IDENTIFICATION DIVISION. *Paragraph-Name.* _____ _____ _____	In this division, the programmer identifies the program by assigning a program name, identifying the author of the program, describing the installation, plus related comments. Most of the information contained in this division is optional. The only required paragraph in this division is PROGRAM-ID.
ENVIRONMENT DIVISION. *Paragraph-Name.* _____ _____ _____	This division describes the hardware that the COBOL program is to run on. This information is usually supplied to the programmer by the particular computer installation.
DATA DIVISION. *Paragraph-Name.* _____ _____ _____	The data that are to be used in the program, including input and output record formats, are defined in this division. Intermediate results (data created by the program but not included in the input or output record definitions) are described in a special paragraph section within this division, called WORKING-STORAGE section.
PROCEDURE DIVISION. *Paragraph-Name.* _____ _____ _____	The processing instructions and program logic are contained in this division. Each sentence within this division begins with a COBOL reserved word *verb* that defines the action to be taken: OPEN, MOVE, READ, PERFORM, WRITE, STOP, and so on.

2. It defines data fields in the CARD-IN-RECORD and names them A-IN and B-IN.

3. It defines the fields in the RESULTS-OUT-RECORD and names them A-OUT, B-OUT, and RESULT-OUT. In order to ensure clarity in the output line of print, FILLER (blank) spaces are also defined between these data fields.

4. It adds the contents of the A-IN and B-IN fields and stores the result in the temporary storage location named RESULT.

5. It moves the contents of A-IN, B-IN, and RESULT to the corresponding output record data fields A-OUT, B-OUT, and RESULT-OUT.

6. It writes the RESULTS-OUT-RECORD.

7. It performs this process until an attempt is made to read another record and no record is found. When this occurs, the TRAILER-VALUE is assigned a value of 1, which leads to the termination of the program. The PERFORM UNTIL COBOL structure is an important type of looping mechanism. The condition specified in the UNTIL clause is tested; if it is *not* satisfied, then the condition in the PERFORM clause is executed. In this example, the set of statements in the paragraph labeled PROCESS-SUBROUTINE will be executed repeatedly, provided that the condition in the UNTIL clause is not true.

COBOL programs tend to be lengthy, follow a rigid format, and include a large number of reserved words and syntactical rules, making COBOL a comparatively difficult language to learn. The novice programmer usually finds COBOL more difficult to master than FORTRAN or many of the other high-level languages. A considerable amount of study is required before the inexperienced programmer can write a nontrivial COBOL program.

```
                    IDENTIFICATION DIVISION.
                    PROGRAM-ID.
                    AUTHOR.
                        LAWRENCE LEFF.

                    ENVIRONMENT DIVISION.
                    INPUT-OUTPUT SECTION.
                    FILE-CONTROL.
                        SELECT CARD-IN-FILE ASSIGN TO UR-2540R-S-SYSIN.
                        SELECT RESULTS-OUT-FILE ASSIGN TO UR-1403-S-SYSOUT.

                    DATA DIVISION.
                    FILE SECTION.
                    FD  CARD-IN-FILE
                        LABEL RECORDS ARE OMITTED.
                    01  CARD-IN-RECORD.
                        05  A-IN            PIC 99V9.
                        05  B-IN            PIC 9V9.
                    FD  RESULTS-OUT-FILE
                        LABEL RECORDS ARE OMITTED.
                    01  RESULTS-OUT-RECORD.
                        05  FILLER          PIC X(10).
                        05  A-OUT           PIC 99.9.
                        05  FILLER          PIC X(10).
                        05  B-OUT           PIC 9.9.
                        05  FILLER          PIC X(10).
                        05  RESULT-OUT      PIC 999.9.
                    WORKING-STORAGE SECTION.
                    01  RESULT              PIC 999V9.
                    01  TRAILER-VALUE       PIC 9.

        1           PROCEDURE DIVISION.
        2               OPEN INPUT CARD-IN-FILE
                            OUTPUT RESULTS-OUT-FILE.
        3               MOVE 0 TO TRAILER-VALUE.
        4               READ CARD-IN-FILE
        5                   AT END MOVE 1 TO TRAILER-VALUE.
        6               PERFORM PROCESS-SUBROUTINE
                            UNTIL TRAILER-VALUE = 1.
        7               CLOSE CARD-IN-FILE, RESULTS-OUT-FILE.
        8               STOP RUN.
                    PROCESS-SUBROUTINE.
        9               ADD A-IN, B-IN GIVING RESULT.
       10               MOVE SPACES TO RESULTS-OUT-RECORD.
       11               MOVE A-IN TO A-OUT.
       12               MOVE B-IN TO B-OUT.
       13               MOVE RESULT TO RESULT-OUT.
       14               WRITE RESULTS-OUT-RECORD.
       15               READ CARD-IN-FILE
       16                   AT END MOVE 1 TO TRAILER-VALUE.


     ***** THERE ARE NO STATEMENTS FLAGGED IN THIS COMPILE


         22.0          5.0          027.0      ⎫
         14.5          3.5          018.0      ⎬   Sample Program Output
                                               ⎭

     COMPILE TIME     0.03 SECONDS TASK;    0.72 SECONDS REAL  ⎫
     EXECUTION TIME   0.00 SECONDS TASK;    0.03 SECONDS REAL  ⎪
     CARDS READ DURING COMPILE        51 DURING EXECUTION    2 ⎬  Run-time
     LINES PRINTED DURING COMPILE     92                        ⎪  Statistics
     PAGES PRINTED DURING COMPILE      2 DURING EXECUTION    0 ⎭
     CORE UNUSED AT COMPILE TIME 891492 BYTES
     CORE AVAILABLE AT ENTRY TO EXECUTION 896232 BYTES
```

PL/1 (PROGRAMMING LANGUAGE 1)

PL/1 is an IBM developed product, introduced in the 1960s and offered as an alternative to COBOL *and* FORTRAN. PL/1 is an extremely rich language, featuring the mathematical power of FORTRAN, the file-handling capability of COBOL, and desirable features not found in either FORTRAN or COBOL. It is more concise and has fewer coding restrictions than COBOL. Like FORTRAN, PL/1 has a large assortment of built-in functions. Compared to many commonly implemented versions of FORTRAN, PL/1 is better suited to interactive processing and to a modular design approach in program development.

The syntax and types of instructions included in PL/1 allow the inexperienced programmer to write simple programs after only a brief exposure to the basic elements of the language. As one's study of PL/1 progresses, the programmer can take advantage of additional features of the language and begin to write more sophisticated programs. As a result of its varied features and the range of its processing capabilities, a PL/1 compiler is relatively large.

PL/C is a student-oriented version of PL/1 developed at Cornell University. PL/C features an enhanced set of error diagnostics and offers faster compilation time than PL/1. Although PL/1 has been promoted as a general-purpose language that combines the best features of FORTRAN and COBOL, it has not enjoyed the widespread support and popularity envisioned by its authors. Nevertheless, it remains a significant programming language, found in educational, scientific, and business environments.

PASCAL

Named in honor of the mathematician Blaise Pascal, Pascal is a relatively new language, which is continuing to grow in popularity, particularly in the educational community. Pascal was developed by Niklaus Wirth in an effort to provide a teaching language that would encourage the development of sound programming practices by including features that permit the unambiguous application of structured programming design techniques.

Standard Pascal was defined in 1973 by the publication of a revised *User Manual and Report* by Kathleen Jensen and Niklaus Wirth. UCSD (University of California at San Diego) Pascal represents another commonly implemented standardized version of Pascal. Some of the popular microcomputers, for example, offer a UCSD Pascal compiler, making Pascal an attractive alternative to BASIC. Although the syntax of Pascal is somewhat more demanding than that of BASIC, Pascal is more powerful than BASIC. The Pascal programmer is free to select variable names of any length and may manipulate a greater variety of data types and structures. The availability of the IF/THEN/ELSE selection sequence and the WHILE/DO repetition structure not only encourages the development of structured programs, but also aids in the problem-solving process by permitting a more direct translation between the developed algorithm (or pseudocode) and the actual program code.

It is not surprising to find that a Pascal program and a PL/1 program designed to accomplish the same processing task bear some resemblance to one another. Both languages provide for the explicit definition of variable data types, a modular structured design approach to program development, the indentation of program statements in order to improve program clarity, and processing in batch and interactive modes. The smaller size of the Pascal compiler, however, makes Pascal better suited to smaller computer systems.

THE OPERATING SYSTEM

The resources of a large modern computer system can be quite extensive. Typically, such computer systems include:

- several I/O devices
- an array of secondary storage devices

- system support software, such as language translators, which must be brought into main memory as needed

- a virtual memory capability (see Chapter 2)

- a multiprogramming capability which allows more than one program to reside in main memory and to be executed concurrently

- a multiprocessing capability (linking of two or more CPUs), permitting the simultaneous execution of two or more instructions

At one time, much of a computer's resources were managed and allocated by a computer operator. As third-generation computers introduced systems of increased capability and complexity, the manual intervention of a computer operator became a significant limiting factor on the overall efficiency of the computer system. In about the mid 1960s, computer manufacturers began to pay increased attention to this problem. The result was the design of a sophisticated package of programs, customized to the particular hardware and overall management requirements of the installation, called the *operating system*. The operating system permits the computer to oversee and distribute its own resources efficiently, regardless of how vast they may be. An operating system consists of three general types of software:

- *Control programs*, the most important of which is called the *supervisor program* and, as its name implies, exercises managerial control over the entire operating system. Control programs are usually written in an assembly language.

- *Language translators*, including both compilers and assemblers.

- *Service programs*, which perform frequently needed system support functions, freeing the programmer from the responsibility of writing these programs each time they are needed. SORT and MERGE programs and a utility program designed to transfer data files from one secondary storage medium to another are examples of service programs.

Language translators and service programs are collectively referred to as the *processing programs* of the operating system.

FUNCTIONS OF AN OPERATING SYSTEM

The operating system is the central nervous system of the computer. Its responsibilities may be likened to those of a traffic officer assigned to direct traffic at a busy intersection as well as to those of a librarian who must catalog, store, and then retrieve reference books when they are needed. The major functions of an operating system are listed below.

Supporting Program Libraries.   Language translators and service programs are brought into main memory only when needed. The operating system must catalog, maintain, and access systems software from the program libraries, which are maintained on a secondary storage device.

Implementing Program Execution.   The operating system orchestrates the source program compilation and the preparation and execution of the object program. It selects and readies the appropriate I/O devices and coordinates all related operations.

Improving System Efficiency.

■ *Overlapped processing.* When a computer is executing the input or output operations associated with the execution of a particular program, the services of the CPU are not required by the program. Rather than allowing the CPU to remain in a wait state until the input or output operations are completed, the operating system directs the CPU to transfer its attention to the execution of another program whose current stage of execution requires processing by the CPU. Thus under the supervision of the operating system, the executions of programs are permitted to overlap in such a way that the amount of idle CPU time is minimized.

■ *Multiprogramming and virtual memory.* Directly related to the concept of overlapped processing is the *multiprogramming* ability of large computer systems. Multiprogramming refers to the *concurrent* execution of two or more programs residing in main memory. Under the supervision of the operating system, two or more programs may be loaded into main memory. Following some established priority system, the CPU alternately executes sets of program instructions associated with different object programs. While the execution of one program sustains an I/O interruption, the operating system directs the CPU to switch its attention to the other programs in memory. In a multiprogramming environment, programs are executed concurrently *not* simultaneously; the computer cannot execute more than one instruction at a time. The supervisor program, however, can direct the CPU to switch back and forth between two or more programs and thereby execute the programs concurrently.

A multiprogramming capability places enormous demands on the storage capacity of main memory. A virtual memory capability helps to relieve the memory requirements created by storing multiple programs in main memory. With virtual memory, the active part of a program is stored in main memory while that part of the program not immediately required is stored on an on-line secondary storage device. The operating system not only protects different programs residing in main memory from interfering with one another, but also coordinates the paging activity in which segments (pages) of the program are exchanged between main (real) memory and secondary (virtual) storage as the execution of the program progresses.

■ *Job scheduling.* Before operating systems existed, a considerable amount of time was needed in order to set up and schedule jobs for processing. The manual intervention of a computer operator was necessary in order for the computer to move from one job to the next. Operating systems allow for *stacked-job (batch) processing* in which system software and hardware, not the computer operator, load jobs that have been accumulated over a period of time and are stored in program libraries. The operating system processes this stack or batch of jobs in a continuous stream by establishing a job queue (waiting line) and selecting jobs to be executed from the queue using the following criteria:

■ The classification (type) of job and its assigned priority level. In the computer system that services a college, for example, a faculty payroll job would carry a higher priority level classification than a student program.

■ The amount of storage space available in main memory versus the amount of storage space required by the program.

■ The availability of any additional computer resources (for example, I/O devices) that are required.

Operating systems also provide for the *dynamic scheduling* of jobs. In addition to using a priority system to schedule jobs, an operating system allows for changes to be made in the job queue on a continuous basis. Jobs may be added or deleted; the position of a job in the queue may be changed by the computer operator; and the current status of jobs may be displayed on the operator's control console. (See Figure 6-6.) The operating system also keeps track of the amount of time a job remains on a queue. The job's priority level may be raised if it has been on the job queue for more than a specified amount of time. This tends to prevent a job from consistently being "bumped" by jobs having a higher priority.

FIGURE 6–6.   *SPERRY-UNIVAC 1100/90 computer with a control console monitor. The system provides for virtual user address space of 268 million words and the ability to connect high-speed scientific processors, permitting hundreds of millions of decimal number operations per second.* (Courtesy of Sperry Corporation.)

Spooling.   Main memory can receive and transmit data at speeds which greatly exceed the capabilities of the corresponding I/O devices. The technique of *spooling* (simultaneous *p*eripheral *o*perations *on-l*ine) is used to help compensate for these discrepancies in speed by routing data awaiting input or printing onto a fast secondary storage medium, such as disk. For example, rather than the computer receiving data directly from a relatively slow input device, the data will first be transferred or spooled onto a disk. When the computer is ready, as determined by the operating system, it may then read the data from disk into main memory, thereby capitalizing on the higher rates of data transfer that are associated with disk devices.

Programs often call for hardcopy output during various phases of their execution. Rather than wait for an available printer, output requiring hard copy printing may be stored temporarily on a secondary storage device. When the program completes execution and a printer becomes available, the output generated by the program may then be printed. This process is known as *print spooling* and is coordinated by the operating system. A print spool job queue may also be formed when several jobs require the same printer because it uses some special type of form. (See Figure 6-7.)

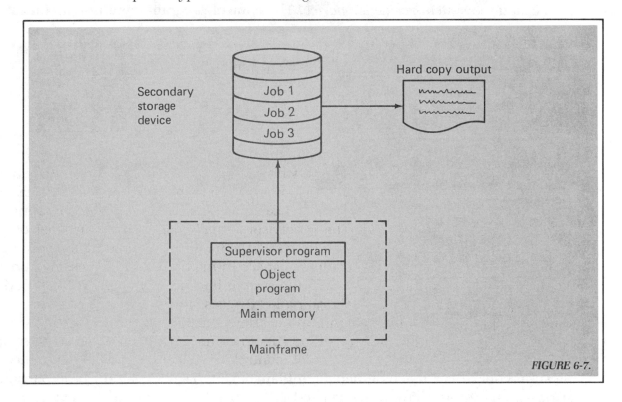

Secondary storage device

Job 1
Job 2
Job 3

Hard copy output

Supervisor program
Object program
Main memory

Mainframe

FIGURE 6-7.

Handling Interrupts. An interrupt is an electronic signal designed to alert the operating system that a certain condition exists. Interrupts may occur for a variety of reasons:

- Machine malfunction.

- A fatal error in program logic, which is detected during program execution. Division by zero, referencing a program statement using a label (e.g., a line number) that does not appear in the program, and incorrectly specifying data (e.g., declaring a numeric data field when the data entered are alphanumeric) are common types of errors that would generate an interrupt condition. Programmers refer to this type of error as a *run-time* error.

- The program's need to suspend processing by the CPU in order to perform an input/output operation.

- An attempt to execute or reference a segment of a program that still resides in virtual memory.

- The computer operator's need to communicate with the operating system. The computer operator, for example, may initiate an interrupt in order to request that the execution of a program be aborted (discontinued).

In each instance, the operating system (usually the supervisor) responds to the interrupt by taking an appropriate action. If the interrupt is the result of some abnormal condition, then the operating system communicates with the operator via the control console monitor.

SOFTWARE COMPONENTS OF AN OPERATING SYSTEM

The software of a disk operating system (DOS) is permanently stored on a disk pack called the *system residence device*. The control program component consists of three major programs:

- the supervisor (monitor or executive) program
- the job control program
- the initial program loader (IPL)

In order to be active in the system, the control programs must reside in main memory. At the beginning of each workday, the supervisor program is loaded into main memory from the system residence device by means of the IPL. Once resident in main memory, the supervisor takes charge, coordinating all operating system functions and programs. The supervisor actually consists of a number of component module programs which have specific functions, including scheduling of jobs, managing the allocation of storage space in main memory, accessing compilers and other service programs from the system libraries which are maintained on the system residence device, allocating I/O devices, and directing virtual memory, multiprogramming, and multiprocessing activities.

In order for the programmer to be able to communicate with the supervisor, a special language must be used. JCL (job control language) is used to command the supervisor. It is a machine-dependent language typically related to the particular operating system software being used. JCL is used to communicate a variety of control information to the computer, including the job name, the location of the program data, the selection of the output device, and directing the supervisor to access a particular compiler from the system residence device. JCL commands must be interpreted for the supervisor by the *job control program*, which must be resident in main memory in order to accomplish its function. (See Figure 6-8.)

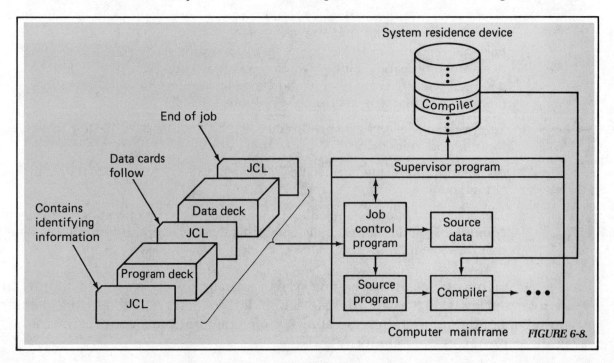

FIGURE 6-8.

The other major software components of an operating system are the processing programs. Generally speaking, processing programs are those programs that perform frequently needed functions which simplify the work of a programmer. All processing programs are accessed, executed, and maintained under the supervision of the control programs. Processing programs consist of language translators and a variety of service programs.

A large computer installation normally maintains a variety of compilers, with the languages offered being dependent on the nature of the installation and on the compilers offered by the computer manufacturer for the particular machine model being used. A computer installation will generally provide a listing of the compiler languages available, the JCL required to execute a program in a particular language, and the corresponding language reference manuals.

The service programs provided by the operating system include:

- the linkage editor
- the librarian
- SORT and MERGE
- Utility programs
- programs that aid in debugging

The *linkage editor program* provides the link between a compiled program and a program that is capable of being loaded into main memory and executed. Although the object program that results from compilation is in machine language, it is not necessarily in a form that can be immediately executed. It normally requires the addition of the precise numeric address that it will occupy in main memory. The linkage editor program processes the object program and adds this information, producing a *load module* that is ready to be executed by the computer.

Service programs are maintained in system program libraries in much the same way that books are stored in reference libraries. The *librarian program* has the responsibility of cataloging and maintaining programs in the system library, which is stored in the system residence device. The system residence device supports three types of program libraries:

- The *source* library stores the original source program.

- The *relocatable* library stores programs whose final main memory addresses have *not* as yet been determined. The object program resides in this library until it is processed by the linkage editor. As its name implies, the relocatable library is a temporary storage area, storing programs that will eventually be relocated.

- The *core-image* library stores programs that are in a form which permits them to be loaded into main memory and executed. The load module (machine language object program with final memory addresses), language translators, and service programs are stored in this library. The name core image is derived from the fact that when computer memory design was based on magnetic core, the terms main memory and core memory were used interchangeably. Hence, programs stored in the core-image library are an exact reflection of their form when executed in main memory.

The steps necessary to compile, link-edit, and execute a program may be summarized as follows:

■ *Compile phase.* The source program and the appropriate compiler are brought from the system residence device into memory, and the resulting object program is stored in the relocatable library. (See Figure 6-9.)

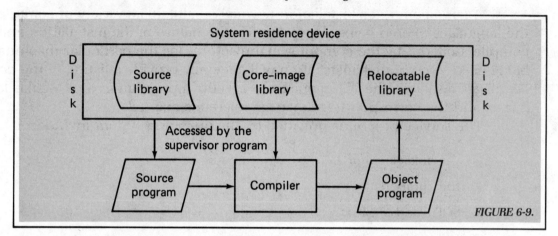

FIGURE 6-9.

■ *Link-edit phase.* The object program and the linkage editor program are called into memory in order to produce a load module, which is then stored in the core-image library. (See Figure 6-10.)

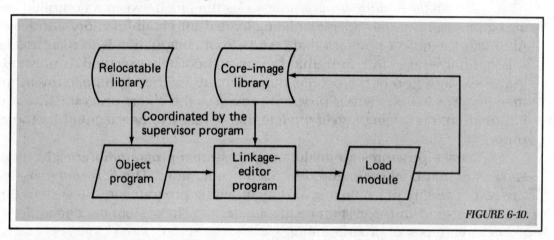

FIGURE 6-10.

■ *Execution phase.* The load module is brought back into memory so that it can be executed by the CPU. (See Figure 6-11.)

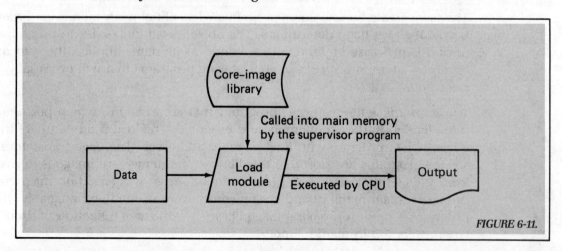

FIGURE 6-11.

A narrative description of a typical sequence of steps that a computer would follow in implementing the compile, link-edit, and execution phases is offered below:

1. A source program and a corresponding set of JCL statements are read.

2. The job control program interprets the JCL commands for the resident supervisor program.

3. The supervisor accesses the appropriate compiler from the core-image library and brings it into memory.

4. The supervisor passes control to the compiler program, which reads and processes the source program. Assuming no errors, an object program is produced and cataloged into the relocatable library.

5. After control passes back to the supervisor, the linkage editor is referenced by the supervisor.

6. The linkage editor processes the object module, creating a load module which is cataloged into the core-image library where it awaits execution. Control passes back to the supervisor.

7. The supervisor calls the load module into main memory.

8. The supervisor passes control to the load module. The machine language version of the original source program (load module) is now executed.

You may have noted that after the linkage editor has created a load module, the load module is stored on disk and subsequently read back into memory. This can be a relatively time-consuming operation and is justified when it is necessary to store a permanent copy of the load module on disk. When no copy is required, a program *loader* may be used. A program loader performs the same function as the linkage editor, except that after it has created the load module, it does not route it to a secondary storage device. Instead, the load module remains in memory and is executed.

MICROCOMPUTERS AND DISK OPERATING SYSTEMS

In order to make the procedure for transferring programs and data between main memory and one or more floppy disk drives as user friendly as possible, each microcomputer system is equipped with its own disk operating system (DOS). A microcomputer-based DOS allows the user to type in simple English-like phrases, called *commands*, which can direct the computer to:

- display the diskette's table of contents, which is sometimes referred to as the diskette's *directory* or *catalog*

- load a particular program from the diskette into main memory

- save a program that is in main memory on a diskette

- make a duplicate copy of a diskette onto another diskette

- send output to an external device such as a printer

Typically a microcomputer requires that as part of a system startup procedure, called *booting up*, the DOS program be available to the computer as the system is powered on. This is a simple procedure. In an Apple IIe, for example, a manufacturer-supplied *system master* diskette must be inserted into the disk drive before the system is turned on. When the *on* switch is activated, the appropriate DOS support programs are automatically loaded into memory. (In some microcomputer systems, such as the COMMODORE PET microcomputers, this is not necessary.)

Each microcomputer system is designed with its own DOS software that is machine dependent. Software packages which are compatible with Apple's DOS 3.3, for example, are not compatible with Radio Shack's TRS DOS, which comes with the Radio Shack TRS-80 models III and IV. There are, however, several standardized DOS packages, such as CP/M which is offered by Digital Research Corporation and MS-DOS which is marketed by the MicroSoft Corporation. In order to increase the versatility of a particular computer, some manufacturers design their machines so that they can be used with different operating systems. The IBM PC personal computer can be used with at least three different operating systems: IBM DOS, CP/M-86, and the University of California at San Diego (UCSD) p-System.

MULTIPROGRAMMING

Multiprogramming is based on the operating system's ability to manage the partitioning of memory so that different programs may be loaded into memory and executed concurrently, thus minimizing idle CPU time. The method of memory partitioning will depend on the particular operating system. Some operating systems may organize memory into partitions of fixed size. Other operating systems will vary the length of the partitions by allocating storage space to the various programs residing in memory according to their individual memory requirements. This dynamic allocation of memory requires a much more sophisticated operating system, but tends to be more efficient, allowing a greater number of programs to be executed concurrently for a given size memory capacity.

In a fixed-length memory partition approach, the number of partitions will depend on the operating system used. The IBM Disk Operating System, for example, can manage six memory partitions: one partition reserved for the operating system and the remaining five partitions allocated to applications programs. In order to simplify the present discussion, we shall restrict our attention to a multiprogramming system in which there are three partitions, one being reserved for the operating system and the other two for applications programs. We shall further assume that the latter two partitions are of equal size, although this need not be true in every multiprogramming environment.

Figure 6-12 illustrates a memory partition in which an applications program is stored in the *foreground* partition and another applications program is stored in the *background* partition. The program stored in the foreground partition has priority over the program that has been loaded into the background partition. If both programs are ready to be executed, the program in the foreground partition will be executed first. When the execution of the foreground program is interrupted (for example, in order to complete an input or output operation), the CPU then devotes its attention to the background program.

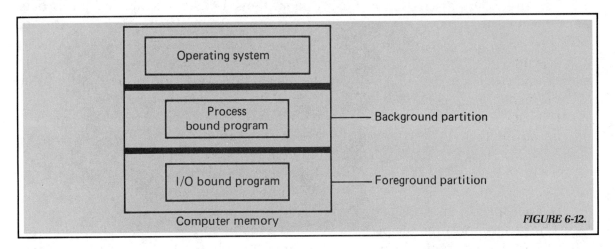

FIGURE 6-12.

Programs can often be categorized by the amount of processing time they require compared to the amount of time required to perform input/output operations. An *I/O bound* program is characterized by extensive input/output operations and relatively few calculations. A *process bound* (or *compute bound*) program has a minimum of input/output interruptions, but involves elaborate data manipulations. Execution time of an I/O bound program is determined by the amount of input/output operations and the speed of the associated input/output devices. With a process bound program, execution time is limited by the volume of data manipulations and by the speed of the CPU. Many business applications programs tend to be I/O bound, while mathematical and engineering applications programs are often process bound.

There is a definite logic that the operating system uses in determining the partition into which a program gets loaded initially. The I/O bound program will be directed to the foreground partition, while programs that are process bound will be loaded into the background partition. The I/O bound program will, therefore, receive priority from the CPU, under the supervision of the operating system. When its execution is interrupted by an input/output operation, control is shifted to the execution of the process bound program that is residing in the background partition. When the input/output operation is completed, control is then passed back to the foreground program. Following this scheme, the CPU allocates its time between the two programs so that it is always occupied. In a *uni*programming system (that is, a single program resides in memory at any one time), much idle CPU time results when execution of an I/O bound program is suspended so that input/output operations can be performed.

To appreciate the logic of this approach fully, consider what would happen if the process bound program were loaded into the foreground partition. The process bound program would always receive priority from the CPU, and due to its sustained processing requirements, would dominate the CPU. The program residing in the background partition would be sufficiently deprived of the attention of the CPU that it would not be able to be executed concurrently with the foreground program, thus defeating the whole purpose of multiprogramming.

TIME-SHARING

The preceding discussion of operating systems focused on stacked-job processing in which the user plays an essentially passive role. In this mode of operation, user jobs are *not* executed as they are submitted but batched and processed in a job stream. Programs are executed according to their job classifications and their assigned priority levels. Many computer users, however, require the ability to communicate directly with the computer at their convenience. For example, banking transactions, inventory control systems, and ticket reservations systems rely heavily on an interactive mode of on-line data processing.

Operating systems make on-line data processing possible by permitting users to submit their jobs directly to the computer, typically using a CRT I/O device (terminal). When functioning in an interactive mode, the user will typically key in an appropriate set of instructions and/or data and then await job execution. The job turnaround time (elapsed time between job submission and output results) will, of course, depend upon the nature of the job, the type of processing required, and the availability of the computer's resources.

The operating system of a large computer will support tens or hundreds of on-line users. In order to ensure that no one user job monopolizes the attention of the CPU, a method for distributing the computer's resources must be established. Many computer systems allow on-line users to interact with the computer in a time-sharing mode, whereby each user is allocated a fixed "slice" of CPU time (typically measured in fractions of a second). After the apportioned time has elapsed, the CPU, under the direction of the operating system, switches its attention to the next job in the time-sharing job queue, regardless of whether it has completed the execution of the previous program. If a job does not complete execution during its allocated slice of CPU time, its execution is temporarily halted and then returned to after the CPU services the remaining time-sharing users. Thus time-sharing is characterized by a cyclic type of processing in which each user receives an equal slice of CPU time. If more CPU time is required for the job, then the user's job is, in effect, placed at the back of the time-sharing job queue where it awaits the allocation of another slice of CPU time. Since each slice of CPU time is small, the CPU returns to each user after a very short period of time, thus creating the impression that he or she is receiving the undivided attention of the computer.

Time-sharing users are often located at sites that are geographically remote from the mainframe computer site. Telecommunications systems allow these users to communicate with the mainframe computer over telephone lines. Data communications will be discussed in more detail in Chapter 8. Rather than purchasing a mainframe computer and maintaining a programming support team, some businesses find it economically advantageous to purchase (or lease) terminals and then to rent computer time from a computer facility that offers a time-sharing service.

MULTIPROGRAMMING VERSUS TIME-SHARING

Time-sharing and multiprogramming are similar in that both provide for the concurrent execution of programs. In multiprogramming, however, the objective is to minimize idle *CPU* time, while in time-sharing the goal is to minimize idle *user* time. In time-sharing an effort is made to try to keep the user occupied by not allowing any single user to receive a disproportionate block of CPU time. This is accomplished by allocating equal increments of CPU time to each user job. In contrast, jobs in a multiprogramming environment are allocated varying amounts of CPU time based on the occurrence of input/output interrupts and the priority of the partition they reside in. In multiprogramming, job queues are usually established based on the priority and classification of the job; time-sharing users typically have access to computer time based on some previously assigned user schedule that may be independent of the nature of the job.

TIME-SHARING VERSUS REAL-TIME PROCESSING

In certain types of on-line processing the system response time is critical. The *response time* of a system refers to the difference between the instant at which a computer completes an input operation and the moment it begins an output operation. In on-line processing, CPU time may be allocated in either a time-sharing mode or a *real-time* processing mode. Although the difference between the two is somewhat hazy, we note that in real-time processing the response time of the system is generally faster than in a time-sharing mode. Real-time processing is essential in computer applications in which a computer is used to monitor, control, or process data received from some on-line physical device that is sending the computer electronic signals on a continuous basis. Real-time processing is characterized by a response time that allows the computer to affect the behavior of the system from which it receives input. Defense systems, control of a spacecraft, and monitoring the mixing of ingredients in a manufacturing environment are some examples of real-time processing applications. Banking and ticket reservation systems usually exist in a real-time processing environment.

State which mode of computer operation (batch, time-sharing, or real-time) you would generally expect to find in each of the following situations.

1. Processing a savings account withdrawal at a bank.
2. Running a student COBOL program.
3. Designing a missile guidance system.
4. Processing a company payroll.
5. Running a student BASIC program on a mainframe computer.

1. Real-time.
2. Batch (stacked-job) mode. (For example, the program may be submitted to the computer installation using punched cards.)
3. Real-time.
4. Batch mode.
5. Batch mode *or* a time-sharing mode via a CRT terminal.

REVIEW EXERCISES

True or False?

1. A computerized missile tracking system would require CPU time on a time-sharing basis.
2. In a uniprogramming environment idle CPU time results from input/output interrupts.
3. Structured programming does not encourage unique and creative short-cut programming solutions.
4. From the computer's standpoint, stacked-job processing is more efficient than processing in a time-sharing mode.
5. The difference between time-sharing and real-time processing is often simply a matter of the length of response time.
6. In time-sharing each user is allocated an equal block of CPU time.
7. Assembly language completely lacks the macroinstruction feature found in high-level languages.
8. Each high-level language requires its own compiler.
9. An assembly language program generally executes more rapidly than a comparable high-level language program.
10. Syntax errors are detected by the computer during program execution.
11. High-level programming languages tend to be general-purpose languages.
12. A programmer inadvertently codes an add instruction instead of a multiplication instruction. The computer will generate a syntax error.
13. Program development and maintenance in an assembly language are typically more time consuming and costly than in a high-level language.
14. In time-sharing, several programs may be executed simultaneously.
15. Operating systems tend to minimize the need for human intervention.
16. Among the high-level languages, COBOL most closely resembles English.
17. In many computer installations a time-sharing user can submit a program coded in the BASIC language.
18. The notion of top-down design is consistent with the principles of structured programming.
19. In machine language, input/output instructions are generally written as macroinstructions.
20. Each time a mainframe computer is powered on, the supervisor must be loaded into memory.
21. Assembly language is a symbolic-oriented language.
22. Compilers are permanently stored in memory, being originally installed by the computer manufacturer.

23. The compilation process does not necessarily produce an object module that can be executed immediately.
24. JCL is universal, being independent of the hardware.
25. Structured programming tries to increase program clarity by imposing rules that force each program written in a particular language to "look the same."
26. A COBOL compiler is larger than a FORTRAN compiler.
27. Structured programming tries to reduce program development costs by encouraging good programming work habits.
28. Virtual memory allows part of a program to reside in main memory and the remaining part to be stored on an on-line secondary storage device.
29. In multiprogramming, programs are executed in an overlapped fashion, with the execution of a program beginning before the execution of a previous program has been completed.
30. All high-level languages have been standardized.

Multiple Choice

31. Which of the following is *not* an advantage of coding in assembly language?
    a. fast execution time
    b. machine independence
    c. ability to access special machine capabilities
    d. none of these

32. Which of the following is a problem-oriented language?
    a. FORTRAN b. COBOL c. RPG d. BASIC

33. Which of the following languages is particularly well suited to the manipulation of character data?
    a. LISP b. FORTRAN c. COBOL d. SIMSCRIPT

34. What is the term used to describe the process by which output is routed to a secondary storage device and printed some time after program execution when an output device becomes available?
    a. stacked-job processing
    b. virtual memory
    c. dynamic scheduling
    d. spooling

35. Which of the following languages would be the best choice to use in a programming course designed to emphasize structured programming techniques?
    a. BASIC b. FORTRAN c. COBOL d. Pascal

36. Which of the following modes of computer processing does *not* necessarily depend on an on-line processing capability?
    a. interactive
    b. batch
    c. time-sharing
    d. real-time

37. Which of the following is *not* a function of the operating system?
    a. allocating I/O devices
    b. scanning a source program in order to determine the appropriate compiler
    c. handling system interrupts
    d. maintaining system program libraries

38. The IF/THEN statement is associated with a(n):
   a. simple sequence   **c.** selection sequence
   b. repetition sequence   **d.** arithmetic sequence

39. Which of the following languages is machine dependent?
   a. assembly   **b.** JCL   **c.** BASIC   **d.** all of these

40. The major goal of time-sharing is to:
   a. minimize response time
   b. keep the computer active   **c.** keep the users active
   d. minimize human intervention in job processing

41. The term stepwise refinement is most closely associated with:
   a. developing a pseudocode solution
   b. program compilation   **c.** program execution
   d. hardware developments

42. Which of the following statements regarding an operating system is true?
   a. the complexity of an operating system will vary from system to system.
   b. operating system software is generally written in an assembly language rather than in a high-level language.
   c. during any given phase of processing, part of the operating system software will be resident in memory while the remaining part will be stored on a secondary storage device.
   d. all of these.

43. Which of the following statements are *false*?
   a. Structured programming frowns on the use of the GO TO statement.
   b. A single computer may be able to support a multitude of programming languages.
   c. A system that supports multiprogramming consequently supports time-sharing.
   d. None of these.

44. Which of the following languages was originally developed as an interactive language?
   a. BASIC   **b.** FORTRAN   **c.** COBOL   **d.** RPG

45. Which of the following languages would least likely be used in a time-sharing environment?
   a. BASIC   **b.** FORTRAN   **c.** COBOL   **d.** Pascal

46. A compiler translates a(n) _____ program into a(n) _____ program.
   a. object, source   **c.** machine language, object
   b. assembly, source   **d.** source, object

47. Which of the following statements are *false*?
   a. Programs which contain a syntax error cannot be compiled.
   b. A COBOL compiler is relatively large, making it impractical for many smaller computer systems.
   c. The execution time for a high-level language program is generally greater than that for a comparable program written in assembly language.
   d. An assembly language program does not require a language translator.

48. Which of the following is *not* a benefit of structured programming?

a. increased program clarity

b. top-down modular design

c. increased programmer productivity

d. the adoption of a standard programming language

49. Which of the following statements are *false*?

a. The same program may exist in some form in each of the three system libraries.

b. The supervisor is called into main memory only when needed.

c. In order for the load module to be executed, the supervisor must relinquish control to it.

d. All operating system software is stored in the system residence device.

50. Which of the following statements are *true*?

a. A system interrupt may only be initiated by an abnormal condition.

b. The first job in a job queue is always the first job to be executed.

c. The linkage editor produces a machine-executable load module.

d. JCL is independent of the computer being used.

51. Which is *not* an advantage of COBOL?

a. its file-handling capability

b. its self-documenting quality

c. its ability to generate large volumes of formatted output

d. the ease with which it can be learned

52. Which of the following statements regarding structured programming is *true*?

a. It emphasizes debugging techniques.

b. It stresses careful planning and program clarity.

c. It was first advanced in the late 1970s.

d. All programming languages are equally well suited to the application of structured programming methods.

53. Which of the following structures is most closely associated with the DO WHILE structure?

a. a block sequence

b. a repetition sequence

c. a selection sequence

d. a simple sequence

54. Which of the following languages is best suited for both scientific and business applications?

a. BASIC **b.** COBOL **c.** PL/1 **d.** FORTRAN

55. Which of the following statements are *false*? In structured programming:

a. Program logic can be read from top to bottom.

b. Each program structure has a single point of entry and exit.

c. Unique short-cut routines that increase program efficiency are permitted, even though they reduce program clarity.

d. Program logic must be expressed in terms of combinations of no more than three distinct structure types.

THE REPETITION SEQUENCE IN BASIC:
THE FOR/NEXT LOOP

In the first section of this chapter the FOR/NEXT loop mechanism was introduced. Let's take a look at how the FOR/NEXT loop may be used to advantage in developing a BASIC solution to a problem that requires a repetition sequence. Keep in mind that each of the major high-level languages has a similar looping mechanism that is able to execute repeatedly a set of statements a specified number of times. In FORTRAN the DO loop is used for this purpose, while in COBOL the PERFORM/UNTIL structure serves to establish a repetition sequence.

FLOWCHART SYMBOLISM

It will be convenient to represent a FOR/NEXT structure as shown in Figure 6-13 by using the flowchart symbolism illustrated in Figure 6-14. It should be noted that the flowchart symbol for this operation is *not* standardized.

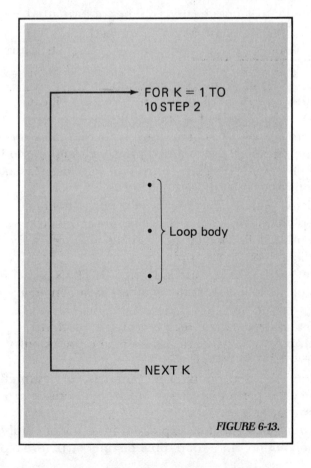

FIGURE 6-13.

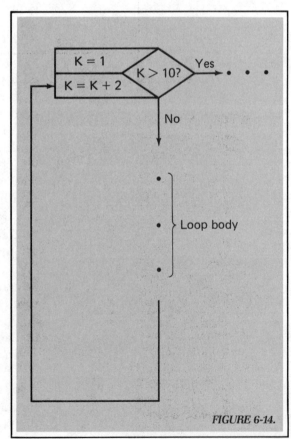

FIGURE 6-14.

EXAMPLE 1

Trace the flowchart illustrated in Figure 6-15 and determine the output.

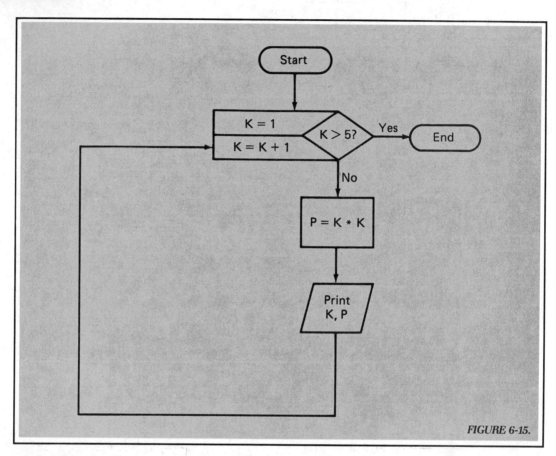

FIGURE 6-15.

SOLUTION

Output	
1	1
2	4
3	9
4	16
5	25

EXAMPLE 2

Print the sum of all even integers from 10 to 30, inclusive.

SOLUTION

Figure 6-16 illustrates the flowchart.

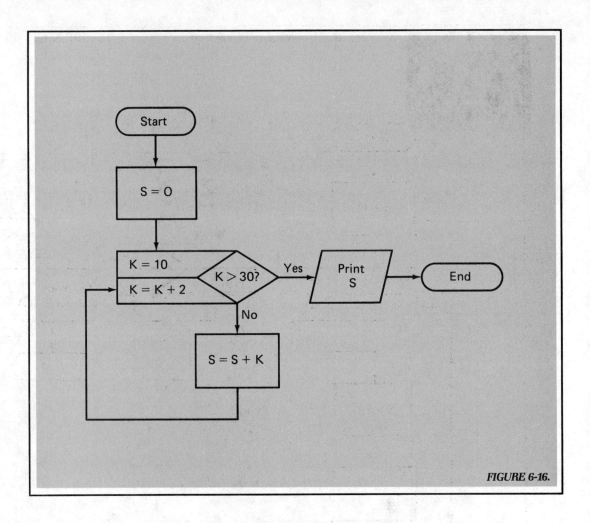

FIGURE 6-16.

	Program

```
10  LET S = 0
20  FOR K = 10 TO 30 STEP 2
30    LET S = S + K
40  NEXT K
50  PRINT S
60  END
```

In this example, the FOR/NEXT loop is used to generate data values.

Use a FOR/NEXT loop to read in exactly six data values from a data list. Determine and print the average of the data set.

Figure 6-17 illustrates the flowchart.

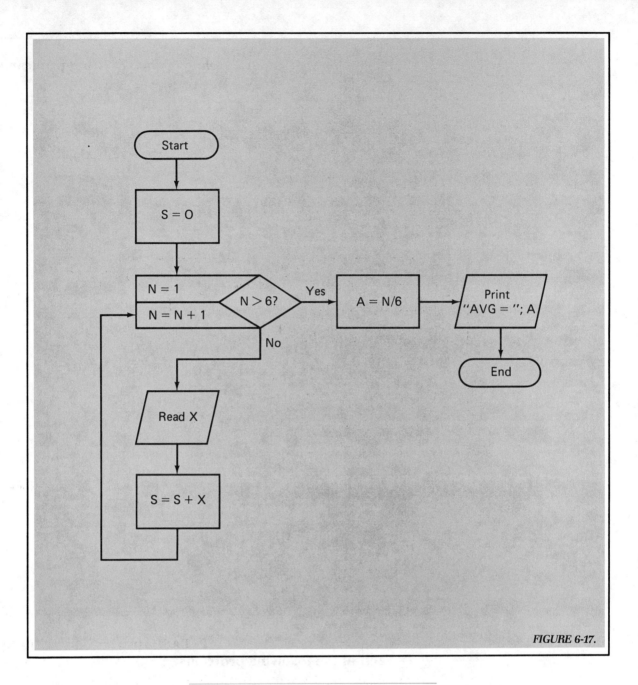

FIGURE 6-17.

Program
10 LET S = 0
20 FOR N = 1 TO 6
30   READ X
40   LET S = S + X
50 NEXT N
60 LET A = N / 6
70 PRINT "AVG ="; A
80 DATA 5, 7, 9, 14, 8, 11
90 END

Note that in line 20, when the step is 1, it may be omitted from the FOR statement.

In this example, the FOR/NEXT loop is used to control the number of times the READ statement is executed.

Determine the output for each of the following programs.

```
1.  10  FOR I = 5 TO 1 STEP -1
    20    PRINT I
    30  NEXT I
    40  PRINT "BOOM!"
    50  END


2.  10  LET P = 1
    20  FOR N = 1 TO 5
    30    LET P = N * P
    40  NEXT N
    50  PRINT "5 FACTORIAL ="; P
    60  END


3.  10  READ N
    20  FOR I = 1 TO N
    30    READ A, B
    40    LET P = A * B
    50    PRINT P
    60  NEXT I
    70  DATA 3, 7, 4, 5, 2, 6, 3
    80  END


4.  10  FOR N = 1 TO 10
    20    LET R = 1 / N
    30    IF R < = 0.2  THEN 50
    40  NEXT N
    50  PRINT N
    60  END
```

Based on a flowchart write a BASIC program solution to each of the following problems.

5. Find the sum of all odd integers from 1 to 25, inclusive.
6. Input a positive whole number N that is greater than 1. Print the sum of all whole numbers from 1 to N.
7. Determine how many numbers in the interval 139 to 497 are divisible by 7. (*Hint*: Use a FOR/NEXT loop to generate the numbers in the interval and the INTeger function to test for divisibility by 7.)
8. The formula to convert from degrees Celsius to degrees Fahrenheit is F = 1.8C + 32. Print a conversion table using Celsius temperatures between 0 and 100 in steps of 5.
9. Use a FOR/NEXT loop to read in ten positive data values. Print the largest value in the data list. (*Hint*: Initially assume that the largest data value is L = 0; compare each data value with L. If L is smaller than the data value, then assign the data value to L.)

ND DATA MANAGEMENT

PRINCIPLES OF FILE OF

GANIZATION AND DATA

MANAGEMENT PRINCIP

ES OF FILE ORGANIZA

CHAPTER

7

PRINCIPLES OF FILE ORGANIZATION
AND DATA MANAGEMENT

PRINCIPLES OF FILE OF

GANIZATION AND DATA

TAPE FILE ORGANIZATION

In order for information to be useful it must be organized so that it can be found and interpreted easily. Regardless of whether information is stored in a file cabinet, on index cards, or on a reel of tape, it must follow the hierarchical arrangement of field, record, and file. A length of tape can store a field, a longer length of tape can store a record, and a file consisting of one or more records would be contained on a still longer length of tape. A single reel of magnetic tape is called a *volume*. Depending on the size of the file, a reel of tape may store exactly one file or several different files. A reel of tape which stores more than one file is called a *multifile* volume. It is also possible that a file may be so large that it extends to more than one reel of tape. This type of file is called a *multivolume* file; the first tape reel is called volume 1, the second tape reel is called volume 2, and so on.

Magnetic tape reels are often stored off-line in libraries and must be handled by people. For example, when they are needed for processing, they must be located and mounted on the tape drive unit. In order to be able to distinguish one reel of tape from another, each tape reel is labeled externally with information such as the name of the stored file or files, the file identification number and creation date, and its volume number if it is a multivolume file. In order for the computer to be able to identify where a particular stored tape file begins and ends, a tape file is preceded by a file *header label* and ends with a file *trailer label*. (See Figure 7-1.) Internal magnetic file labels also serve to guard against problems that might arise as a result of a human error in the external labeling of the tape file. Control information, such as a count of the number of records in the file, is also included on the stored magnetic file label.

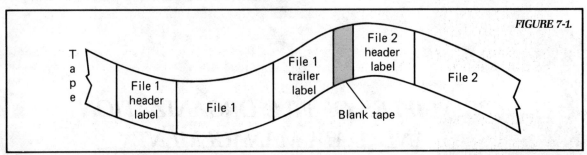

FIGURE 7-1.

Much of tape file processing is characterized by a stop and go tape motion. Just as a moving car cannot "stop on a dime," moving tape cannot be stopped at the precise beginning of a desired record—there must be some allowance for the distance a tape travels when the braking mechanism is applied. Furthermore, when a tape starts up, it does not instantly attain its normal transport speed. The tape travels some small distance in the time it takes the tape to accelerate to its normal operating speed. These problems are unavoidable and are inherent in the design of the *mechanical* tape drive unit. In order to overcome these difficulties, gaps of blank tape are used to separate records. Each such gap is referred to as an *interrecord gap* (IRG) and is typically between 0.3 and 0.75 inch in length. In order to conserve tape, records are usually stored with gaps, called *interblock gaps* (IBG), inserted at the end of a group or *block* of consecutive records. The number of records within a block is called the *blocking factor*. Each individual record is referred to as a *logical* record, while the information between two IBGs represents a single *physical* record. Figure 7-2a shows a strip of unblocked records, while Figure 7-2b illustrates the blocking of tape records using a blocking factor of 3.

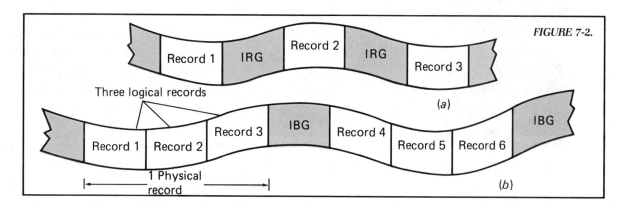

FIGURE 7-2.

Blocking records also increases processing efficiency. Unblocked records are read into main memory one record at a time, with the tape stopping momentarily after each individual record has been read. Blocked records are transmitted to the main memory as a unit (physical record). If the blocking factor is 5, then five logical records are read into main memory during the same read operation. One may wonder why the entire tape file is not read into main memory at one time. The answer is quite simple: the size of the tape file may easily exceed the available storage space in main memory.

As the following examples illustrate, the length of the tape gap and the size of the blocking factor will affect the storage capacity of a reel of tape.

On a particular standard 2400-foot reel of magnetic tape, each stored record has a fixed length of 400 bytes. The tape density is 1600 bytes per inch and the length of an IRG is 0.75 inch.

a. Determine the length of tape required to store a single record.
b. Determine the maximum number of records that can be stored on this tape reel.

a. The tape length for one record is calculated as follows:

400 bytes per record ÷ 1600 bytes per inch = 0.25 inch per record

Since an IRG of 0.75 inch is associated with each record, the total tape length required to store one record is

0.25 + 0.75 = 1.0 inch per record

b. To determine the maximum number of stored records, one must express the tape reel length in inches and then divide by the record length:

$$\text{number of records} = \frac{2400 \text{ feet} \times 12 \text{ inches}}{1.0 \text{ inch per record}} = 28{,}800 \text{ records}$$

Note that this is a maximum number. Some of the tape's length must be devoted to storing internal file labels.

EXAMPLE 2

Suppose that in the preceding example a blocking factor of 3 is used and that the IBG is also 0.75 inch. Determine the maximum number of records that can be stored.

SOLUTION

Step 1. Determine the length of tape required for each physical record and its associated IBG:

each physical record
= 3 logical records × 0.25 inch per record = 0.75 inch

The corresponding tape length is

$$\begin{array}{r} 0.75 \text{ inch (physical record length)} \\ + \ 0.75 \text{ inch (IBG length)} \\ \hline 1.50 \text{ inches each physical record with IBG} \end{array}$$

Step 2. Divide the tape reel length expressed in inches by the length of the physical record (with IBG) to obtain the number of *physical* records:

$$\frac{2400 \text{ feet } \times \ 12 \text{ inches}}{1.5 \text{ inches per physical record}} = 19{,}200 \text{ physical records}$$

Step 3. Multiply the number of physical records by the blocking factor to obtain the number of *logical* records that can be stored:

$$19{,}200 \ \times \ 3 \ = \ 57{,}600 \text{ logical records}$$

Note that with all other things remaining the same, a change in the blocking factor from 1 (Example 1) to 3 doubles the storage capacity of this particular tape reel.

TAPE FILE PROCESSING

Records stored on a tape file must be organized and processed in sequential fashion, following the order in which they were written to the tape file. What types of processing applications lend themselves to this type of file organization? Perhaps it would be better to indicate first when a sequential file organization is *not* appropriate.

Searching for a particular record in a sequential file can be a relatively time-consuming process since each record must be examined in turn, beginning with the first record in the file. Clearly such a file organization does not benefit a user communicating with the computer in a time-sharing mode who wishes to reference a particular record in the file. The desired record may be the fifth record or the five thousandth record in the file; while the computer is searching, the time-sharing user must wait patiently. Consider another situation in which an office manager drops by a computer installation each Monday, with three or four transactions to be processed against a master file that contains 10,000 records. The office manager says that she is not in a hurry but needs the transactions processed by Wednesday. From the computer's standpoint, processing three or four transactions against a sequential file having 10,000 records is a very inefficient use of its time, since in searching for a particular record to update, many other records may have to be looked at before the desired record is found. The sequential file organization that the tape medium requires is therefore inappropriate for those processing applications which emphasize the speed at which a particular record may be located, or which processes a very small proportion of the records contained in the file.

This implies that tape file organization is suitable for applications in which the nature of the processing task depends on each record of the file being read, with a significant proportion of the records in the file requiring further processing. A master file updating cycle, for example, is typically based on a sequential file organization. In master file updating, changes, deletions, and additions to the master file are accumulated over a period of time and batched to form a transaction file. The transaction file is then processed against the master file at regular time intervals. Examples of this type of processing include producing customer account statements and payroll processing.

At the end of each semester a college performs a student master academic file update.

1. What data might you expect to be included in the transaction and master files?
2. What reports might be produced as a result of a master file update?

1. The *master student academic file* would include the cumulative academic record for each active student. Each record would also contain identifying and biographical information, such as student name, identification number, and address. The *transaction file* would include data to initiate additions and deletions of student master records as well as changes to existing student master records as a result of changes in biographical information (for example, change of address) or in academic information (for example, changing an *incomplete* student grade to a valid grade). At the end of each semester, a set of subject class grades must be added to each student's master academic record as part of a master file updating procedure.
2. After student grades have been updated at the end of a semester, the following documents might be generated: a complete set of student transcripts, a listing of student grades by subject class/instructor, a honor roll list, and an academic warning report listing those students with failing grade averages.

Suppose that a college has an enrollment of 5000 active students. At the end of a semester, grades are submitted for each student requiring each student's master record to be updated. What would happen if we attempted to update the master file *without* first arranging the 5000 transaction records in some logical sequence? For each transaction record the master file would have to be searched, beginning with the first record, resulting in many master records being examined repeatedly. To give a more concrete illustration let's assume for simplicity that a student master file consists of five records that are sorted according to the student identification number which serves as the key identifying field of each record:

Unsorted Transaction File	Master File
[2564]	[1121]
[1829]	[1137]
[2901]	[1829]
[1137]	[2564]
[1121]	[2901]

When records are processed in an unsorted transaction file against a master file, each time a transaction record is processed, the master file must be read from the beginning until the desired (that is, matching) record is found. Thus in updating the unsorted transaction file, transaction record 2564 requires that four master records be examined; for transaction record 1829, the file must be read from the beginning with three master records examined before the desired record is located; in processing transaction record 2901, the file must once again be read from the beginning, with each record in the file being examined before master record 2901 is located. This is an extremely time-consuming and repetitious process, yet there are only five records in the file. Imagine if the master and transaction files contained 500, 5000, or 50,000 records!

Suppose that the transaction file has been sorted previously on the same key field as the master file. It is now possible to read from both files and match record keys so that it is *not* necessary to read from the beginning of the master file each time the next transaction record is to be processed. Figure 7-3 outlines the general steps typically found in a master file updating cycle using our college grade reporting example.

Typically there are fewer records in the transaction file than in the master file. During master file processing, the transaction record and the corresponding master record must be paired in some systematic fashion. The matching process is usually based on first reading a record from the sorted transaction file and then reading records from the master file until the record keys match. The master record is then updated, and another record from the transaction file is read. The process continues until all transaction records have been processed. In order to maintain the established sequence of the records in the master file, *each active master record, regardless of whether there is a corresponding transaction record, is written to the new updated master tape file.*

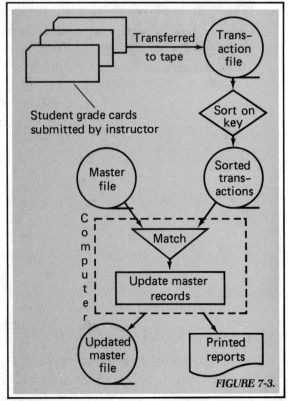

FIGURE 7-3.

To illustrate the updating process when the transaction file contains fewer records than the master file, consider a master file that consists of five records and a transaction file that contains three records. (See Figure 7-4.) (In reality, files with a small number of records can usually be handled more efficiently using a direct access file organization.) Each transaction record includes a code to indicate whether a record is to be updated, added to the file, or deleted from the file:

Transaction Code	Nature of File Activity
C	Record is to be updated (modified)
A	Record is to be added to the master file
D	Record is to be deleted from the master file

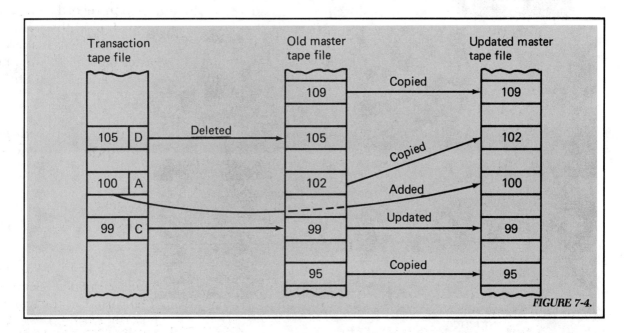

FIGURE 7-4.

In Figure 7-4, the processing begins when the first transaction record (key 99) is read into main memory. Next the first record from the master file (key 95) is read into main memory. The record keys are compared. Since the key of the master *is less than* the key of the transaction record, the master record is written to the updated master tape file and the next master record (key 99) is read into memory. The record keys are again compared and since they are *equal*, the transaction code is inspected. The transaction code of C indicates that the master record having key 99 is to be updated and then written to the updated master tape file.

The next transaction record (key 100) is read into memory followed by the next master record (key 102). Since the key of the master record is *greater than* the key of the transaction record, and the transaction code is A, the transaction record represents a master record to be added to the master file. The master record (key 102) is then written to the updated master file.

The next transaction record (key 105) followed by the next master record (key 105) are read into memory. The keys are compared. Since they are *equal*, the transaction code is examined, and the master record having key 105 is deleted from the file. With the transaction file exhausted, the remaining master records (key 109) are written to the updated master tape file.

EXAMPLE

During master file updating the keys of the transaction and master records are compared. Discuss the action taken when the key of the transaction record is:

1. equal to the key of the master record
2. greater than the key of the master record
3. less than the key of the master record

SOLUTION

1. The master record is updated (or deleted, depending on the transaction code).
2. The master record is written to the new master tape file. The next master record is then read into main memory, and the record keys are again compared.
3. There are two possibilities: (a) the transaction record represents an addition to the master file, in which case the transaction record followed by the master record that was also in memory are written to the updated master tape file; or (b) one of the files is out of sequence, in which case an appropriate error message is generated.

In order to summarize the steps followed in a master file update procedure, we consider a typical payroll processing application designed to update employee payroll master records and produce the weekly payroll.

▪ The source documents (e.g., time cards, changes in employee biographical data, changes in wage rate, etc.) are batched to form a transaction file and stored on magnetic tape via a key-to-tape data entry device.

▪ Prior to processing, the transaction file is sorted using the same key field as the master tape file. If records in the master tape file are arranged in Social Security number order, then records in the transaction file must be sorted in the same sequence.

▪ An *edit program* is run, which verifies that the records are properly sorted and that each field on the transaction record contains a legal data entry. For example, a record which contains an invalid transaction code would be flagged in the output of the edit run.

▪ Processing commences and key matching is performed as previously described. In the case of payroll processing, the master record may indicate the employee's wage rate, the number of dependents, and summary totals such as year-to-date accumulated earnings and withholding taxes previously deducted. The transaction record may include data such as the number of hours worked during the previous payroll period, a change in the employee's wage rate, or some change in biographical information such as a change in marital status. A transaction record may initiate the addition or deletion of a master file record.

  When an employee's master record is updated for purposes of producing a payroll check, the amount of hours worked is obtained from the transaction record and the wage rate is read from the master record; the gross and net salaries are calculated and, together with summary totals, are posted on the master record.

▪ The output generated by the master tape file update generally includes the following:

1. An *updated master tape file* in which each active master record from the previous master file has been written, regardless of whether there was a corresponding transaction record for the master record.

2. A *summary report*, which may include information such as total employee wages and total overtime pay. In addition, the printing of payroll checks is part of a summarizing operation.

3. *Control information*, such as the number of records processed, the number of records added, and the number of records deleted.

We stress that at the conclusion of the master file update procedure there are *three* distinct tape files present:

1. The transaction tape file.

2. The old master tape file.

3. The new (updated) master tape file.

The transaction and old master tape files are usually maintained and serve as a backup in the event that the updated master tape file is misplaced or damaged.

Before considering other types of file organizations, we note that there are both advantages and disadvantages associated with sequential tape file organization. The advantages of sequential tape file processing include the following:

■ Sequential file organization represents the simplest type of file organization, resulting in uncomplicated file creation and maintenance procedures.

■ The low cost of magnetic tape permits appropriate types of large-volume batch processing jobs to be handled economically and efficiently.

There are, however, several factors which impact on these advantages:

■ The transaction file must first be sorted, which can be a relatively time-consuming and costly operation.

■ If only a few records are to be updated, then the cost advantage of tape storage and processing is considerably diminished.

■ Since there is usually a time lag between the receipt of a transaction and its processing, the master tape file does not reflect current information.

DISK FILE ORGANIZATION

The physical design of a disk drive makes several types of file organization possible, including:

■ *Sequential file organization*, which is exactly the same as found with magnetic tape.

■ *Direct file organization*, in which records are located directly, without the need to examine any other records in the file.

■ *Indexed sequential file organization*, which represents a compromise approach. Records in an indexed sequential file may be processed either sequentially or directly.

Before elaborating on these different types of file organizations, we pause to indicate briefly how stored records are located on the disk surface. Recall that a disk surface consists of a set of concentric circles, called tracks, along which information is recorded. The tracks are labeled sequentially, beginning with the outermost track. Disk storage usually consists of a vertical stack of magnetic disks, called a disk pack. The disk pack is supported by a central rotating spindle (see Figure 2-8b). Read/write heads are provided for each disk recording surface and are supported and moved by a set of comb-like access arms, which are attached to an erect mechanism which in turn controls the in and out movement of the arms over the disk surface. The access arm assembly moves as a unit so that at any given access arm position, each read/write head is aligned over the same number track on all the disk surfaces. The set of vertically aligned tracks of a disk pack that have the same track number is referred to as a *cylinder*. Cylinder 002, for example, will consist of the set of all tracks numbered 002 on each disk surface. If the disk pack consists of ten recording surfaces, then cylinder 002 will consist of the ten surface tracks numbered 002. The cylinder concept is essential for understanding how records are addressed (located). Figure 7-5 illustrates the cylinder concept with a disk pack containing four disks (and six recording surfaces). Note that the two outermost disk surfaces are not used for storing data.

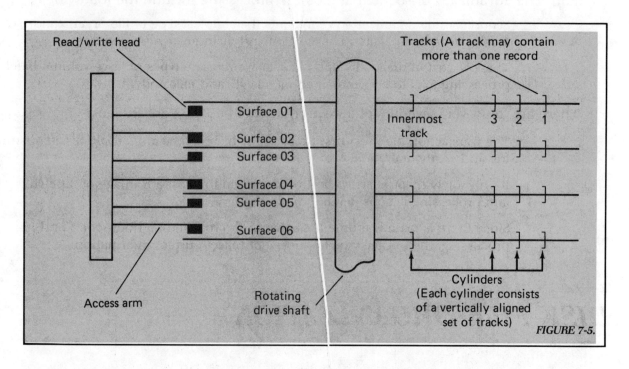

FIGURE 7-5.

In order to locate a particular record that is stored on one of the disk surfaces of a disk pack, it is necessary to know three items:

- The particular disk surface, which is identified by its number. Disk surfaces are sequentially numbered beginning with the top recording surface.

- The cylinder number, so that the read/write head assembly can be moved in or out from its previous position and aligned over the desired track.

- The record number, since a surface track may contain more than one record. Figure 7-6 illustrates addressing a record.

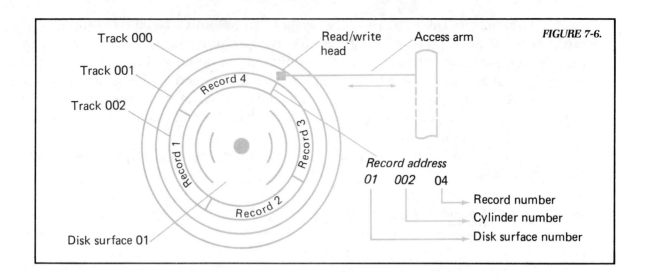

FIGURE 7-6.

Track 000
Track 001
Track 002
Record 4
Record 1
Record 3
Record 2
Disk surface 01

Read/write head
Access arm

Record address
01　　002　　04
→ Record number
→ Cylinder number
→ Disk surface number

SEQUENTIAL DISK FILE ORGANIZATION

In order to minimize the movement of the access arm assembly, records are stored sequentially on a disk pack by filling up the available space on a cylinder rather than by filling up consecutive tracks of the same disk surface and then going on to the next disk surface. For the sake of simplicity, assume that the first record of a sorted file is stored on track 001 of recording surface 01. Assuming that one record is to be stored per track, then the second record of the file will be stored on track 001 of disk surface 02; the third record is stored on track 001 of disk surface 03, and so on. The access arm assembly remains stationary until all disk surfaces are exhausted. When this occurs, the access arm assembly moves the read/write heads and positions them over the next cylinder (that is, over the next higher surface track number).

A simple example will further illustrate this process. Suppose that a disk pack consists of four recording surfaces and a file consists of ten sorted records having the following key fields: 118, 123, 150, 175, 199, 200, 210, 215, 249, and 300. Further assume that each surface track will store two records. Table 7-1 indicates how these records may be assigned storage locations on the disk surfaces.

TABLE 7-1

	Record Address		
Record Key	Disk Surface	Cylinder Number	Relative Record Number
118	01	001	1
123	01	001	2
150	02	001	3
175	02	001	4
199	03	001	5
200	03	001	6
210	04	001	7
215	04	001	8
249	01	002	9
300	01	002	10

Note that in Table 7-1 the read/write head assembly remains stationary while the first eight records are stored. In order to store the ninth record of the file (record key 249), the read/write head assembly must be moved to the next cylinder since the last record surface of the cylinder has been used. If these records had been stored on the same disk surface, then the read/write head assembly would have had to be moved after every two records stored, which is a relatively time-consuming operation.

Sequential file processing with disks is essentially indistinguishable from tape processing.

DIRECT ACCESS DISK FILES

In on-line systems where the user may wish to make an inquiry into a file in order to read a particular record, it would be too inefficient to search for the record sequentially, beginning with the first record in the file. A direct access file organization permits any record in the file to be located in the same amount of time as any other record in the file, regardless of their locations on the disk surface. This implies that a direct access file organization does not require that inquiries (that is, transactions) be batched or organized into any particular sequence. An addressing scheme is used which randomly assigns disk storage locations to records in a file, but which permits any record in the file to be accessed directly.

In a direct access disk file, the locations of stored records are determined by the key fields of the records rather than by their relative positions in a sorted file. In one common approach the address of a record is determined by subjecting the record key to a mathematical randomizing formula. The formula operates on the record key and translates it into a number which can then be transformed easily into the number of the disk surface and cylinder to which the record will be assigned. This randomizing operation, sometimes referred to as *hashing*, is accomplished by a programming routine. Each time the randomizing formula is applied to a given record key, the identical record address is generated. This permits a stored record to be located by repeating the identical mathematical procedure that was used to determine the record's address at the time when the record was originally written to the disk. Figure 7-7 outlines the randomization process.

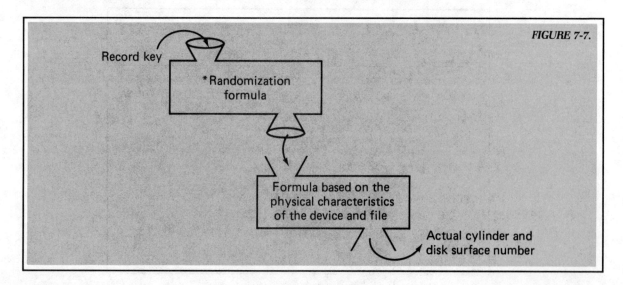

FIGURE 7-7.

Record key

*Randomization formula

Formula based on the physical characteristics of the device and file

Actual cylinder and disk surface number

A common randomization technique is based on a division and remainder algorithm:

1. Determine the prime number (number divisible only by itself and 1) closest to, but not exceeding the number of tracks allocated to the file.

2. Divide the key by this number. The remainder in this division example gives the relative position of the stored record in the file.

For example, suppose that a record key is 2934 and 100 tracks are to be allocated to the file.

1. The prime number closest to 100 is 97.

2.
$$
\begin{array}{r}
30 \\
97\overline{)\,2934} \\
291 \\
\hline
24 \text{ remainder}
\end{array}
$$

24 represents the relative position of the stored record in the file. Based on the number of disk surfaces and the assigned address of the first record in the file, the actual surface and cylinder number of the record can be determined.

It is possible that two or more record keys will randomize into the same address; two such record keys are called *synonyms*. Sometimes synonyms will fit on the same calculated cylinder (track) address. In the event they do not, the programmer provides for an overflow area. It should be noted that there are a number of different randomizing formulas that are available to the programmer. If the application of one formula produces an uneven distribution of record keys on the available disk surfaces, then the programmer will usually experiment with other randomizing formulas.

Updating a direct access file is considerably different from processing a sequentially organized file. The advantages of a direct access file update include the following:

- Individual transactions need not be sorted since the corresponding master records may be addressed directly.

- Transactions may be processed on-line rather than in a batch processing mode as with a tape file.

- Only those records that are to be updated are read and written. In a tape master file update, each record in the file is read and written onto a new master tape file, resulting in an increased expenditure of time and money.

- Record additions are placed in an area of the disk reserved by the programmer for this purpose. Records to be deleted from the disk file are typically read into memory and a special code is inserted in a field of the record to indicate that it is an inactive record. The inactive record is then stored in its original location on the disk. In a tape file, additions and deletions of records require a new master tape file to be written.

Direct access disk file organization does not make as economical use of the storage space on the medium as does sequential file organization. With disk storage, the randomization process often leads to an uneven distribution of records on the allocated disk surface. Additional unused space on the disk surface is intentionally created by the programmer since he or she must anticipate record additions to the file and accordingly reserve storage space. Often the programmer will overestimate in order to provide for unexpected additions. Furthermore, inactive records remain on the disk surface, at least for a time.

When a direct access file is processed, the records are read into main memory, updated, and then rewritten back to the *same* physical location as the old record, thus destroying a potential backup record. With tape processing, the old master file together with the transaction file form a backup. A more subtle disadvantage of an *on-line* direct access file is that with many different users having access to the same file, there is a greater danger that the file may be tampered with and its contents corrupted, either intentionally or unintentionally.

ISAM FILES

Indexed sequential access method (ISAM) files offer greater flexibility than sequential or direct file organizations by permitting records to be accessed sequentially or directly. To contrast the difference between the three file organizations, consider the problem of locating a particular topic in a textbook, which was given as a homework assignment in a data processing class. One approach would be to begin with page 1 and examine each consecutive page until the desired topic is located; this is an example of sequential access. Another method would be to ask the instructor on what page number the topic is located and then to turn directly to the page without examining each page that precedes it; this is an example of direct access. The most familiar approach would be to inspect the index at the rear of the book for the page of the topic and then to turn directly to the appropriate topic. The latter approach corresponds to how a record may be accessed directly in an indexed sequential file organization.

In creating an indexed sequential file, records are stored following a sequential file organization. In addition, an index or "table of contents" is maintained on the disk, which lists each record key and its address on the disk. In a textbook the topic would correspond to the record key and its page number to the record's address.

For sequential processing, the records are read in the same sequence that they were stored. In direct accessing of an indexed sequential file, the index is first examined in order to determine the address of the record; the record may then be located without having to process the preceding records on the disk file sequentially. After the initial creation of the file it may be necessary to add records to the file. New records are usually stored on overflow tracks with appropriate entries made to the file index. Periodically a file maintenance procedure is performed in which inactive records are deleted, and active records stored on the overflow tracks are copied onto the primary data tracks.

The ability to process records stored in an indexed sequential file either sequentially or directly is a compelling advantage to this type of file organization. There are many applications in which this flexibility in accessing is preferred. For example, consider a college which maintains computer files on its students. At the end of each semester each student's transcript must be updated to reflect the previous semester's grades. Sequential processing would be appropriate in this instance. At unpredictable times during the school year an inquiry or update to a particular student's record may be initiated. Interrogation of the student academic file in this case would be most efficient with direct accessing. There is, however, a distinct disadvantage associated with this type of file organization. Since the file's index must be read by the computer before file processing can begin, direct accessing under this file organization is slower compared to a direct file organization in which a randomizing formula is used to determine a record's location.

Another major weakness of ISAM is that record addresses are expressed in terms of cylinder and disk surface numbers, making this type of file organization only suitable for disk devices. The virtual storage access method (VSAM) is an alternate type of file organization that also permits the sequential and direct accessing of stored records. VSAM, however, uses an addressing scheme in which records are assigned to fixed-length storage areas that are independent of a cylinder and surface number. VSAM is therefore compatible with *any* secondary storage device. Under ISAM record additions are accommodated through the use of special overflow tracks. VSAM provides for record additions by allocating "free space" *throughout* the file, thereby allowing record additions and rearrangements to be handled more efficiently.

DATA BASE MANAGEMENT

In the infant stages of electronic data processing, computerization tended to filter through a business organization in such a way that each department shared the same computer mainframe but otherwise functioned as an autonomous data processing unit. Each department collected its own data and organized its own set of computer files. It was not uncommon to find several departments maintaining files that contained many of the same data items. This type of overlapping in information is referred to as *data redundancy*.

The efficiency gained in business operations, which was attributed to the implementation of computer systems, was offset to some extent by this problem of data redundancy. For example, if an employee's address was stored in several different department files that maintained employee-related data, then a change in his or her address would necessitate the updating of *several* different files. Furthermore, if one of these files were not updated, then the integrity (accuracy) of the data would be in question since different data entries would appear for the same data item (i.e., address) in different places.

In recognition of these problems, the concept of a *data base* evolved. A logical approach, for example, would be to have all the data related to an employee located in a single place. This would not only minimize data redundancy, but it would allow any changes in employee data to be processed once, thus assuring the integrity of the data. All authorized departments would then have access to this file and would be able to access selectively the information they required from it. Furthermore, this centralization of data allows the various department users to be free of the technical details relating to how the file is organized (for example, sequential versus indexed sequential). The job would fall to a special data base manager. This is the essence of a data base approach to the organization and maintenance of information within a business organization.

In general, a data base consists of a related set of files and exhibits the following characteristics:

- The files are consolidated so that data redundancy is minimized.

- The data base is made available to a variety of different users who may require the data for a number of different applications.

- The organization of the records and files that make up the data base reflects the logical relationships inherent in the data being stored rather than the particular needs of the various people who will use the data. As a result, each department or user can retrieve the data with equal effort, the organization of the data being independent of the nature of the applications programs that will access the data.

The supervision of requests for data from the data base is handled by a sophisticated software system known as data base management system (DBMS). A DBMS is usually supplied by the computer manufacturer or a specialized software vendor. The programs that make up the DBMS are written in a special data base language such as CODASYL (a COBOL-like language) or DL/1 (an IBM data language). In many larger computer systems, a separate memory partition is assigned to the DBMS where it interfaces between the operating system and the applications program. With a DBMS the programmer need not be concerned with the details of how a particular file is organized. Regardless of the data accessed, the programmer's request for data usually takes the same general form, which is dictated by the particular DBMS that has been installed.

A variety of microcomputer-compatible DBMS software packages are available. Essentially these programs function as electronic filing systems, offering the user varying degrees of versatility in organizing and then selectively retrieving stored information. The *Personal Filing System** offered by Software Publishing Corporation is a small-scale DBMS. *VisiFile** from VISICORP is a versatile and easy to use filing system which allows files to be easily organized, scanned, and manipulated. Another sophisticated data base manager is *DB Master** offered by Stoneware. Like VisiFile, DB Master permits the user to specify multiple criteria in selectively accessing information.

After a DBMS software package has been acquired, it must be implemented according to the particular needs of the user. Typically, this consists of three general steps:

- *Deciding upon the type and structure of each file.* Each file must be described so that the contents and record layout are defined, including a description of the type of data item that will be entered in each field. In designing a payroll file, for example, the information that each employee record will contain and its format must be planned by the end user, often in conjunction with a computer consultant.

- *Keying in data.* Once the format of a record in a particular file has been established, the corresponding data can be entered. In a payroll file, the required data for each employee must be entered (e.g., name, address, social security number, payroll deductions, and wage rate). This is easy to do but can be time consuming.

*Names are copyrighted trademarks of the indicated software vendors.

■ *Learning to use the system.* Some amount of study is needed in order to exploit the capabilities of the system fully. Many systems, for example, permit various types of sorting, calculations between specified fields, merging files, using multiple criteria to access certain records selectively (for example, scanning an employee payroll file for workers who have been with the firm for less than two years *and* who are earning more than $25,000 a year), and printing various types of formatted reports (including mailing labels).

More sophisticated data base managers are also available for microcomputers. The Ashton-Tate *dBase II* is a popular *relational* data base management software system which offers increased flexibility in operating on stored data files. A relational data base system is usually written in a specialized data base programming language which permits the user to modify individual data items as well as to update the entire data base at once by using a single command. As with a DBMS that is used in a commercial environment with larger computer systems, each data base is created independent of the programs that will use the data.

Most relational data base systems offer a *query language* facility which enables the user to request information by using simple English phrases or commands. Less sophisticated file management systems tend to be *menu driven.* In menu driven systems the user expresses requests for information by selecting an option from a prepared list or menu of choices, which are displayed on the CRT screen. Systems which support a query language tend to be more powerful and versatile than systems in which system commands can be selected only from a supplied menu of options.

The typical user of a data base management system finds it easier to retrieve information from the data base by making appropriate selections from a planned menu. Many relational data base systems allow a programmer to create customized menu driven systems.

MIS

In larger organizations, data are often required by management in order to make decisions. A management information system (MIS) is a data processing structure that is designed to provide accurate information to management so that decisions can be made in a timely fashion. An effective MIS requires:

■ A comprehensive DBMS

■ A sufficiently large computer system, which supports on-line CRT terminals that are strategically located throughout the business organization

■ Trained personnel and, in very large organizations, an in-house technical support team

■ A hierarchical managerial structure in which decision-making responsibilities and communication lines are clearly defined

■ A strong commitment, financial and otherwise, to electronic data processing (EDP) by management

■ Provision for the planning of new projects, the monitoring of current projects, and the periodic evaluation of current systems

DATA PROTECTION AND SECURITY

A DBMS also serves another important function—data security. Within any organization it is necessary to take precautions to guard against the unauthorized accessing of confidential data files. Since each request for data must be handled by the data base management system, it is also a function of the DBMS to protect its data files against unauthorized use. A *password* system is typically found on on-line computer systems. In order to use the system or access particular data files, the user must first supply the correct password. The password may simply be an authorized account number, or it may be a secret word that only the authorized user knows. More sophisticated schemes are in use, but it is generally acknowledged that no security system is foolproof.

It is a standard data processing practice to take steps to protect stored program and data files against losses resulting from accidental erasure, mishandling, theft, or some natural disaster such as fire. A routine practice is to make *backup* copies of important files and then to store them in vaults or at locations distant from the computer site at which the original copies are being used.

In sequential master file updating, the previous master and transaction files form a natural backup to the newly written master. If the newly created master is destroyed, then the master can be recreated from the old master and transaction files. Frequently at least the previous two master files are maintained. If we consider the most current master file to be the "son," then the "father" and "grandfather" master tape files are also stored.

In updating a direct access file, the previous master becomes the new master, with each updated record replacing the original record in the same storage location on the disk surface. In order to provide a backup of the most current master file, it would be necessary to copy the file after each update job run. Utility programs are available which copy from disk to disk or from disk to tape. Since tape is less expensive than disk storage, the contents of a disk file are frequently "dumped" onto tape rather than on a removable disk pack. In some installations, large direct access files are not copied each time the file is updated. Instead, only the updated records are copied, resulting in a less costly and time-consuming backup procedure. The entire master file would then be copied according to some established schedule, often on a weekly basis.

SOME SAFEGUARDS IN HANDLING TAPE

Tapes and disks are labeled externally to protect against inadvertently picking up the wrong tape or disk and recording over its stored contents. Machine-readable labels that precede stored files also provide identifying information.

Suppose that a tape reel has been left on a tape drive and contains vital information that is to be stored permanently. A careless operator may forget to remove the tape from the tape drive unit and then direct the computer to write onto the tape, thus destroying its previous contents. In order to protect against this type of disaster, a plastic file protection ring is used. The file protection ring must be inserted in the center of the tape reel in order for a write operation to commence using the tape. If the tape reel does not have the protection ring inserted, then the tape drive permits the tape to be used exclusively for read operations.

PROTECTING DATA STORED ON CASSETTES AND DISKETTES

In microcomputer systems, auxiliary storage is provided by cassette tapes and diskettes. In order to protect program and data files stored on these media, certain precautions in the care and handling of these items should be observed.

- Since both are magnetic-based media, tapes and diskettes should not be subjected to magnetic fields, excessive heat, direct sunlight, or static electricity.

- The magnetic surface coating should not be touched.

- The stored contents of tape and diskette can be protected against accidental erasure resulting from recording over existing files by *write-protecting* the tape and diskette. A write-protect notch is located on the side of the disk jacket. When the notch is covered with a foil tab, the diskette cannot be written on. A cassette tape has two write-protect notches located in the corners opposite the tape access opening of the cassette frame sides. Punching out the tabs prevents the tape from being written on. If a cassette tape is write-protected, the user may write onto the tape only by first covering the notches with a piece of tape. (Actually, each notch corresponds to a different side of the tape.)

- Less tape is better than more tape; that is, when purchasing cassette tapes, select tapes that offer no more than 30 minutes of recording time. Longer tapes can increase the amount of time it takes to locate a stored file. In addition, there is a greater tendency for longer tapes to stretch, particularly in climates that suffer from high humidity.

- With respect to diskette storage:
  1. Never remove the diskette from its protective jacket.
  2. Do not remove the diskette when the red "in use" light is on.
  3. In labeling the diskette, use the labels supplied with the diskette. Never write on the label with a pencil or ball point pen. Instead, write gently using a felt-tip pen.
  4. Never bend the diskette.
  5. Unused disks should be stored in an upright position. (Special diskette storage cases can be purchased for this purpose.)

Both cassettes and diskettes provide the ultimate form of protection against their unauthorized use—they are light and compact enough to enable the user to walk away with them at the end of a work session, thus preventing anyone else from having access to their contents.

Due to the susceptibility of magnetic storage media to accidental erasure and physical damage, as well as to loss due to misplacement or theft, the importance of making backup copies of important files cannot be overemphasized.

REVIEW EXERCISES

True or False?

1. A tape file may exceed the capacity of a single reel of magnetic tape.
2. A blocking factor of 5 means that after every five consecutive logical records there is a gap of blank tape.
3. In master file updating with tape, the master file is written onto another reel of tape.
4. As the blocking factor increases, the storage capacity of the tape reel decreases.
5. A file protection ring prevents unauthorized read operations from being made from a tape file.
6. A master file updating procedure in which a relatively large number of transactions are processed at regular time intervals usually depends on a sequential file organization.
7. Direct accessing is fastest with an indexed sequential file organization.
8. A cylinder consists of the set of all tracks on a given disk surface.
9. Additions of records to a file is more efficient with respect to processing time in a direct access file organization than in a sequential file.
10. A data base seeks to minimize data redundancy while maximizing data integrity.
11. The most economical use of space on a storage medium is achieved through a direct access file organization.
12. With direct access master file updating, a new master file is written.
13. DBMS not only simplifies data updating, but also reduces the effort required in writing applications programs that use the data base.
14. Retrieving information from an indexed sequential file organization is called hashing.
15. In direct access master file updating, updated records are placed into an overflow area.

Multiple Choice

16. Which file organization offers the greatest flexibility?
    a. sequential b. direct c. ISAM d. VSAM
17. Which is a function of a DBMS?
    a. to minimize data redundancy
    b. to provide data security
    c. to simplify a programmer's work in accessing data
    d. all of these
18. Which of the following statements are *false*?
    a. MIS is essentially synonymous with DBMS.
    b. In direct file organization keys may randomize into the same address.

c. An indexed sequential file organization is created by sequentially storing records.

d. A tape file is labeled internally and externally.

19. Which is a disadvantage of tape file processing?

    a. The transaction file must first be sorted.

    b. A master tape file usually does not reflect the most up-to-date information.

    c. It is relatively expensive to process a low proportion of transaction records.

    d. All of these.

20. The use of computers as an aid in decision making is most closely associated with:

    a. DBMS **b.** MIS **c.** ISAM **d.** CODASYL

21. Which of the following statements regarding a data base is *false*?

    a. The overlapping of the contents of data files is reduced.

    b. Data are organized based on application areas.

    c. It may be used in batch and on-line processing.

    d. None of these.

22. In sequential file updating:

    a. New records are added to the end of the file.

    b. An entire new master file is created each time an individual record is changed.

    c. Efficiency increases as the number of processed records decreases.

    d. The new file must be written on magnetic tape.

23. Which of the following is *not* true when updating a direct access file?

    a. The transaction file does not have to be sorted.

    b. Updating usually takes place in a batch processing mode.

    c. Each updated record is written back into the same location as the original record.

    d. All of these.

24. Which of the following file organizations are possible on a disk medium?

    a. direct   **d.** a and c

    b. sequential   **e.** all of these

    c. indexed sequential

25. A sequential file organization:

    a. is typically found in on-line systems

    b. yields faster access times than a random access file in locating a particular record

    c. is typically used in a batch processing environment

    d. is never more efficient than a random access file organization.

26. A data base management system is:

    a. a group of computer programs

    b. a management plan for organizing and distributing information within an organization

    c. based on an indexed sequential file organization

    d. recommended only for very large organizations

27. In an indexed sequential file organization:
   a. records are stored randomly, but are accessed either directly or sequentially
   b. records are stored sequentially, but are accessed either directly or sequentially by applying a randomizing formula to the record key
   c. records are stored sequentially, but are accessed either directly or sequentially by referring to a stored index
   d. records are stored randomly, but are accessed either directly or sequentially by referring to a stored index

28. The application of a randomizing formula:
   a. guarantees that each record key will generate a unique address
   b. guarantees that record locations will be uniformly distributed
   c. establishes a predictable mathematical relationship between a record key and its address
   d. is used in indexed sequential files

29. What is a typical size of an IRG?
   a. 0.06 inch   c. 6 inches
   b. 0.6 inch   d. 60 inches

30. Record addresses in a sequential access disk file are based on cylinder numbers in order to:
   a. minimize the movement of the read/write head assembly
   b. maximize the storage capacity of the disk
   c. minimize the number of synonyms
   d. all of these

31. In a direct access file organization, a record is located based on:
   a. examining previous records in the file
   b. manipulating the contents of a particular field
   c. its position in the index
   d. its length

32. In a student academic file, the record key selected might be the:
   a. students' last names   c. students' grade point
   b. students' ID   averages
      numbers   d. length of the record

33. Which of the following file organizations is available on both tape and disk?
   a. direct   c. indexed sequential
   b. sequential   d. none of these

34. All of the following statements are true except:
   a. A DBMS function is to provide data security.
   b. An underlying theme of organizing a data base is that data are an organizational resource that should be shared.
   c. DBMS and MIS are completely independent concepts.
   d. Hashing is applied to a record key in order to determine its storage location.

35. The key of a particular record to be updated in a direct access file is 4321. There are 200 tracks allocated to the file. Using the prime number division and remainder algorithm, determine the relative location of the record in the file.

a. 21 **b.** 142 **c.** 121 **d.** 200 **e.** none of these

 # EXCURSION INTO BASIC

This section offers a brief and somewhat simplified introduction to sequential disk file processing in BASIC using a microcomputer. Unfortunately, the set of system commands used to create and retrieve externally stored files varies sharply from manufacturer to manufacturer. The discussion that follows is based on the Apple IIe microcomputer manufactured by Apple Computer, Inc. Although the syntax and structure of input/output disk file commands generally vary from machine to machine (being dependent on the particular disk operating system that is used by the microcomputer), the underlying concepts are the same regardless of the particular microcomputer which is used.

Frequently, the number of program statements or the volume of data that is to be periodically processed by a program is so great that it becomes a significant chore to type the information manually each time the program is run. It may then be worthwhile to save the program and data on a diskette and retrieve them at some future date when they are needed. Programs and data are maintained on a diskette as *files*. To save a *program* that has already been typed in and is stored in main memory:

▪ Insert a previously *initialized* diskette (see the user's manual of the microcomputer being used) into the disk drive.

▪ Decide upon a program *filename*.

▪ Type the (Apple IIe) system command, SAVE *filename*.

▪ Press the RETURN key.

The SAVE command is fairly universal. Some computers require that the filename that appears in DOS (disk operating system) commands be enclosed within quotation marks. *Note:* all system commands must be followed by hitting the RETURN key.

If you now type the system command NEW, the program will be erased from main memory. You may verify this by typing the command LIST. No program statements will appear on the screen. To retrieve the program from the disk, type the command, LOAD *filename*. The filename must be exactly the same as the name given to the program file when it was originally saved on the disk. After some disk drive activity, a copy of the program that is stored on the disk under the filename entered will be placed into main memory. (If the filename given in the LOAD command does not match a program filename that is stored on the disk, then a FILE NOT FOUND error will occur). You may verify that the program has been loaded into main memory by once again typing the command LIST. A listing of program statements should appear on the screen. With the Apple IIe, the program may be loaded into main memory and executed using the single command, RUN *filename*.

A single disk may contain many different files. If you forget what has been stored on the diskette, type the command CATALOG which will display the disk's "table of contents," which for some microcomputers is called a *directory*.

Creating a *data* file is considerably more involved. To write a data file we must first establish an electronic "pipeline" so that data entered via the keyboard can be routed to the appropriate disk file *rather than to the display screen*. This is accomplished by using the DOS OPEN and WRITE commands. The OPEN statement includes the programmer-determined name of the data file and serves to establish a communications link between the data keyed in and the disk file that will store the data. The WRITE statement instructs the computer to write all program output (that is, data) that follows to the disk file and *not* to the CRT display screen. The specific commands that are used with the Apple IIe are:

PRINT CHR$(4); "OPEN *filename*"
PRINT CHR$(4); "WRITE *filename*"

Although DOS OPEN and WRITE commands are found in all microcomputer systems, the syntax of the OPEN and WRITE commands illustrated above is peculiar to the Apple II family of computers. CHR$(4), for example, is the *Apple* BASIC language representation of the control keys, CONTROL-D. In general, all Apple IIe I/O disk file commands take the form:

PRINT CHR$(4); *"file command"*

The Apple IIe, like other microcomputers, requires that data be supplied to the disk data file from within a program. The following program creates a sequential data file whose filename is GRADES. Each data record consists of a student's name (N$) and two exam grades (X1 and X2).

```
2    REM   *****************************************************
4    REM   ***      PROGRAM CREATES A SEQUENTIAL DATA FILE      ***
5    REM   *                                                       *
6    REM   *         CHR$(4) = A SPECIAL CONTROL SIGNAL            *
7    REM   *         DATA FILE NAME IS GRADES                      *
8    REM   *                                                       *
9    REM   *****************************************************
10   PRINT CHR$(4); "OPEN GRADES"
20   PRINT CHR$(4); "WRITE GRADES"
30   READ N$, X1, X2
35   REM TO WRITE DATA TO THE DISK DATA FILE USE:
40   PRINT N$; "," ; X1; "," ; X2
50   IF N$ = "EOF" THEN 70 : REM NO MORE DATA
60   GO TO 30 : REM RETURN TO READ NEXT DATA RECORD
70   PRINT CHR$(4); "CLOSE GRADES"
80   REM DATA RECORDS FOLLOW
91   DATA "JON AMES", 90, 84
92   DATA "TIM BOSTON", 74, 93
93   DATA "MIKE CHARLES", 48, 75
94   DATA "EOF", 0, 0
99   END
```

After keying in this program, the command RUN is used to execute the program.

PROGRAM COMMENTARY

Line Numbers	Explanation
10–20	The file GRADES is "readied" on a disk which should be inserted into the disk drive before the program is executed.
30	A single data record is read.
40	Output is written to the disk file and *not* to the screen. The commas are used to separate (that is, to distinguish between) stored data items in the diskette data file. The punctuation that is illustrated is mandatory.
50 and 70	A trailer record identified by EOF is tested for. If encountered, program control is transferred to statement number 70 which closes the file. Before any program that involves disk I/O operations is terminated, all files that were opened must be closed.
60	If the trailer record is not present, then program control is transferred back to the READ statement in order to process the next data record.
80–94	This section of the program contains the data that are to be stored on the disk in the data file having the name GRADES.

After this program is executed, a data file with the name GRADES is stored on the disk with an appropriate entry automatically made on the disk's catalog. To verify that the file has been stored on the disk, type the command CATALOG. The disk's table of contents should show the addition of a data file having the name GRADES.

Suppose we now wish to retrieve the data and actually use them in a program designed to serve some data processing function. For instance, let us prepare a program that retrieves the data and then supplies them to a program that is designed to print the name of each student, the average of the student's two exam scores, and the number of data records processed. In order to accomplish this, we must OPEN the data file, and then READ from the file. After processing is finished, the file must be CLOSED. (See Figure 7-8 and the program on page 230.)

The pipeline that connects the disk data file with the area in main memory that will store the retrieved data is established when the OPEN statement is executed. Data flow from the data file into main memory whenever a BASIC input statement is executed, provided it is preceded by a DOS READ statement. When the CLOSE statement is executed, the pipeline between the disk data file and main memory is severed.

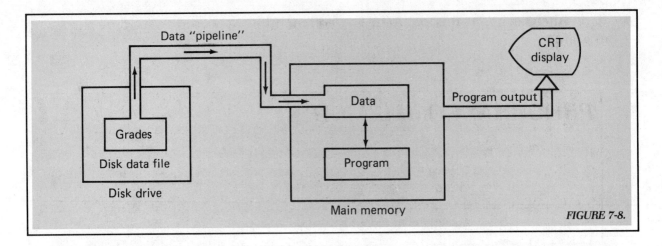

FIGURE 7-8.

In this program, lines 20–40 have the effect of instructing the computer to read data from the disk file GRADES (not from the keyboard console) and then to assign the first three data values read to variables N$, X1, and X2.

As can well be imagined, there is considerably more than this involved in the creation and manipulation of program and data files. For example, we have not mentioned how to add data to a data file that has already been stored on the disk or how to create and process *random access* data files. These topics are addressed in microcomputer user manuals and specialized textbooks.

```
1    REM*******************************************************************
2    REM****          PROGRAM PROCESSES DATA FROM A              *****
3    REM****             SEQUENTIAL DATA FILE                     *****
4    REM*                                                            *
5    REM*             FILE NAME IS GRADES                           *
6    REM*                                                            *
7    REM*          PROGRAM VARIABLE NAMES:                          *
8    REM*             N$ = STUDENT NAME                             *
9    REM*             X1 AND X2 = EXAM SCORES                       *
10   REM*             C  = COUNT OF DATA RECORDS                    *
11   REM*             AV = EXAM AVERAGE                             *
12   REM*                                                            *
13   REM*******************************************************************
15   C = 0
20   PRINT CHR$(4); "OPEN GRADES"
30   PRINT CHR$(4); "READ GRADES"
40   INPUT N$, X1, X2
50   IF N$ = "EOF" THEN 100 : REM NO MORE DATA
60   C = C + 1
70   AV = (X1 + X2) / 2
80   PRINT N$, "AVERAGE = "; AV
85   PRINT
90   GO TO 40 : REM RETURN TO READ NEXT DATA RECORD
100  PRINT CHR$(4); "CLOSE GRADES"
110  PRINT
120  PRINT C;" STUDENT RECORDS WERE PROCESSED"
130  END
```

MMUNICATIONS DATA
COMMUNICATIONS DAT
ATIONS DATA COMMU
A COMMUNICATIONS D
ATA COMMUNICATIONS

CHAPTER

8

DATA COMMUNICATIONS

DA
MU
AT

TA
M
IC

CATIONS DATA COMMU
UNICATIONS DATA COM

DATA COMMUNICATIONS

The need to transmit data and jobs to a central computer site from geographically distant locations has become a major consideration in the overall design of the data processing systems of large business organizations. *Data communications* is the general term used to describe the transmission of information from one location to another so that the information remains intact. Communication of data over long distance, for example via telephone, radio, television, or satellite, is referred to as *telecommunications*. It is sometimes convenient to describe data processing that is dependent upon telecommunications systems as *teleprocessing*.

Several aspects of data communications have already been encountered in previous discussions relating to on-line processing and time-sharing. In general, the practice of initiating a data processing job from a location that is remote from the mainframe and then telecommunicating it to the mainframe for processing is referred to as remote job entry (RJE). The RJE terminal (I/O device) may be either a CRT type of keyboard device with a display or a batch-oriented device such as a card reader and printer. When received at the central computer site, the job or data may be processed in a time-sharing mode, stored on an on-line secondary storage device and placed on an active job queue, or stored off-line and processed at some established time intervals in a batch processing mode.

DATA COMMUNICATIONS LINES

Exactly how is information transported over long distances? Without getting too technical, the answer in the majority of situations is: in much the same way as words spoken into a telephone receiver at one end of a conversation are transmitted to the person at the other end. In fact, ordinary telephone lines are a commonly used medium for the transmission of computer data from one location to another. There are, however, some complications. Computers represent information in digital form as *on* (binary 1) and *off* (binary 0) electrical pulses. Most telephone lines, however, are not capable of carrying either sound or digital signals, being able to send electrical *waveforms* only. (See Figure 8-1.)

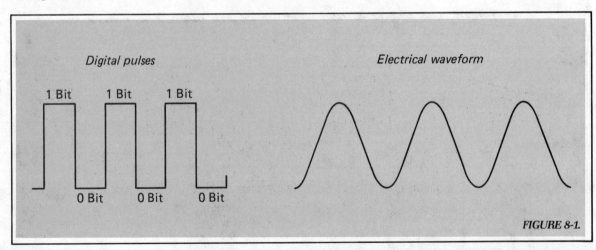

FIGURE 8-1.

In voice communication, information in the form of sound waves is first converted into an equivalent (i.e., analog) electrical waveform. The information is then transmitted over the telephone lines in this analog waveform. At the receiving end the electrical waveform is converted back into the corresponding sound waves. Thus, this form of transmission is based on making an analogy between sound and electrical waves, with appropriate signal conversions being made at both ends of the transmission. (See Figure 8-2.)

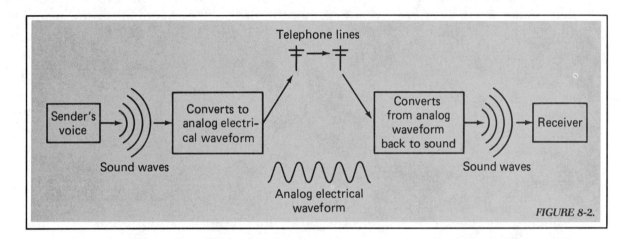

FIGURE 8-2.

In an effort to make the transmission of computer-related data as economical as possible, telecommunications systems seek to capitalize on the existence of telephone lines. In order to make the digital computer signal compatible with the analog electrical wave transmission required by telephone line communication, special encoding (digital to analog wave) and decoding (analog wave to digital) devices are placed at either end of the data communications line. The devices which perform this critical signal conversion are called *modems* (*modulator/demodulator*). Sometimes the term *data set* is used to refer to the device that performs this function. (See Figure 8-3.)

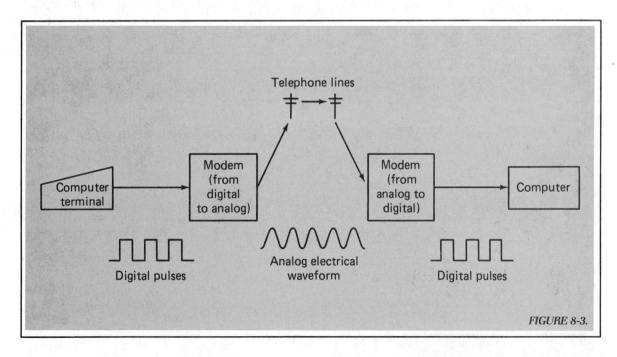

FIGURE 8-3.

Two types of telephone lines are generally available with modems: dial-up and leased (dedicated) lines. With dial-up, each time a communications link is to be established the remote user dials a special telephone number, supplied by the central computer site, in much the same way that one would dial the home telephone number of an acquaintance. After the number has been dialed, the telephone company uses its switching circuits to choose a telephone line path that will complete the connection. Typically, a different path is followed each time the number is dialed. Since a computer will usually have only a few lines available for dial-up service, it is entirely possible that the user will occasionally get a busy signal when dialing, indicating that all the lines are engaged. This situation is avoided when a leased line is used. With a leased line a single telephone line is dedicated to servicing a particular user; that is, a permanent connection represented by a reserved telephone line path exists between the user and the computer. For the privilege of having this private line to the computer, the user pays a fixed monthly charge, which varies according to the geographic locations of the sites and their distances apart. Dial-up charges are based on a unit message rate. Dial-up charges will therefore depend on the extent of use of the equipment.

The monthly flat fee of a leased line tends to be higher than charges associated with a dial-up installation, particularly for low to moderate use. A leased line is often more reliable, less subject to noise (interference), and more convenient than a dial-up line since it is not shared (i.e., no busy signals occur). The choice of which of the two types of line to rent will usually depend upon the volume and urgency of the data communications. Installations which communicate frequently with the mainframe, which cannot tolerate the potential delays inherent in a dial-up system, and which require special modems offering higher speeds of data transfer, will generally opt for a leased line.

Modems tend to be stationary, being wired on one end to the telephone communications cable and on the other end to the terminal. An *acoustic coupler* offers greater flexibility than a modem, allowing the communications link between mainframe and terminal to be established using any standard telephone handset. The acoustic coupler requires no special wiring since the modem is contained within the unit. (See Figure 8-4.) Using this device, one merely dials the special

FIGURE 8–4. Radio Shack TRS-80 MODEM 1, with acoustic coupler.
The suction cups are the receptacles for the telephone receiver. (Courtesy of Radio Shack, a division of Tandy Corporation.)

telephone number supplied by the computer center, waits for the computer to acknowledge as indicated by a high-pitch audio signal, and then inserts the telephone handset into the acoustic coupler which completes the communications link. (See Figure 8-5.)

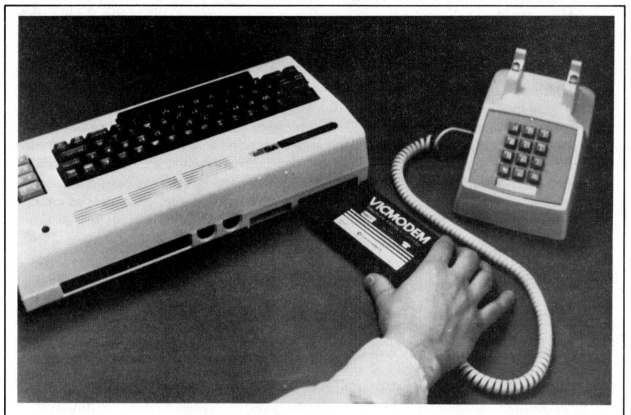

FIGURE 8–5. *Commodore VIC-20 MODEM. The VICMODEM provides an alternate means for establishing a communications link based on using the modular connector from the telephone handset which plugs directly into the VICMODEM, thereby eliminating the need for an acoustic coupler. The modem, in turn, plugs into a receptacle in the back of VIC-20 personal microcomputer.* (Courtesy of Commodore Business Machines, Inc.)

Once the data communications link is made, the transmission of data may take one of three forms, depending on the type of equipment:

- *simplex,* in which data communication proceeds in only one direction (for example, from the terminal to the central computer)

- *half-duplex,* in which data communication may take place in either direction but not at the same time

- *full-duplex,* in which data communication may occur in both directions at the same time

In addition to classifying data communications lines according to the direction of information flow, communications lines may be categorized according to the speed of data transmission. *Narrowband* channels, such as telegraph lines, transmit data at a rate of from 75 to 300 bits per second or 75 to 300 *baud,* where 1 baud equals 1 bit per second.

Telephone lines are an example of a *voice-grade* line that typically has a transmission rate of 2,400 baud. Higher rates, usually in multiples of 2,400, are available, but require special modems and a leased line. The fastest rates of data transmission are available with *wideband* channels, which offer speeds as high as one million bits per second. Microwave (radio wave) and satellite communications systems are based on wideband channel communications. Each of the three types of communications channel supports both dial-up and leased-line services. Most teleprocessing is performed over voice-grade lines. Modems which allow microcomputers to transmit or receive data over ordinary telephone lines typically operate at speeds of 300 or 1,200 baud.

Digital-to-digital communications lines requiring no modems are available on a relatively small scale, primarily due to economic rather than technological reasons. The ability for data communications systems to use existing digital/analog communications lines gives this mode of data communications a cost advantage over implementing new digital-to-digital communications systems. As new communications systems are introduced to handle the increasing demands placed on existing systems, many rely on digital data transmission.

DATA COMMUNICATIONS NETWORKS

A planned system of data communications in which two or more computers are linked by communications channels is referred to as a data communications *network*. A data communications network may take several different forms. Two of the most common arrangements are the *star* and the *ring* networks. In a star configuration a large mainframe serves as the nucleus of the network, with smaller satellite computer installations (terminals or minicomputers) telecommunicating with it. All centralized processing must pass through the main computer. Since this computer mainframe services all other data processing components that are linked to it, the central computer is sometimes referred to as the *host* computer. (See Figure 8-6.) In a ring network, computers of approximately equal power are intercon-

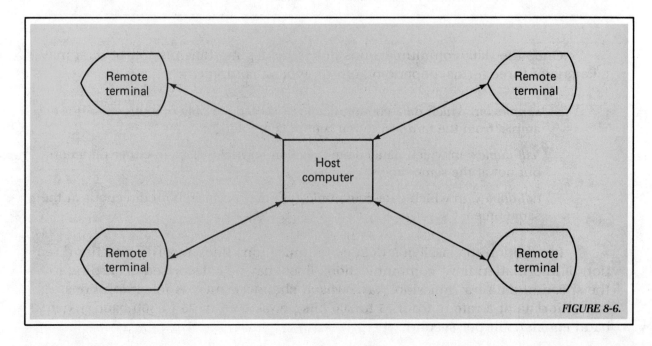

FIGURE 8-6.

nected in a circular fashion. (See Figure 8-7.) In a star configuration, if the main computer goes down, all processing is suspended; in a ring grouping, it is possible to bypass a malfunctioning member of the network.

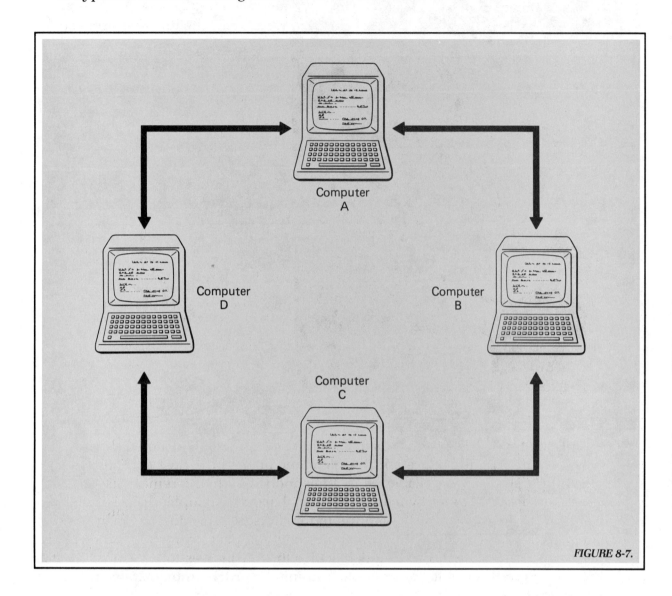

Computer A

Computer D

Computer B

Computer C

FIGURE 8-7.

In the establishment of a data communications network in which one computer "talks" to another computer, a question of hardware compatibility arises. The set of rules which must be obeyed in the encoding and decoding and the transmission of data so that the information that is transmitted between the communicating computers is understood at both ends of the transmission line is referred to as a line *protocol*. Programs called *emulators* are sometimes used to enable computers of different designs to communicate. A remotely located minicomputer, for example, will execute the emulator (usually supplied by the manufacturer of the minicomputer) so that during data transmission it is able to conform to the protocol of the data communications network associated with a particular host computer.

Figure 8-8 features the Texas Instruments SILENT 700 portable terminal, a full-function battery-powered teleprinter that fits into half of a standard size briefcase. The SILENT 700 model 707 may be plugged into a modular telephone jack,

FIGURE 8–8. *Texas Instruments SILENT 700 portable terminal. A full-function light-weight teleprinter that is particularly well suited for salespeople and commercial data base users.* (Courtesy of Texas Instruments, Inc.)

eliminating the need for an acoustic coupler. Data can then be entered via the keyboard and transmitted over standard telephone lines to the host computer. When a telephone jack is not available, as in a telephone booth, the remote user may access the host computer by using an optional acoustic coupler accessory. The host computer communicates with the terminal user by producing a computer-generated response that silently prints on the nonimpact printer. Portable terminals, such as the Texas Instruments model, allow businesses to extend their offices into the field. Salespeople, for example, can initiate orders immediately and access data bases from a telephone booth or hotel room.

COMPUTER CLASSIFICATIONS AND SYSTEMS

Throughout this book we have referred to computers in general terms, using adjectives such as "large," "small," and "micro." It is very common to distinguish between computers by categorizing them according to their sizes: micro, mini, small, medium, large, and superlarge. *Size* in this instance does not simply refer to the physical dimensions of the box that houses the computer. Instead, it is determined by the following factors:

- The storage capacity and speed of main memory

- The number and types of I/O devices that the computer can support

- The cost of a typical configuration

- The nature, quality, and variety of compatible applications and systems software that is commercially available

MICROCOMPUTERS AND MINICOMPUTERS

The first minicomputer, the PDP-8, was introduced by the Digital Equipment Corporation (DEC) in 1965. The popular PDP-11 minicomputer series was introduced by DEC in 1970. (See Figure 8-9.) The memory organization of the PDP-11 is based on a 16-bit computer word, which is typical of minicomputers. The relatively low price tag of a typical minicomputer system ($20,000–$125,000) provides small businesses with the incentive to introduce an electronic data processing system within their business organizations. As a result of VLSI technology, many minicomputers now offer power and flexibility that a decade ago were associated with medium to large computer systems.

The quality of software available for minicomputers continues to grow. Many companies which market minicomputers will package a minicomputer system with all the software necessary to satisfy the customer's needs. Essentially, all the customer need do is turn on the machine and enter data. This approach to data processing is referred to as a *turnkey* computer system. The minicomputer enjoys

FIGURE 8–9. PDP-11 minicomputer system. (Courtesy of Digital Equipment Corporation.)

great popularity, as evidenced by the number of different companies that offer excellent products designed to capture a share of this highly competitive market.

Some of the manufacturers of minicomputers are Digital Equipment Corporation, Hewlett-Packard, Texas Instruments, Data General, Mohawk Data Sciences, Prime Computer, and Wang Laboratories. Manufacturers of larger computer systems, such as IBM, Honeywell, NCR, Burroughs, and Amdahl, also market competitive minicomputer systems.

The CPU of a *microcomputer* is the microprocessor, developed in the early 1970s. A microprocessor includes both the arithmetic logic unit and the control unit on a square integrated circuit chip less than $\frac{1}{4}$ inch on a side. For this reason a microcomputer is sometimes referred to as a computer on a chip. Originally, the design of microprocessors was based on an 8-bit computer word. Recently some manufacturers have been incorporating 16-bit microprocessors into the design of their microcomputers. A machine based on a 16-bit microprocessor can address a larger memory than an 8-bit machine and has the potential for achieving increased economies in processing speed. Apple Computer's newest design, called the Macintosh, is based on the 32-bit Motorola 68000 microprocessor. Although 32-bit chunks of data residing in memory can be addressed by the microprocessor, external busses permit data to be transferred only in 16-bit blocks.

With some microcomputers a CRT display monitor is an integral part of the unit, while with other (personal) microcomputers the user is given the flexibility of purchasing a monitor or using the screen of a home television set by making a simple hookup. Microcomputers support a variety of peripherals, including a cassette and disk drive, a hard copy printer, and data communications device (modem).

Most of the manufacturers of microcomputers, as well as special software vendors, offer the purchaser of a microcomputer a great deal of software support. Commercially available software ranges from business-oriented applications programs to recreational game programs. In addition, a variety of computer compiler languages are available for many of the better known microcomputers. The computing power, flexibility, ease of operation, and price of the current crop of microcomputers make them suitable for personal use at home as well as for assisting the small businessperson in conducting office operations, particularly in the area of record keeping. The microcomputer market is very competitive and is shared by a number of companies, including Apple Computer, IBM Personal Computer, Radio Shack, Commodore Business Machines, Atari, North Star, Epson, and a host of others.

The proliferation of mini- and microcomputers at work, at home, and at school may prove to have a greater impact on the manner in which we conduct our daily lives than any other modern technological advance. As a billion-dollar industry, microcomputers have had a profound effect on the economy. Their use as an instructional tool in the secondary and primary schools has served as a catalyst in the upgrading of curricula in many school systems. The continued growth in the sales of microcomputers for home use, coupled with the availability of telecommunications devices, increases the likelihood of the following labor- and/or time-saving functions eventually being performed routinely in the home:

■ Initiating the transfer of personal monetary funds electronically. Electronic funds transfer (EFT) is the general term applied to this type of activity. This capability would allow a person to conduct all of his or her banking and shopping transactions without leaving home.

- Sending and receiving electronic mail (assuming, of course, that both correspondents have the appropriate hardware).

- Working for an employer, with the employee's home computer communicating, when necessary, with the office's mainframe.

These activities are currently being performed at home with microcomputers and terminals, but on a limited scale.

MAINFRAME COMPUTERS

Small, medium, and large computers are collectively referred to as *mainframe* computers, emphasizing their ability to support a wide variety of input/output devices in different configurations. Differences between mainframes usually exist in their effective memory capacities (main, virtual, and auxiliary), in their processing speeds, and in the complexity of the data communications networks which they are able to support. In addition to offering processing speeds in the nanosecond range, large mainframes typically feature a sophisticated disk operating system, which supports virtual memory, multiprogramming, time-sharing, and a DBMS that permits the implementation of an elaborate data base approach to data collection, organization, and retrieval. Small to medium mainframes share many of the features of large mainframes, but on a reduced scale, offering less elaborate computer configurations with increased system response time.

It is common to find in the product lines of the major computer manufacturers a computer series or a family of computers which includes one or more representative models in the small, medium, and large categories. All models in the series share a common design philosophy as well as performance characteristics, but are graded in price to reflect increased capabilities in memory capacity, speed, and possible input/output configurations. The IBM System 370 series, for example, was a family of computer models that formed the flagship of the IBM product line in the mid-1970's. (A number of these computers are still in use.) It included model 138 (small), model 148 (small to medium), model 158 (medium to large), and model 168 (large). The IBM 370 series was succeeded by the 303X family (models 3031, 3032, and 3033). The IBM 308X series of computers, which are capable of executing between 1.5 and 7.5 million instructions per second (MIPS), represent the most recent addition to IBM's high-end product line. IBM product sizes and typical price ranges are given in Table 8-1. Companies that offer mainframes designed to com-

TABLE 8-1

Mainframe Size	Purchase Price[a]	Some Representative IBM Models
Mini to small	$20,000–$250,000	Systems 34, 36, and 38
Small to medium	$200,000–$750,000	4300 series; 3031
Medium to large	$750,000–$1,500,000	System 370/158; 3032; 308X
Large	$1–7 million	System 370/168; 3033; 3033MP 308X

[a]Prices are approximate and will vary according to the particular model and the nature of the configuration.

pete across the board with IBM's mainframe product line include Control Data Corporation, Sperry (UNIVAC), Honeywell, NCR, and Burroughs. (See Figure 8-10.)

FIGURE 8–10.   IBM 3084 computer system, a large computer system. (Courtesy of IBM Corporation.)

The concept of a company offering a family of computers has proven to be an extremely effective marketing strategy. Software written for one model in a given series will usually run with little or no modification on a more powerful model in the same series. Thus, as the data processing requirements of businesses expand, customers may upgrade their mainframes by purchasing (or leasing) more powerful models in the same series without fear of rendering their software libraries obsolete. In addition, the computer series concept makes the *path* for upgrading apparent to the customer. System components are also designed by computer manufacturers to be *upward compatible*, with improved or more powerful peripheral devices designed to be compatible with several models in a family of mainframes.

In order to encourage a customer using brand X computer to switch to brand Y computer when upgrading, some companies have adopted an effective computer design and marketing strategy based on offering *plug-compatible mainframes* (PCM's). PCM's permit software written for a competitor's hardware to run with little or no modification on their own equipment.

SUPERCOMPUTERS

In 1976 the Cray-1 supercomputer was delivered to the Los Alamos Scientific Laboratory in order to facilitate research and development in nuclear defense weapons and energy. The Cray-1 established new standards for supercomputers, offering from 10 to 15 times the computing power of a typical large mainframe at a base price of about $4 to $5 million for the CPU. (See Figure 8-11.) In addition to Cray Research, Control Data Corporation offers supercomputers of the Cyber series. A typical supercomputer configuration costs between $9 and $17 million and is generally found in special defense, weather, aerospace, and government information processing installations.

FIGURE 8–11. *Cray-1 supercomputer mainframe. The 6.5-foot-high semicircular mainframe includes over 200,000 integrated circuits, 3400 printed circuit boards, and over 60 miles of wire, yet occupies less than 70 square feet of floor space. The upholstered benches which surround the CPU include the power supplies of the Cray-1.* (Courtesy of Cray Research, Inc.)

The Cray-1 is capable of executing a machine cycle in 12.5 nanoseconds, achieving computational rates exceeding 140 million floating point operations per second. The Cray operating system can support up to 63 jobs in some stage of concurrent processing in a multiprogramming batch environment. The Cray X-MP computer system is the fastest general-purpose computer that is commercially available. It is rated at over 200 million instructions per second, has a machine cycle time of 9.5 nanoseconds, achieves computational rates exceeding 400 million floating-point operations per second, and executes combined arithmetic and logic operations at rates which may exceed 1,000 million operations per second. The largest Cray X-MP system CPU has a price tag of about $11 million and a main memory capacity of 4 million 64-bit words.

Recently the Japanese have announced an eight-year national superspeed computer project whose goal is to produce machines having speeds up to 1,000 times faster than current supercomputer designs. The Japanese also intend to intensify their research efforts in the area of artificial intelligence. Some experts believe that the achievement of these goals would signal the beginning of the fifth generation of computers.

MULTIPROCESSING

In order to increase the computing power of a computer system, two or more CPUs may be linked together while sharing a common memory unit. This approach to improving system efficiency is referred to as *multiprocessing* (or *parallel processing*). In a multiprocessing system the computer is able to execute two or more sequences of program instructions *at the same time* since there is more than one CPU. If a multiprocessing system consists of two CPUs, then two different programs can be executed *simultaneously*. Be careful not to confuse this term with multi*programming*. In a multiprogramming system two or more programs are executed *concurrently;* the CPU can execute only a *single* series of instructions at a time, but it switches its attention back and forth between two or more programs. (See Figure 8-12.)

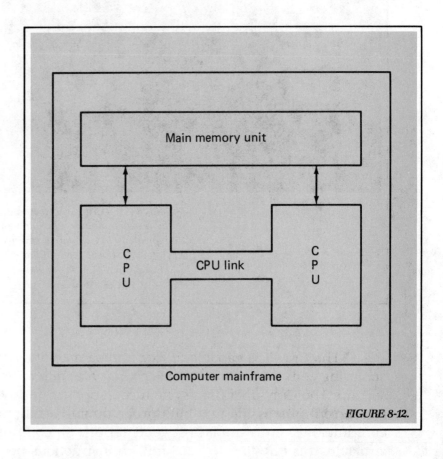

FIGURE 8-12.

The IBM 3033MP, for example, is a multiprocessor version of the uniprocessor IBM 3033, and consists of two identical CPUs that work in parallel in order to increase system throughput. Supercomputers such as the Cray X-MP are based on a multiprocessing design approach. The Cray X-MP includes two identical CPUs each of which is more powerful than the single CPU used in the Cray-1 Supercomputer.

In some multiprocessing environments the CPUs are not identical. A smaller CPU serves as a front-end processor, coordinating all input and output operations and data communications; the larger CPU is then free to handle the more complex processing operations.

MICROCOMPUTERS AND SOFTWARE SYSTEMS

MICROCOMPUTERS AND WORD PROCESSING

Looking at a microcomputer's typewriter-like keyboard immediately suggests yet another application of microcomputers: to prepare written documents that otherwise might be prepared using an ordinary typewriter. Attach a disk drive and a printer to a microcomputer, purchase one of the many excellent word processing software packages that are supplied on a diskette, and the microcomputer is ready to perform sophisticated word processing functions.

When a microcomputer is used as a word processor, text is entered at the keyboard and displayed on the screen; at the same time the text is stored in main memory. The screen serves as a "scratch pad" as the user composes, revises, and corrects the text electronically. A typical word processing program includes an array of commands which allows the user to:

- Reformat text. New paragraphs can be inserted easily into the text and existing paragraphs can be rearranged.

- Correct typographical errors. Characters, words, and sentences, individually or in groups, can be modified, deleted, or inserted into the text without the need to retype the surrounding text.

- Search for a specified word or phrase and then replace it with another word or phrase that is designated by the user. At the conclusion of a word processing session, for example, the user may realize that throughout the text the word "environment" has been spelled incorrectly as "enviornment." A single command can be used to search the text for the word "enviornment," and each time it is found to replace it with the word "environment."

- Create a glossary in which expressions that frequently appear in the text can be defined using a single character. Whenever the expression is needed, the character representing the expression can be typed instead of the original expression. When the document is printed, the actual phrase will be called from the glossary and printed.

- Prepare sections of the text in the order that is most convenient to the author rather than in the sequence in which they will appear in the finished document. The individual sections are stored on disk and at some future time can be combined in any desired order so that when the document is printed the sections appear in the correct logical sequence.

When the author is satisfied with the content and appearance of the document that has been prepared, parameters such as margin and line spacing can be indicated. A single command will produce one or more printed copies of the document. The contents of a document can also be written to a disk where they can be conveniently stored as a file, thereby providing an alternative to storing printed matter on reams of paper. Some word processing programs such as the Apple Writer II which is offered by Apple Computer, Inc., feature their own word processing language which enables users to customize word processing functions further in order to meet their individual needs.

A commonly used word processing application is the preparation of form letters. After a form letter template is created, it is stored on disk and retrieved when needed. Using the facilities of the word processing program, variable items such as the name of the receiving correspondent can be changed easily without affecting the remaining text. This provides a convenient means by which a small organization can prepare "personalized" form letters. Some word processing software packages include a spelling checker program, while others allow for one to be added. A spelling checker program features a dictionary of words, typically including between 20,000 and 50,000 words. With a single command, each word of a document is looked up in the dictionary. Any word that is not found is flagged. Words in the document can be scanned by the spelling checker program at a rate of about 4,000 words per minute. The speed will vary according to the particular spelling checker program used and will largely depend on the number of words contained in the dictionary; the larger the dictionary, the longer it will take to check the document for spelling errors. Many spelling checker programs allow the user to supplement the built-in dictionary with special words or terms that are used in the document but that are not contained in the supplied dictionary. This is important, for example, when preparing a technical document that may use certain jargon. If a word processor and spelling checker program were used in preparing this manuscript, then the terms pseudocode and multiprocessing would be added to the dictionary so that when the text was scanned for spelling errors, the spelling checker would recognize these words and not highlight them.

A program which prepares mailing labels is also commonly linked to word processing programs. Some word processing packages include the ability to interface with a mailing label program so that prepared letters can be merged with selected information gathered from a mailing list. Word processing systems are sometimes used in a data communications environment in order to help create and transmit mail electronically from one location to a geographically different location.

INTEGRATED SOFTWARE SYSTEMS

A current trend in microcomputer-based software is to offer the end user an integrated software package that includes a collection of commonly purchased applications programs. Software packages such as Lotus' 1-2-3 and MBA by Context Management Systems typically include those programs that form the nucleus of a business data processing system: a data base management system to store and retrieve data; some form of spreadsheet package (that is, an electronic worksheet that is often patterned after VisiCorp's VisiCalc program) to manipulate and process data; a word processor and graphics program to produce formatted reports, letters, bills, and display charts and graphs. The main advantage of using an integrated software system is convenience. Since the applications programs tend to share a number of commands, the variety of commands that the user must learn in order to use and switch between the various applications is minimized. Furthermore, the various applications programs are able to share and transfer information between each other. A change made in the price of an item that is maintained in a data base can be automatically reflected in a spreadsheet which involves that variable and in a bill prepared by the word processing program.

There are, however, one or two disadvantages associated with integrated systems. Some of the programs included within an integrated package may not be as powerful as stand alone applications programs that are marketed by other software vendors. Integrated software packages also place an increased demand on main memory, typically requiring at least a 256K main memory capacity.

Programs such as VisiCorp's *Visi On* are designed to create an operating environment in which popular business applications programs may coexist in memory and interact with one another. Imagine several television sets standing side by side and each being tuned to a different broadcasting station. The analogous computer concept is called *windowing*. Each application program may be displayed on the same CRT screen in its own window. A hand-held mechanical pointer and cursor mover (called a "mouse") is used in conjunction with a self-explanatory set of commands to access an application program ("open" a window) and to transfer data from one window to another (for example, to transfer data from a spreadsheet to a letter which is being created with a word processing application program).

While computer windows provides the user with simultaneous *visual* access to several applications programs, Digital Research's Concurrent CP/M *operating system* provides for the concurrent *processing* of up to four different applications programs.

The motivating idea behind integrated software packages and concurrent operating systems is to have the computer resemble an "electronic desktop." A worker sitting at his or her desk often has several different file folders, each corresponding to a different task or project. The worker may wish to transfer or exchange information between these file folders. It may be preferable to work on one file folder, then on another, and then return to the first. The trend in microcomputer based hardware and software is for computers to be able to perform these desktop chores as easily and efficiently as possible.

The trend in many scientific and business data processing environments is away from mainframes and toward creating individual workstations that are equipped with desktop computers. Nevertheless, important and large data bases will usually be maintained on a mainframe computer system. In recognition of this, hardware manufacturers are showing increased attention to micro-to-mainframe communication and software compatibility. IBM, for example, has introduced the IBM 3270 Personal Computer which has the ability to communicate with several of IBM's larger mainframes, including the IBM 370 family and the 308X series. Another IBM product, the PC XT/370 is a desktop computer which can run programs developed for IBM PC personal computer. What makes this product special is that it can also simulate a mainframe by running software that is compatible with the IBM system 370.

Software is becoming available which when used in conjunction with a voice recognition hardware device will allow the user to control the execution of an applications program either manually (e.g., using the keyboard) or verbally! *VoiceDrive* is a software interface offered by SuperSoft which allows their spreadsheet software package, called ScratchPad, to be controlled using either voice or keyboard commands. In addition to the software, all that is needed is a compatible computer such as the IBM PC, a compatible voice recognition plug-in card, and a microphone. The variety of computer environments and the applications programs which support voice commands, can be expected to grow rapidly.

BUNDLED PACKAGES

A *bundled* hardware or software package refers to a marketing strategy rather than to a technological advance. Some companies will authorize their dealers to offer a special package price if the consumer purchases a complete system from the same manufacturer, usually consisting of the microcomputer, a disk drive, and a monitor or printer. Other companies will try to entice customers to purchase their systems by bundling software. The computer manufacturer will market their computer systems with a popular operating system such as Digital Research's CP/M and will include some of the more commonly purchased applications programs that run under CP/M. The bundled software package will typically include a file management system, a spreadsheet package, and a word processing program. The bundled software package is not only attractive from an economic standpoint, but also greatly simplifies matters for the consumer. After purchasing such a system, the consumer does not have to shop around for compatible software. An assortment of high quality software is included which should satisfy most, if not all, of the purchaser's data processing needs.

DISTRIBUTED DATA PROCESSING

At one time management believed that the most efficient approach to data processing was to direct all the processing activities of its main and branch offices through a large central computer installation, usually located at the site of the home office. As the information processing needs of its branch offices expanded, the increased demands placed on the central computer led to increased turnaround time and an overall reduction in system efficiency. In response to these problems, the concept of *distributed data processing* evolved.

Distributed data processing seeks to allocate or distribute appropriate data processing responsibilities to personnel working at locations that are geographically remote from the main computer, but which are closer to the places where the data are collected. In the most common approach to distributed data processing, relatively inexpensive yet powerful minicomputers having a data communications capability are installed at the remote sites. The minicomputer functions in two basic modes:

- as a computer in performing local processing jobs, such as capturing and storing formatted source data on disk(ette), updating locally maintained files, and producing summarizing reports

- as a terminal in telecommunicating transaction files to the central computer and in receiving reports and electronic mail generated by the central computer

A typical minicomputer configuration at the local site might feature:

- a CPU having a main memory capacity of from 128K to 512K bytes and the ability to run several programs concurrently

- a CRT operator station that permits a human operator to communicate with the various system components

- a key-to-tape or key-to-disk data entry device

- multiple CRT terminals (typically 4 to 12) and data communications equipment that allow the minicomputer to send and receive data to and from the host computer located at the central site

- printers (typically one to four) having an operating speed of 250–350 lines per minute

- diskette storage used to load programs, store local files, and temporarily store data files for transmittal to the main computer; it is not uncommon to find one to four floppy disk drives per system

- additional mass storage using large disks (10 to 40 megabyte capacity is typical) and/or magnetic tape drive units.

Although each branch office may develop its own computer routines and create a local data base, distributed data processing does not seek to establish a completely autonomous data processing unit at each branch office. Its primary aim is to relieve the main computer of those data processing activities that could be performed more efficiently at the point where the transaction data originate and are used.

In addition to office locations, the concept of distributed data processing can be extended to any remote site where there is information processing. Many businesses, for example, install terminals at warehouse locations for the purpose of capturing data related to inventory control and customer billing. As merchandise is moved in and out of the warehouse, the corresponding transaction data are keyed in and stored on a diskette. At the end of each workday, the day's transaction files are telecommunicated to the central computer.

The following advantages are associated with distributed data processing:

- reduction in the data processing load of the central computer

- reduced turnaround time, since much of the processing occurs locally, thereby minimizing the need to telecommunicate with a potentially overburdened mainframe

- reduced data transmission between branch and main offices resulting in lower operating costs

- increased accuracy, since the data can be more closely monitored, being processed and used where the data originates

- increased accountability and productivity of branch office personnel, since they are given greater responsibility in the management of the business activities that directly affect their own operations

THE DATA PROCESSING STAFF

Regardless of how sophisticated the computer or how "intelligent" the peripheral device, a trained data processing staff is required for the efficient operation of a computer installation. A data processing staff typically consists of three distinct groups, headed by a department director. (See Figure 8-13.)

Operations Personnel. There is a certain amount of physical effort required in order for a computer system to function. *Key data entry operators* are needed in order to store source data on an appropriate input medium for subsequent com-

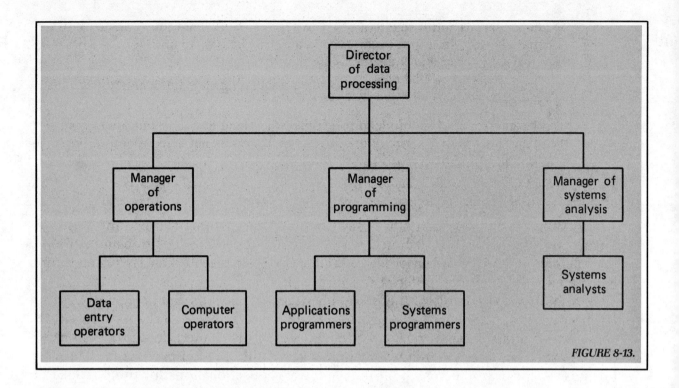

FIGURE 8-13.

puter processing. *Computer operators* are needed to supervise and handle the equipment. Their responsibilities include:

- monitoring the computer control console display, being alert to any abnormal operating conditions

- mounting and dismounting tapes and disks

- loading and changing paper forms in printers

- removing printed output from the printer

- assisting in the handling of card, OCR, and MICR documents

Programmers.   There are two general types of programmers: applications programmers and systems programmers. *Applications* programmers typically write programs in a compiler language that are designed to accomplish a specific data processing task. An applications programmer may be required to author an original program or to modify an existing program. *Systems* programmers tend to be more specialized, preparing and maintaining systems and utility software written in an assembly language.

Systems Analysts.   A *systems analyst* takes a general description of a problem, arrives at a clear definition of it, and then determines whether a computer solution is feasible. If it is, he or she works with the various interest groups (management, programmers, customers, hardware and software vendors) in making the computer solution a reality. The systems analyst may be given the responsibility of evaluating an existing system and, if the findings warrant, of developing a new data processing system or modifying an existing one. Throughout the design and development process, the systems analyst is confronted with a myriad of decisions, including:

- What size system is required?

- What type of hardware configuration is needed?

- What steps should be taken in order to ensure that the system is implemented without exceeding the project's allocated budget?

- What timetable should be established?

- What are the software requirements of the system? Will the software be leased, purchased, or written by the programming staff employed by the business?

- Which computer vendor should be selected? Is compatibility with the hardware and software currently being used a consideration?

- Should the hardware be leased or purchased?

- Where will the hardware be located? Are any special room ventilation or electrical modifications necessary?

- How will the implementation of the new system impact the various departments within the business organization? Is any special staff and/or customer training required?

- Is the program and system documentation being prepared on an ongoing basis? Is it sufficiently detailed?

- Does the newly installed system work? Has it been adequately field tested under all potential operating conditions and system parameters?

Above all, the systems analyst must constantly reflect on whether the proposed system represents a worthwhile and cost-effective improvement over the existing system.

REVIEW EXERCISES

True or False?

1. In a data communications network, data are usually transmitted over ordinary telephone lines.
2. Most telephone lines transmit data in digital form.
3. The Cray-1 is an example of a minicomputer.
4. A PCM is an essential telecommunications device.
5. The linking of two or more CPU's for parallel processing is referred to as multiprogramming.
6. The simplex mode is the most flexible data communication line.
7. A distributed data processing system would most likely be based on a star type configuration.
8. A data processing staff consists of both programming and nonprogramming personnel.
9. With a leased line it is possible to get a busy telephone signal.
10. A modem includes an acoustic coupler.

Multiple Choice

11. Which of the following terms implies the simultaneous execution of program instructions?
    a. RJE **b.** multiprogramming
    c. multiprocessing
    d. telecommunications

12. The term *turnkey* computer system refers to a system's ability to:
    a. protect its stored contents through the use of a key protection system
    b. operate under the control of supplied software simply by turning the system on
    c. telecommunicate
    d. be used with a variety of different software

13. The device that converts from digital to analog form and vice versa is a:
    a. modem **b.** PCM **c.** ring network
    d. multiprocessor

14. The individual whose responsibility is to determine the feasibility of a computer solution to a problem is the:
    a. programmer
    b. computer operator
    c. systems analyst
    d. data base manager

15. Which of the following is *not* an advantage of distributed data processing?
    a. reducing communications costs
    b. offloading jobs from the main computer
    c. centralizing data processing operations
    d. reducing turnaround time

16. In which of the following modes of operation can data communication proceed in either direction between two points?
    a. simplex **b.** half-duplex **c.** full-duplex
    d. choices b and c

17. PCMs are designed to:
    a. facilitate communication between two different-size computer systems
    b. allow software written for one computer to run on a different computer system
    c. increase computer security
    d. replace microprocessors

18. A minicomputer may:
    a. support a variety of peripherals
    b. have a multiprogramming capability
    c. have a data communications capability
    d. all of these

19. Which of the following statements are *true*?
    a. general-purpose computers represent data in analog form.
    b. a dial-up telephone communications line is more reliable than a leased line.
    c. an acoustic coupler is more flexible than a modem.
    d. all of these.

20. Which of the following statements are *false*?
  a. An RJE terminal is a CRT keyboard terminal.
  b. Distributed data processing assigns specific data processing responsibilities to remote sites in order to reduce the workload of the main computer installation.
  c. A series or family of computers is offered by a computer manufacturer in order to encourage customers not to switch manufacturers when upgrading their equipment.
  d. PCMs allow smaller and less well known computer manufacturers to compete more effectively with the larger and more established companies.

21. An acoustic coupler:
  a. amplifies audio signals
  b. converts only analog to digital signals
  c. converts only digital to analog signals
  d. converts either from analog to digital form or from digital to analog form

22. A voice-grade line typically may have a transmission rate of any of the following *except*:
  a. 1,200 bits per second   **b.** 2,400 bits per second
  c. 4,800 bits per second   **d.** 1,800 bits per second

23. In order for a computer to communicate with a host computer, the remote computer must:
  a. have the same modem as the host computer
  b. have the same manufacturer as the host computer
  c. follow the same protocol as the host computer
  d. all of these

24. Which type of communications channel offers the highest transmission speed?
  a. narrowband   **b.** voice grade   **c.** broadband
  d. telephone line

25. Which of the following types of data communications network is least affected by central computer downtime?
  a. star   **b.** ring   **c.** distributed   **d.** all equally affected

 # EXCURSION INTO BASIC

As has already been indicated, a key consideration in planning for efficient data processing is deciding how data are to be organized and structured for subsequent processing. In this section we look at a powerful method for storing and referencing a group of related data items—data arrays and subscripted variables.

In processing a list of related data items it is often desirable to be able to describe the data set by using a single variable name rather than introducing a distinct variable name for each individual data item. For example, suppose we wished to analyze the quantities of an item sold by 100 different salespeople. First let us write a program to determine the average number sold, where variable X represents the amount sold by each salesperson:

```
1  LET S = 0
10 FOR K = 1 TO 100
20    READ X
30    LET S = S + X
40 NEXT K
50 LET AV = S / 100
60 PRINT "AV ="; AV
70 DATA 23, 4, 18, 31, 19, . . . , 27
80 END
```

Suppose that the sales manager also wanted to know the difference between each sales figure and the average. It would be much too inefficient to write a second program and again read in 100 data items. How can the original program be modified to determine this additional quantity? Since each of the 100 data values must be saved for subsequent processing (subtraction from the average figure), one approach would be to have a READ statement with 100 distinct variable names representing each data value. Clearly this approach is not satisfactory. The preferred method is to use the same variable X to represent the entire data list. To distinguish between individual data items in the list, the position of each data item is included in its variable name: X(1), for example, represents the first data value in the list.

X(1)	X(2)	X(3)	X(4)	X(5)	. . .	X(100)
23	4	18	31	19		27

Array X

The variable X is said to define an *array* of data values, with each individual data item [for example, $X(5) = 19$] representing an *element* of the array. The variable $X(5)$ is an example of a *subscripted* variable. The number in parentheses refers to the position of the data value in the list and is called the *subscript* of the variable. The subscript of the variable $X(5)$ is 5; $X(5)$ represents the fifth data value in the list of data values. The number of data values in the list is called the *dimension* of the list. The dimension of the list we are talking about is 100.

In order to be able to assign variable names in this fashion, the computer must be informed that it is to store the data values associated with the subsequent input operation to a block of adjacent memory cells. This is accomplished by the DIMension statement: DIM X(100). The DIMension statement is a program statement that precedes the input operation and that declares that the data values are to be stored as an array, with the maximum number of elements specified by the number within the parentheses. If the actual number of data values exceeds the declared dimension value, then an error condition results. On the other hand, if the number of actual data values is less than the declared dimension value, an error will not necessarily result. The program solution follows:

```
1    LET S = 0
5    DIM X(100)
10   FOR K = 1 TO 100
20     READ X(K)
30     LET S = S + X(K)
40   NEXT K
50   LET AV = S / 100
60   PRINT "AV ="; AV
70   REM ***TO FIND DIFFERENCES FROM THE AVERAGE***
80   FOR L = 1 TO 100
90     LET D = X(L) - AV
100    PRINT "DIFFERENCE ="; D
110  NEXT L
120  DATA 23, 4, 18, 31, 19, . . . , 27
130  END
```

EXAMPLE

Read in a list of six data values and print them in reverse order. For example, if the data list inputted consists of 2, 9, 7, 16, 1, and 5, then print the sequence 5, 1, 16, 7, 9, 2.

SOLUTION

```
10   DIM X(6)
20   FOR K = 1 TO 6
30     READ X(K)
40   NEXT K
50   FOR K = 6 TO 1 STEP -1
60     PRINT X(K)
70   NEXT K
80   DATA 2, 9, 7, 16, 1, 5
90   END
```

BASIC Exercises

Determine the output in Exercises 1 to 3.

```
1.  10   DIM A(6)
    20   FOR K = 1 TO 6
    30     READ A(K)
    40   NEXT K
    50   FOR L = 1 TO 3
    60     LET P = A(2 * L)
    70     LET Q = 2 * A(L)
    80     PRINT P, Q
    90   NEXT L
    100  DATA 5, 9, 3, 8, 12, 10
    110  END
```

```
2.  10   DIM X(5)
    20   FOR N = 1 TO 5
    30     READ X(N)
    40   NEXT N
    50   FOR N = 1 TO 4
    60     LET X(N) = X(N + 1)
    70     PRINT X(N)
    80   NEXT N
    90   DATA 6, 10, 2, 7, 1
    100  END


3.  10   DIM A(5)
    20   FOR I = 1 TO 5
    30     READ A(I)
    40   NEXT I
    45   REM*****ILLUSTRATION OF A SORT ALGORITHM*****
    50   LET C = 0
    60   FOR K = 1 TO 5
    70     IF A(I) > = A(I + 1) THEN 90
    80     GO TO 130
    90     LET Z = A(I + 1)
    100    LET A(I + 1) = A(I)
    110    LET A(I) = Z
    120    LET C = C + 1
    130  NEXT I
    140  IF C > 0 THEN 50
    150  FOR I = 1 TO 5
    160    PRINT A(I);
    170  NEXT I
    180  DATA 5, 2, 19, 24, 10
    190  END
```

Note Lines 90–140: Adjacent elements in the list are being interchanged. Each time there is a switch, 1 is added to the counter C. The list is sorted when the value of the counter in line 140 is 0, indicating that no swapping of elements was necessary. A number of more efficient sorting algorithms are available.

4. Modify the program given in Exercise 3 so that the data values are sorted in *descending* order, yielding 24, 19, 10, 5, 2.

Write a BASIC program to accomplish each of the following tasks. Make up your own test data.

5. Read in 10 data values and store them in an array Z. Use the INPUT statement to enter then a single number X. Determine how many times, if any, the number X appears in the array Z. [*Hint:* Use a FOR/NEXT loop to compare each element of the array with X; use a counter to tally the number of times, if any, that X = Z(K).]

6. Read in 12 data values and store them in an array T. Use the INPUT statement to enter two numbers, L and H (L < H). Compare each element of T with L and H, forming a new array, say B, whose elements consist only of those elements of T that are in between L and H (greater than L but less than H). Print arrays B and T.
7. Read in a list of six last names. Print the original list of six names and the name that would go first if the names were listed in alphabetical order. (*Hint:* Recall that an A is considered to be less than a B.)

BASIC FILE PROGRAMMING

The following program creates the same sequential data file (called GRADES) that was developed in the Excursion Into BASIC at the end of Chapter 7. This program, however, features the use of subscripted variables. In addition, the INPUT statement is used to enter the data interactively.

```
1     REM*******************************************************
2     REM***       PROGRAM CREATES A SEQUENTIAL DATA FILE      ***
3     REM*                  IN APPLE BASIC                        *
4     REM*          CHR$(4) = A SPECIAL CONTROL SIGNAL            *
5     REM*                                                        *
6     REM*          VARIABLE NAMES:                               *
7     REM*               N$(I) = STUDENT'S NAME                   *
8     REM*               X1(I) = FIRST EXAM GRADE                 *
9     REM*               X2(I) = SECOND EXAM GRADE                *
10    REM*******************************************************
20    INPUT "HOW MANY NAMES? "; K
25    DIM N$(K), X1(K), X2(K)
30    PRINT CHR$(4); "OPEN GRADES"
40    FOR I = 1 TO K
50        INPUT "NAME: "; N$(I)
60        INPUT "EXAM 1: "; X1(I)
70        INPUT "EXAM 2: "; X2(I)
80        PRINT CHR$(4); "WRITE GRADES"
85    REM       THE FOLLOWING SET OF PRINT STATEMENTS WRITE
86    REM       THE VARIABLE VALUES TO THE DISK DATA FILE
90        PRINT N$(I)
100       PRINT X1(I)
110       PRINT X2(I)
120   REM       THE FOLLOWING STATEMENT TERMINATES THE WRITE
121   REM       COMMAND SO THAT ANOTHER DATA RECORD CAN BE READ
130       PRINT CHR$(4)
140   NEXT I
150   PRINT CHR$(4); "CLOSE GRADES"
160   END
```

Line Numbers	Explanation
20	The program requests that the user enter the number of data records to be inputted.
25	The appropriate arrays are dimensioned.
30	The data file GRADES is opened.
40–140	A FOR/NEXT loop is used to control the number of times the set of statements that reads the data entered at the keyboard and writes it to the disk file are executed.
150	The data file is closed.

The following sample program is designed to retrieve the data entered from this file and use it to print the name of each student and the average of the two test scores.

```
1      REM**********************************************************
2      REM***    PROGRAM PROCESSES DATA FROM A DATA FILE ***
3      REM*      VARIABLE NAMES                                   *
4      REM*          N$(I) = STUDENT'S NAME                       *
5      REM*          X1(I) = FIRST EXAM GRADE                     *
6      REM*          X2(I) = SECOND EXAM GRADE                    *
7      REM*          AV(I) = AVERAGE EXAM GRADE                   *
8      REM**********************************************************
10     INPUT "ENTER THE NUMBER OF DATA RECORDS "; K
20     DIM N$(K), X1(K), X2(K), AV(K)
30     PRINT CHR$(4); "OPEN GRADES"
40     PRINT CHR$(4); "READ GRADES"
50     FOR I = 1 TO K
60         INPUT N$(I), X1(I), X2(I)
70         AV(I) = ( X1(I) + X2(I) ) / 2
80         PRINT N$(I), AV(I)
90     NEXT I
100    PRINT CHR$(4); "CLOSE GRADES"
110    END
```

RY NUMBERS AND DATA

BINARY NUMBERS AND

DATA REPRESENTATION

NARY NUMBERS AND DA

ATA REPRESENTATION

CHAPTER

9

BINARY NUMBERS AND DATA REPRESENTATION

NARY NUMBERS AND D

REPRESENTATION BINA

POWERS AND EXPONENTS

In preparation for our discussion of how numeric data are represented and stored in main memory, we now present a convenient method for expressing numbers in a compact form. Products of *identical* numbers, such as $10 \times 10 \times 10 \times 10$, may be expressed using a concise notation called *exponential notation*. The number that is being multiplied repeatedly (10 in this example) is called the *base*; the number of times it is being multiplied (4 in this case) is called the *exponent*:

$$10 \times 10 \times 10 \times 10 = \overset{\text{exponent}}{\underset{\text{base}}{10^4}}$$

In general,

$$b^N = \underbrace{b \times b \times b \times \cdots \times b}_{b \text{ appears } N \text{ times}}$$

For example, $5^3 = 5 \times 5 \times 5 = 125$. We also note the following:

$$b^1 = b$$

that is, any number having an exponent of 1 (raised to the first power) is merely the number itself; for example, $10^1 = 10$, $2^1 = 2$, and so on.

$$b^0 = 1$$

that is, by definition, any number raised to the zero power is equal to 1; for example, $10^0 = 1$, $2^0 = 1$, $8^0 = 1$, and so on.

For convenience, some powers of 10 are listed in Table 9-1.

EXAMPLE
SOLUTION

Evaluate: **1.** 2^5 **2.** 13^0 **3.** 16^1

1. $2^5 = 2 \times 2 \times 2 \times 2 \times 2 = 32$
2. $13^0 = 1$
3. $16^1 = 16$

TABLE 9-1

Power of 10	Description	Expansion
10^0	one	1
10^1	ten	10
10^2	one hundred	100
10^3	one thousand	1,000
10^4	ten thousand	10,000
10^5	hundred thousand	100,000
10^6	one million	1,000,000
10^7	ten million	10,000,000
10^8	hundred million	100,000,000
10^9	one billion	1,000,000,000

Referring to Table 9-1, notice that each time the exponent is *reduced* by 1, the corresponding power expansion is divided by 10. This pattern allows us to give meaning to *negative* exponents:

$$10^0 = 1$$

$$\div 10$$

$$10^{-1} = \frac{1}{10(=10^1)}$$

$$\div 10$$

$$10^{-2} = \frac{1}{100(=10^2)}$$

This suggests the following general principle:

$$b^{-e} = \frac{1}{b^e}$$

where *b* can be any number; for example,

$$10^{-3} = \frac{1}{10^3} = \frac{1}{1,000} = 0.001$$

Table 9-2 lists the decimal representations of some negative powers of 10.

TABLE 9-2

Power of 10	Decimal Representation
10^{-1}	0.1
10^{-2}	0.01
10^{-3}	0.001
10^{-4}	0.0001
10^{-5}	0.00001
10^{-6}	0.000001
10^{-7}	0.0000001
10^{-8}	0.00000001
10^{-9}	0.000000001

EXAMPLE

Express each of the following parts of a second as a power of 10 and also give its decimal equivalent.

1. 1 millisecond **2.** 1 microsecond **3.** 1 nanosecond

SOLUTION

1. 1 millisecond = 1 thousandth of a second = 10^{-3} = 0.001 second
2. 1 microsecond = 1 millionth of a second = 10^{-6} = 0.000 001 second
3. 1 nanosecond = 1 billionth of a second = 10^{-9} = 0.000 000 001 second

REPRESENTING NUMBERS IN DIFFERENT BASES

In modern computers, numbers are stored by electronic devices. Electronic devices are two-state (*on* or *off*) devices. Computers must therefore represent numbers by sequences of on/off circuits. It would seem logical that a computer would operate more efficiently if rather than using our familiar base 10 number system, which uses ten different digits (0–9), a number system were used in which each number is represented as a sequence in which each place value position is occupied by one of *two* digits, say, 0 and 1: one digit, say, 0, would correspond to an *off* state, while 1 would correspond to an *on* state. The *binary* number system, based on powers of 2, is such a number system. Although computer data entry devices accept base 10 numbers (and alphanumeric characters) as input, all data values are subsequently translated (as an internal machine function) into a binary code that is consistent with the electronic design of the computer.

In order to give you a feeling for binary numbers, in this section we look at how to express a base 10 number in binary and vice versa. In addition, another commonly used system, hexadecimal or base 16, will also be discussed. You should keep in mind that *we* associate the binary digits 0 and 1 to a computer's OFF and ON circuit conditions. The computer has *no* intrinsic mathematical knowledge or aptitude. It is only capable of representing sequences of *logical* states which, through proper design and implementation, can be used to accomplish mathematical operations.

BINARY REPRESENTATION

Any base 10 number may be expressed as the sum of powers of 10:

$$246 = 2 \times 100 + 4 \times 10 + 6 \times 1$$
$$246 = 2 \times 10^2 + 4 \times 10^1 + 6 \times 10^0$$

Thus the digits 2, 4, and 6 in the number 246 may be interpreted as the coefficients of descending powers of 10, ending with the exponent 0.

EXAMPLE

SOLUTION

Represent 5,704 as the sum of powers of 10.

$$5{,}704 = 5 \times 1000 + 7 \times 100 + 0 \times 10 + 4 \times 1$$
$$5{,}704 = 5 \times 10^3 + 7 \times 10^2 + 0 \times 10^1 + 4 \times 10^0$$

Note in the preceding example that:

$$
\begin{array}{llll}
5\ 7\ 0\ 4 & & & \\
& 4 \times 10^0 = 4 \times 1 & = & 4 \\
& 0 \times 10^1 = 0 \times 10 & = & 0 \\
& 7 \times 10^2 = 7 \times 100 & = & 700 \\
& 5 \times 10^3 = 5 \times 1000 & = & 5000 \\
\hline
& & & 5704
\end{array}
$$

Next let us consider the binary number 1101, which is not to be confused with the decimal number one thousand one hundred and one. In order to differentiate between numbers expressed in different bases it is often convenient to write the base one-half line below the last digit: 1101_2. Since the base is 2, the digits 1, 1, 0, and 1 represent the coefficients of descending powers of 2:

$$1101_2 = 1 \times 2^3 + 1 \times 2^2 + 0 \times 2^1 + 1 \times 2^0$$
$$= 8 + 4 + 0 + 1$$
$$1101_2 = 13$$

The base 10 equivalent of 1101_2 is 13.

For your convenience, Table 9-3 lists some frequently encountered powers of 2.

Determine the base 10 equivalent of 10110_2.

The following format is recommended for conversion into base 10:

TABLE 9-3

Power	2^0	2^1	2^2	2^3	2^4	2^5	2^6	2^7	2^8	2^9	2^{10}
Result	1	2	4	8	16	32	64	128	256	512	1024

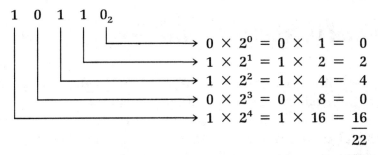

In order to convert a given decimal (base 10) number into base 2, a convenient divide-and-remainder-method is used, in which 2 is divided successively into the original number and its resulting quotients until a quotient of zero is obtained. The resulting sequence of 1s and 0s, which are obtained as the remainders in each division, represents the binary equivalent of the original decimal number. The algorithm used is as follows:

Step 1. Divide the original number (dividend) by 2.

Step 2. Record the remainder (which must either be a 1 or a 0).

Step 3. Let the quotient become the new dividend. Repeat steps 1 and 2.

Step 4. If the quotient is 0, then go to step 5; otherwise go to step 3.

Step 5. The binary equivalent of the original number is formed by writing the remainders in the reverse sequence in which they were recorded.

To illustrate, let us convert the base 10 number 27 into its binary equivalent form:

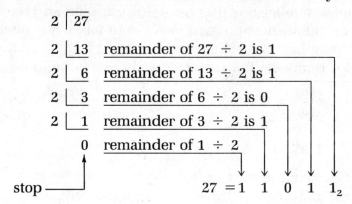

$$27 = 1\ 1\ 0\ 1\ 1_2$$

Convert 56 from base 10 into base 2.

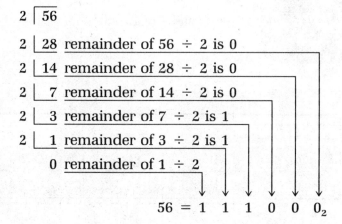

$$56 = 1\ 1\ 1\ 0\ 0\ 0_2$$

HEXADECIMAL REPRESENTATION

As you can well imagine, large base 10 numbers would require long sequences of 1s and 0s in their binary representations. It is sometimes convenient to express base 10 numbers in a number system related to the binary number system. This system is based on the number 16 (2^4) and is called the *hexadecimal* system. Sometimes numbers are represented in an *octal* or base 8 (2^3) system. We shall restrict our discussion to hexadecimal numbers. It should be stressed, however, that both hexadecimal and octal number systems are convenient shorthand notations for binary; computers must ultimately work in binary.

    In hexadecimal, the digits 0 through 9 are expressed in exactly the same form as in base 10. However, in hexadecimal the base 10 numbers 10, 11, 12, 13, 14, and 15 must be represented as *single* hexadecimal digits. The letters A, B, C, D, E, and F are used to represent the decimal numbers 10, 11, 12, 13, 14, and 15, respectively. Thus there are 16 hexadecimal digits: 0, 1, 2, 3, 4, 5, 6, 7, 8, 9, A, B, C, D, E, F. A single hexadecimal digit can be used to represent any whole number between 0 and 15. On the other hand, four binary digits are needed to express any whole number between 0 and 15. Hexadecimal is therefore a much more compact notation than binary, with four binary digits equivalent to a single hexadecimal digit.

Computers display their internal contents in hexadecimal (or octal) rather than in binary notations. The relationship between hexadecimal, binary, and decimal digits is illustrated in Tables 9-4 and 9-5.

TABLE 9-4

Hexadecimal (Base 16)	Binary (Base 2)	Decimal (Base 10)
0	0000	0
1	0001	1
2	0010	2
3	0011	3
4	0100	4
5	0101	5
6	0110	6
7	0111	7
8	1000	8
9	1001	9
A	1010	10
B	1011	11
C	1100	12
D	1101	13
E	1110	14
F	1111	15

TABLE 9-5

	Decimal	Binary	Octal	Hexadecimal
Base	10	2	8	16
Digits	0–9	0 and 1	0–7	0–9, A–F

To convert a given hexadecimal into a decimal (base 10) number, a power expansion method, similar to the one used to convert from binary into decimal form, is followed. For example, to convert $A9F_{16}$ into decimal form, we note that the hexadecimal digits A, 9, and F represent the coefficients of descending powers of 16. Table 9-6 lists some powers of 16 that will be useful in this conversion process.

$$A \quad 9 \quad F_{16}$$

$$F \times 16^0 = 15 \times 1 = 15$$
$$9 \times 16^1 = 9 \times 16 = 144$$
$$A \times 16^2 = 10 \times 256 = 2{,}560$$
$$A9F_{16} = 2{,}719$$

EXAMPLE

Convert $1C2B_{16}$ into decimal form.

We use the more convenient vertical arrangement of the powers of 16:

$$1 \quad C \quad 2 \quad B_{16}$$

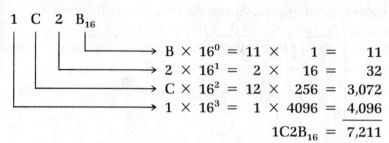

$$
\begin{aligned}
B \times 16^0 &= 11 \times 1 = 11 \\
2 \times 16^1 &= 2 \times 16 = 32 \\
C \times 16^2 &= 12 \times 256 = 3{,}072 \\
1 \times 16^3 &= 1 \times 4096 = 4{,}096 \\
\end{aligned}
$$

$$1C2B_{16} = 7{,}211$$

TABLE 9-6

Power	16^0	16^1	16^2	16^3	16^4	16^5
Result	1	16	256	4,096	65,536	1,048,576

To convert a decimal number into hexadecimal form, a divide and remainder method may be used similar to the one used to convert from decimal into binary form. However, in the present case the divisor is 16 and the remainder may be any *hexadecimal* digit, from 0 to F. For example, let us convert the base 10 number 1,514 into hexadecimal form:

$$
\begin{array}{rl}
16 \, \overline{|\, 1514} & \\
16 \, \underline{|\quad 94} & \text{remainder of } 1514 \div 16 \text{ is } 10 \\
16 \, \underline{|\quad 5} & \text{remainder of } 94 \div 16 \text{ is } 14 \\
16 \, \underline{|\quad 0} & \text{remainder of } 5 \div 16 \text{ is } 5 \\
\end{array}
$$

$$1514 = 5 \ E \ A_{16}$$

Convert 9,998 into hexadecimal.

$$
\begin{array}{rl}
16 \, \overline{|\, 9998} & \\
16 \, \underline{|\quad 624} & \text{remainder of } 9998 \div 16 \text{ is } 14 \\
16 \, \underline{|\quad 39} & \text{remainder of } 642 \div 16 \text{ is } 0 \\
16 \, \underline{|\quad 2} & \text{remainder of } 39 \div 16 \text{ is } 7 \\
16 \, \underline{|\quad 0} & \text{remainder of } 2 \div 16 \text{ is } 2 \\
\end{array}
$$

$$9998 = 2 \ 7 \ O \ E_{16}$$

We have converted from binary to decimal and from hexadecimal to decimal. To convert a binary number such as 11010100_2 into hexadecimal will be our next concern. One approach would be to convert from binary to decimal and then from decimal to hexadecimal. A more elegant method is based on the fact that every group of four binary digits is equivalent to a single hexadecimal digit. For example, using Table 9-4, we may write:

$$\underset{D \quad\; 4}{\underbrace{1101}\,\underbrace{0100_2}} = D4_{16}$$

Convert from binary into hexadecimal.

1. 01110010_2 **2.** 110110_2

1. $01110010_2 = \underset{7 \quad\; 2}{\underbrace{0111}\,\underbrace{0010}} = 72_{16}$

2. $110110_2 = 11\,0110_2 = \underset{3 \quad\quad\; 6}{\underbrace{0011}\,\underbrace{0110}}$

$110110_2 = 36_{16}$

Note: The insertion of leading zeros does not change the value of the number.

This technique may be reversed so that any hexadecimal number may be immediately expressed as an equivalent binary number. For example,

$$B5_{16} = \underset{B \quad\; 5}{\underbrace{1011}\,\underbrace{0101}} = 10110101_2$$

Convert from hexadecimal into binary.

1. $8C_{16}$ **2.** $F0E_{16}$

1. $8C_{16} = \underset{8 \quad\quad\; C}{\underbrace{1000}\,\underbrace{1100}} = 10001100_2$

2. $F0E_{16} = \underset{F \quad\quad 0 \quad\quad E}{\underbrace{1111}\,\underbrace{0000}\,\underbrace{1110}} = 111100001110_2$

Exercises

1. What is the maximum decimal value of:
   a. 6-digit binary number **b.** 3-digit hexadecimal number
2. Convert each of the following to base 10:
   a. 110101_2 **c.** 213_{16}
   b. 1001011_2 **d.** $ACE1_{16}$
3. Convert each of the following base 10 numbers to base 2:
   a. 29 **b.** 60 **c.** 157
4. Convert each of the following base 10 numbers to hexadecimal form:
   a. 271 **b.** 1983 **c.** 5912

5. Convert from binary to hexadecimal:
   a. 11010100_2 **b.** 0110101110_2 **c.** 1001111_2
   d. 1110110101001_2
6. Convert from hexadecimal to binary:
   a. $C7_{16}$ **b.** BAD_{16} **c.** $9F04_{16}$

CODING ALPHANUMERIC CHARACTERS

Digits, letters, and special characters are internally represented and stored in main memory according to some established binary-based code. Two of the most widely used translation codes are the extended binary coded decimal interchange code (EBCDIC) and the American standard code for information interchange (ASCII-8). EBCDIC was devised by IBM and is used on IBM equipment as well as on other manufacturers' computers whose designs seek to emulate those of IBM. ASCII-8 is also a popular code and is used in most, if not all, personal microcomputers. Each code uses a block of 8 bits, called a *byte*, to represent a single character. Hence 1 character equals 1 byte equals 8 bits equals a sequence of eight consecutive 1s and 0s. Each code has the potential of representing 256 distinct characters ($2^8 = 256$).

In each code, the first 4 bits are called the *zone bits* and identify the *type* of character; the following 4 bits are called the numeric or *digit bits* and identify the specific character within the stated type. (See Table 9-7.) For example, in EBCDIC each decimal digit is translated into an 8-bit binary code:

Character	EBCDIC Code
1	1111 0001
A	1100 0001

The zone 1111 defines the character as a digit, while the zone 1100 defines the character as a letter. The digit bits identify the particular decimal digit or alphabetic letter. The space between the zone and digit bits is inserted for clarity only. In ASCII-8, a zone of 0101 immediately identifies a character as a digit. (See Table 9-7.)

TABLE 9-7

Format of an 8-Bit Character Code							
Zone Bits				Digit Bits			

← ————————— 1 byte ————————— →

For reference, Table 9-8 gives a partial listing of EBCDIC and ASCII code representations for letters, digits, and some special characters. Notice that the zone bits are *not* the same for each letter within the same code. This is because the digit bits are capable of representing only 16 distinct characters ($2^4 = 16$), each having the same zone bits. Since there are 26 letters in the alphabet, the zone bits must change. In EBCDIC, the alphabet is partitioned by assigning letters A through I a zone of 1100; J through R a zone of 1101; and S through Z a zone of 1110. The digit bits are then used to identify a particular letter within the range of letters having the same zone bits. For example, 1101 0010 is the EBCDIC code for K, while 1101 0111 is the EBCDIC code for P. It is useful to keep in mind that the binary digits in each group of 4 bits serve as a binary place value. (See Table 9-9.)

TABLE 9-8

EBCDIC Code			ASCII-8 Code	
Zone Bits	Digit Bits	Character	Zone Bits	Digit Bits
1100	0001	A	1010	0001
1100	0010	B	1010	0010
1100	0011	C	1010	0011
1100	0100	D	1010	0100
1100	0101	E	1010	0101
1100	0110	F	1010	0110
1100	0111	G	1010	0111
1100	1000	H	1010	1000
1100	1001	I	1010	1001
1101	0001	J	1010	1010
1101	0010	K	1010	1011
1101	0011	L	1010	1100
1101	0100	M	1010	1101
1101	0101	N	1010	1110
1101	0110	O	1010	1111
1101	0111	P	1011	0000
1101	1000	Q	1011	0001
1101	1001	R	1011	0010
1110	0010	S	1011	0011
1110	0011	T	1011	0100
1110	0100	U	1011	0101
1110	0101	V	1011	0110
1110	0110	W	1011	0111
1110	0111	X	1011	1000
1110	1000	Y	1011	1001
1110	1001	Z	1011	1010
1111	0000	0	0101	0000
1111	0001	1	0101	0001
1111	0010	2	0101	0010
1111	0011	3	0101	0011
1111	0100	4	0101	0100
1111	0101	5	0101	0101
1111	0110	6	0101	0110
1111	0111	7	0101	0111
1111	1000	8	0101	1000
1111	1001	9	0101	1001
0100	1110	+	0010	1011
0110	1110	>	0011	1110
0111	1110	=	0011	1101

When a programmer wishes to "see" the contents of memory, he or she calls for a computer *dump*. Although the computer represents characters in binary form and calculates in binary, it does not display the contents of memory in binary form, since a binary representation would prove too long and cumbersome to read. The contents would not be displayed in decimal form, since the conversion from binary to decimal form would require too much time. Furthermore, under certain circumstances a binary-to-decimal conversion does not always give an exact representation of the contents of memory, with the possibility of some decidedly small round-off error creeping in. The memory contents are displayed to the "outside world" in hexadecimal (or octal) form, since this form provides a compact and precise conversion from and to binary. We therefore note that each EBCDIC and each ASCII binary code has a corresponding hexadecimal representation.

TABLE 9-9

Binary EBCDIC Code								
Zone Bits				Digit Bits				
2^3	2^2	2^1	2^0	2^3	2^2	2^1	2^0	←—Binary place value

←——4 bits——→   ←——4 bits——→

EXAMPLES

Determine the hexadecimal representation for the following:

1. An L coded in EBCDIC.   **2.** The digit 9 coded in ASCII-8.

SOLUTIONS

1. L = 1101 0011 = D3 (by referring to Tables 9-8 and 9-4).
       D   3

Hence the hexadecimal EBCDIC representation of L is D3.

2. 9 = 0101 1001 = 59 (by referring to Tables 9-8 and 9-4).
        5   9

Hence the hexadecimal ASCII representation of 9 is 59.

Exercises

7. Find the hexadecimal representation of each of the following EBCDIC characters:
   a. all digits 0–9   **b.** all letters A–Z
8. Find the hexadecimal representation of each of the following ASCII-8 characters:
   a. all digits 0–9   **b.** all letters A–Z

PARITY BITS AND DATA TRANSFER

In order to minimize the possibility that binary coded data may be inaccurately transferred to and from memory, modern computers come equipped with a built-in self-checking mechanism. To ensure that a particular combination of 0 and 1 bits remains intact, an additional *check* or *parity* bit is added to the coded character. If the character is coded using an 8-bit code, such as EBCDIC or ASCII-8, then the parity bit occupies a *ninth* bit position:

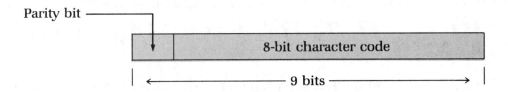

A machine may be designed to operate with either *even* or *odd* parity. Under even parity, the computer automatically chooses the parity bit (a 0 or a 1) so that the resulting number of 1 bits in the transmitted character code (the 8-bit code plus the parity bit) is an even number; with odd parity, the total number of 1 bits must be an odd number. (See Table 9-10.)

TABLE 9-10

Character	EBCDIC Code	With Even Parity	With Odd Parity
I	1100 1001	0 1100 1001	1 1100 1001
W	1110 0110	1 1110 0110	0 1110 0110
3	1111 0011	0 1111 0011	1 1111 0011

As coded characters are moved within the computer, the parity is checked. If there is a change in parity, then an error signal is generated. It should be stressed that the check for correct parity does not detect errors in the logic of an operation or computation; it merely checks whether a bit has been "lost" (1 to 0) or "added" (0 to 1).

DATA TRANSMISSION

Data is transmitted over telephone lines as a stream of characters represented in digital form as a binary sequence of numbers. Typically, ten bits are used to represent a character. The first bit position is used to alert the receiving computer that a character code follows. The next 8 bits are used to represent the character. Depending on the data communications protocol, the character will be represented using either an 8 bit character code such as ASCII-8, or as a 7 bit ASCII code (an information code which we have not presented) plus a parity bit. The last bit position is used to signal the end of the transmission of a character.

Assuming that data is transmitted after being coded in ASCII-8, the letter "T" would be represented as follows:

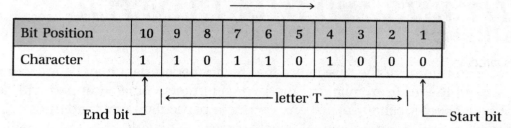

Bit Position	10	9	8	7	6	5	4	3	2	1
Character	1	1	0	1	1	0	1	0	0	0

End bit — |←————— letter T —————→| — Start bit

A typical rate of data transmission between microcomputers is 300 baud or 300 bits per second. At this rate, 30 characters can be transmitted per second.

REPRESENTING DATA ON MAGNETIC TAPE

Information is stored on magnetic tape as a sequence of magnetized spots. A magnetized spot represents a 1 bit, while the absence of a magnetized spot indicates a 0 bit. A reel of magnetic tape is organized into either seven or nine horizontal rows, called *tracks*. The particular tape drive will determine the number of tracks, with nine-track models being the most common. A byte (character) is represented by a combination of bits encoded in a single vertical column, with one track holding a parity bit. Figure 9-1 shows a segment of a seven-track tape.

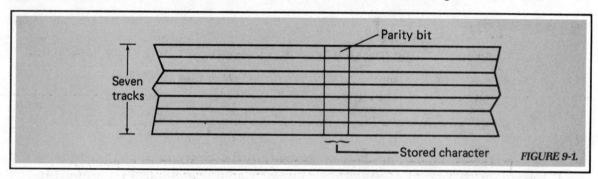

Seven tracks · Parity bit · Stored character · FIGURE 9-1.

A nine-track tape will typically represent data using an 8-bit information code, such as EBCDIC or ASCII-8; the ninth track is reserved for the parity bit. A seven-track tape will use a 6-bit information code, the seventh bit serving as the parity bit. One such commonly used 6-bit code is BCD (*binary-coded decimal*). In this code there are two zone bits and four digit bits. The zone bits define the type of character, while the digit bits are used to identify a particular character within the stated type or group. The zone bits 00 define a numeric character, while other combinations of zone bits are used to partition the alphabet into three groups. (See Table 9-11.)

TABLE 9-11

6-Bit BCD CODE		Zone	Character Type
Zone	Digit	11	Letters A–I
		10	Letters J–R
		01	Letters S–Z
		00	Digits 0–9

Table 9-12 gives a partial listing of BCD codes.

TABLE 9-12

Character	BCD	Character	BCD
0	00 1010	J	10 0001
1	00 0001	K	10 0010
2	00 0010	L	10 0011
3	00 0011	M	10 0100
4	00 0100	N	10 0101
5	00 0101	O	10 0110
6	00 0110	P	10 0111
7	00 0111	Q	10 1000
8	00 1000	R	10 1001
9	00 1001		
A	11 0001	S	01 0010
B	11 0010	T	01 0011
C	11 0011	U	01 0100
D	11 0100	V	01 0101
E	11 0101	W	01 0110
F	11 0110	X	01 0111
G	11 0111	Y	01 1000
H	11 1000	Z	01 1001
I	11 1001		

Figure 9-2 compares XYZ encoded on seven- and nine-track tape using BCD and EBCDIC, respectively. Odd parity is assumed.

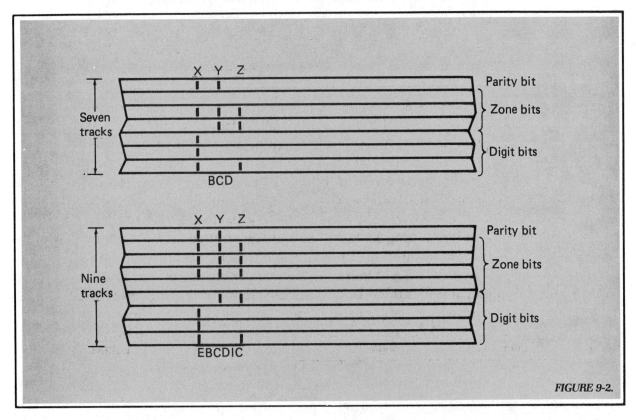

FIGURE 9-2.

Given the following table:

	Character	Computer Code	With Even Parity	With Odd Parity
a.	P			
b.	D			
c.	1			
d.	9			

9. Complete the table using EBCDIC.
10. Complete the table using ASCII-8.
11. Complete the table using BCD.

INTERNAL DATA REPRESENTATION

STORING ALPHANUMERIC DATA

The byte represents the smallest unit of information that can be addressed (fetched) from main memory. When an alphanumeric character is coded into, say, EBCDIC, each character is given its own byte representation. The word LET, for example, would require 3 bytes, while the word DATA would require 4 bytes when coded into EBCDIC:

L	E	T
1101 0011	1100 0101	1110 0011
1st byte	2nd byte	3rd byte

D	A	T	A
1100 0100	1100 0001	1110 0011	1100 0001
1st byte	2nd byte	3rd byte	4th byte

One may wonder how the computer distinguishes between character data and program instructions. The answer is, it can't! It must have help. It is the job of the programmer to identify and describe data types as well as to use the facilities of the particular programming language to allocate storage space for data and for program instructions. Recall that in BASIC the characters that are to be treated as data are defined by the DATA statement; the storage locations that will be allocated to these data items are identified by the READ statement. Furthermore, nonnumeric data items must be distinguished from numeric data by following the variable name with a $ symbol. In COBOL there are distinct divisions which alert the computer as to what are data definitions and what are program instructions. The DATA DIVISION in a COBOL program provides a complete description of the nature of the data while the PROCEDURE DIVISION includes the processing instructions (calculations, decisions, and input and output operations).

STORING NUMERIC DATA

Storing numeric data is a little more complicated. In storing integer values there are two basic approaches. The first is based on giving each digit a byte representation and then processing the number by manipulating each byte while maintaining the positional significance (place value) of each digit (byte). In this method, the number of bytes used to represent the number will vary according to the length of the original number. In contrast, the second approach gives a *fixed-length binary* representation of each integer value. The number is processed intact, as a single numerical quantity rather than digit (byte) by digit (byte) as in the first method. (See Figure 9-3.)

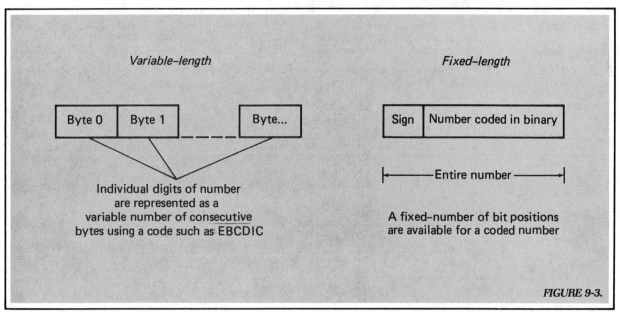

FIGURE 9-3.

In storing integer values using a variable-length format, each individual digit of the number is given a byte representation. To illustrate, consider the EBCDIC coding of 349:

Decimal digits	3	4	9
EBCDIC code	1111 0011	1111 0100	1111 1001
	1st byte	2nd byte	3rd byte

Notice the inefficient use of storage space with half of each byte containing exactly the same information. It is common for computers to *pack* numeric data by dropping the common numeric zone bits (1111), thus allowing each byte to represent a maximum of *two* digits rather than a single digit:

Decimal digits	3 4	9	
Packed code	0011 0100	1001	
	1st byte	2nd byte	3rd byte

Until now we have not considered the possibility that the number may be negative. The half-byte immediately following the final digit of the number being stored is reserved for the sign of the number. The sign of the number may be coded in EBCDIC as shown in Table 9-13.

TABLE 9-13

Sign of Number	EBCDIC Representation	
	Binary	Hexadecimal
Positive (+)	1100	C
Negative (−)	1101	D
Unsigned (+)	1111	F

The numbers +349, −349, and 349 are binary coded below in packed form. Note that the sign of the number *follows* the number:

+349:

3	4	9	+
0011	0100	1001	1100

1st byte   2nd byte

−349:

3	4	9	−
0011	0100	1001	1101

1st byte   2nd byte

349:

3	4	9	No sign
0011	0100	1001	1111

1st byte   2nd byte

This form is sometimes referred to as the *packed* BCD or, more simply, packed decimal form. In packed decimal form, the number 1234567 would require 4 bytes, with the rightmost half-byte being reserved for the sign of the number. On the other hand, the number 9753 would require 3 bytes in packed decimal form with the *leftmost* half-byte containing zeros. That is, when representing numbers in packed decimal form, the numbers are right-justified, with the sign of the number occupying the rightmost half-byte. The packed decimal representation of an integer having an *even* number of digits will always require a leading half-byte of zeros (0000):

9753:

0	9	7	5	3	No sign
0000	1001	0111	0101	0011	1111

1st byte   2nd byte   3rd byte

Represent each of the following numbers in packed decimal form:
1. +43 **2.** −516 **3.** 6,901

1.

0 4	3 +
0000 0100	0011 1100
1st Byte	2nd Byte

2.

5 1	6 −
0101 0001	0110 1101
1st Byte	2nd Byte

3.

0 6	9 0	1 No sign
0000 0110	1001 0000	0001 1111
1st Byte	2nd Byte	3rd Byte

COMPUTER WORDS

It would be costly in terms of time and speed for data to be fetched from memory one character (byte) at a time. Many computers have the ability to address and move groups of characters at a given time. A *computer word* is the number of bits that can be moved as a unit to and from memory. The number of bits which form a computer word varies from machine to machine. In smaller computers it is common to find word lengths of 8, 12, and 16 bits. In larger computers, no standard exists; 32- and 36-bit words are the most common. In IBM mainframes, bytes are consecutively numbered beginning with 0; four consecutive 8-bit bytes form a word. Thus, in an IBM computer a word has a fixed length of 32 bits:

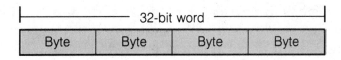

For increased flexibility, words of variable length may also be addressed. For example, IBM's approach permits the manipulation of individual bytes, units of 2 bytes (a halfword), units of 4 bytes (a fullword, or word), and units of 8 bytes (a doubleword). IBM's word configuration is shown in Figure 9-4. The address of a word is the address of the leading byte. The address of the word in the diagram is 8, the number of its beginning byte. In some computers the largest addressable unit is the byte; in others it is the word. It should be noted that a byte *typically* consists of 8 bits. It is possible to find computers in operation which are based on a byte having 6 bits.

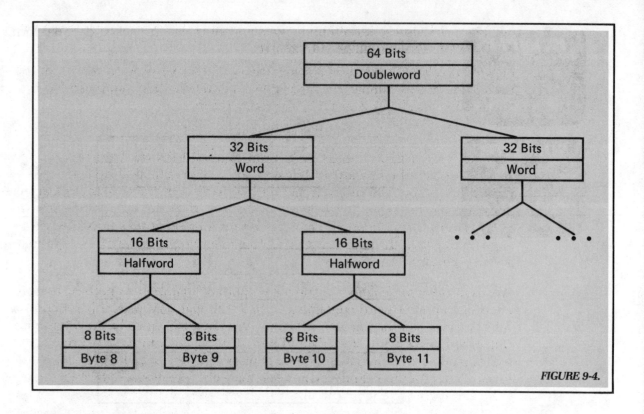

FIGURE 9-4.

Exercises   **Express each of the following in packed decimal form.**

12. a. 918 **b.** +918 **c.** −918
13. a. 1463 **b.** +1463 **c.** −1463

FIXED-LENGTH REPRESENTATION OF NUMERIC DATA

Although many computers can manipulate integer values stored in packed decimal form, this form of data representation is not particularly well suited to arithmetic calculations since the number must be manipulated by the individual byte (digit) rather than as a single numerical quantity. In a second approach the integer is coded directly into binary form and then entered in the first 31 bit positions of a 32-bit word, the last bit position being reserved for the sign of the number. Figure 9-5 illustrates the fixed-length representation of an integer.

With regard to this form of data storage, the following points should be noted:

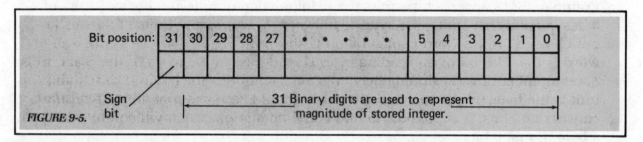

FIGURE 9-5.

- *Sign bit.* A 1 bit is entered in the sign bit position if the number is negative; a 0 is entered if the number is positive.

- *Maximum value of the stored integer.* Since 31 bits are used to represent the magnitude of the number, the largest decimal number that can be coded into this fixed-length block is given by the relationship

$$2^{31} - 1 = 2{,}147{,}483{,}647$$

This implies that every integer having nine or less digits can be precisely represented in this form. Any attempt to store an integer value that exceeds the value 2,147,483,647 will result in an overflow error, with the loss of the leading (most significant) digits.

On the other hand, if the binary representation of the stored integer requires fewer than 31 binary digits, then the binary representation is right-justified, with leading zeros entered.

- *Words of different lengths.* Again we emphasize that there is nothing sacred about a computer word containing 32 bits. Although IBM uses this scheme, other manufacturers may use different word lengths. Typically, however, computers are designed to store data in both fixed-length addressable units (e.g., words) and variable-length addressable units (e.g., one or more bytes). Provision for the latter method is necessary since increased processing efficiency may result from requiring the programmer to specify the length of data items (as in COBOL), with the computer having to allocate the appropriate storage space.

EXAMPLE

SOLUTION

Give the 32-bit word representation of -318.

Using the division and remainder method developed in an earlier section, the binary representation of 318 is 100111110_2. A negative number is coded as a 1 bit. The coded representation of -318 would be as follows:

31	30	29	28	27	26	25	24	. . . . .	10	9	8	7	6	5	4	3	2	1	0
1	0	0	0	0	0	0	0		0	0	1	0	0	1	1	1	1	1	0

← ——————— Leading zeros ———————→ ← ——————— 318 ———————→

The top row of numbers corresponds to the position number of each binary digit used in the 32-bit word representation of the integer value.

FLOATING-POINT DECIMAL REPRESENTATION

Floating-point numbers (also referred to as real numbers) are numbers which have a decimal part. The values 98.6, -18.109, and 24.0 are examples of floating-point numbers. Computers store integer and floating-point numbers differently. Integer values are given an exact binary representation in memory, while floating-point numbers are generally approximated when expressed in binary form. (Some floating-point values do have exact binary representations.) Floating-point numbers are stored using a 32-bit fixed-length format. The leading bit is devoted to representing the sign of the number, while the remaining 31 bits are used to express the number in *exponential* form. Although the computer will represent the stored floating-point number in *binary* exponential form, for simplicity we shall illustrate the process while working in base 10. The principles involved, however, are the same.

We begin by noting that multiplying a floating-point number by a power of 10 merely affects the position of the decimal point. For example,

$$
\begin{array}{llll}
31.415 & \times\ 10^2 & = 31.415 & \times\ 100 & = 3141.5 \\
5.982 & \times\ 10^{-1} = & 5.982 & \times\ 0.1 & = 0.5982 \\
0.00643 & \times\ 10^3 & = \quad 0.00643 & \times\ 1000 & = 6.43
\end{array}
$$

Multiplying by a positive power of 10 moves the decimal point to the right, while multiplying by a negative power of 10 moves the decimal point to the left. The number of decimal positions moved depends on the magnitude of the exponent. An exponent of 4 will move the decimal point four places to the right, while an exponent of -2 will move the decimal point two places to the left. By making a suitable choice for the exponent, we may express any floating-point number N in the form $N = m \times 10^e$, where

◼ m is a decimal number between 0.1 and 1 if N is positive; or

◼ m is a decimal number between -1 and -0.1 if N is negative.

When a number is expressed in this form, the decimal part m is called the *mantissa*, and the number is said to be expressed in *standard exponential form*.

EXAMPLES

Express each of the following in standard exponential form.

1. 74.93 **2.** 0.0166

SOLUTIONS

1. *Step 1* Determine the mantissa:

mantissa = 0.7493

Step 2 Determine the exponent:

think: $74.93 = 0.7493 \times 10^?$

What exponent will give us back the original number? (answer: 2)

answer: $74.93 = 0.7493 \times 10^2$

2. *Step 1* Determine the mantissa:

mantissa = 0.166

Step 2 Determine the exponent:

think: $0.0166 = 0.166 \times 10^?$

answer: $0.0166 = 0.166 \times 10^{-1}$

Table 9-14 gives some additional examples.

TABLE 9-14

Decimal Number	Standard Exponential Form	Exponent	Mantissa
18.6	0.186×10^2	2	0.186
−512	-0.512×10^3	3	−0.512
0.25	$0.25 \ \times 10^0$	0	0.25
64,000	$0.64 \ \times 10^5$	5	0.64
0.00947	0.947×10^{-2}	−2	0.947
−0.0103	-0.103×10^{-1}	−1	−0.103

Computers represent floating-point numbers in standard (binary) exponential form using the fixed-length format illustrated in Figure 9-6.

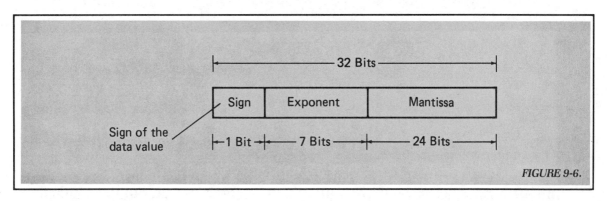

FIGURE 9-6.

In the preceding examples we saw that the exponent could be either positive or negative. So that they will not have to provide for a storage location of the sign of the exponent, many computers *bias* the exponent by adding a fixed constant to the value of each exponent. Then the resulting exponent values fall all within a positive range. For example, suppose that in a certain computer the limiting magnitude of the numbers that can be stored is represented by exponent values in the range of −64 to 63. A bias constant of 64 would then be added to *every* exponent of each data value stored. The range of the stored exponents would now be from 0 to 127. For example:

Actual Exponent	Bias Value	Stored Exponent
10	64	74
−31	64	33
0	64	64

The exponent which is stored after having been biased is called the *characteristic*.

The range of possible exponent values used in the preceding discussion (−64 to 63) was not selected arbitrarily. Assuming a 32-bit word format, 7 bits are reserved for representing the stored exponent. Since bit 1 is needed for the sign of the exponent, 6 bits are used to represent the value of the exponent. The maximum value of the stored exponent is 63 ($2^6 - 1 = 63$). Thus the nonnegative exponents may range from 0 to 63. Since we have provided a bit position for the sign of the exponent, the exponent may take on values between −1 and −64. A *7-bit* exponent allows values of the exponent to range from −64 to +63.

We once again stress that both the exponent (characteristic) and the mantissa are represented in memory in binary form. The *smallest* floating-point number that can be stored will have a minimum binary mantissa value of 0.10000 ... 0 and a true exponent of -64, yielding an approximate value of 2.7×10^{-20} ($\approx 0.1000 \ldots 0_2 \times 2^{-64}$). The *largest* floating-point number that can be stored will have a maximum binary mantissa value of 0.11111 ... 1 and a true exponent of 63, yielding an approximate value of 9.2×10^{18} ($\approx 0.11111 \ldots 1_2 \times 2^{63}$).

When a data value exceeds the maximum value that the design of the particular computer allows, an "overflow" error message is generated. If the data value is less than the smallest number that the computer can represent, an "underflow" error results, and a value of zero is usually stored instead of the actual data value.

DATA PRECISION

In the following BASIC program, what decimal number would be stored in memory cell A?

```
10  READ X, Y
20  LET A = X / Y
30  DATA 2, 3
40  END
```

The quotient of 2 divided by 3 is a nonterminating decimal number, 0.666666 ...; the three dots indicate that the digit 6 repeats endlessly. All computers, regardless of their size, must impose a limit on the number of decimal positions of a number that can be stored. The number of *significant* digits of a number that a computer can store is referred to as data *precision*. When expressed in scientific notation, leading zeros are *not* significant. For example,

$$0.0706 \quad = 0.706 \quad \times 10^{-1}$$

not significant

significant

Actually, there is considerably more to determining whether a digit is significant. However, such a discussion would be beyond the scope of this book. Suppose that the previous program is run on a certain computer that has a precision of 8 significant digits; that is, it can store a mantissa having a maximum of 8 significant digits. What number would be stored in memory cell A? There are two possibilities:

$$\overset{7}{} $$
0.66666666 6̸ 6̸   or   0.66666666̸ 6̸ 6̸

In the first case all 6s which followed the eighth 6 were merely chopped off; this is called *truncation*. In the second case, the digit in the eighth position was rounded off. Since the digit to its right is 5 or more (6 in this case), the last significant digit is rounded up from 6 to 7. Some computers truncate, while others round off in the last decimal position that can be stored by the computer. The manual of the particular computer being used should be checked in order to determine its precision and whether truncation or rounding off is performed. Table 9-15 contrasts truncation and rounding off for a given level of precision.

TABLE 9-15

Number	Mantissa	Precision	Truncated	Rounded off
8.120492	0.8120492	6	0.812049	0.812049
157.97528	0.15797528	7	0.1579752	0.1579753
21.485	0.21485	8	0.21485	0.21485

Exercises

14. Represent each of the following integer values in binary form using the 32-bit fixed-length representation.
   a. 219   **b.** −111

15. Fill in the following table, which indicates the floating-point representations of the given decimal numbers. In each case assume that the *bias* value is 64 and the precision is 8 significant digits.

	Number	Standard Exponential Form		Characteristic	Stored Mantissa	
		Exponent	Mantissa		Truncation	Rounding Off
a.	1.02514637	1	0.102514637	65	0.10251463	?
b.	815.093214	?	0.815093214	?	?	?
c.	0.000123987	?	?	?	?	?
d.	−12.90913756	?	?	?	?	?
e.	11519.0005	?	?	?	?	?
f.	1.33333333	?	?	?	?	?

REVIEW EXERCISES

True or False?

1. A block of 8 bits is referred to as a byte.

2. When expressed in standard exponential form, the mantissa of 8154 is 4.

3. Assuming a bias constant of 64, when expressed in standard exponential form, the characteristic of 0.000712 is 61.

4. The base 10 representation of 111011_2 is 59.

5. The base 10 representation of $FA1_{16}$ is 400.

6. A 1 bit is used to denote a *positive* number expressed using a fixed-length format.

7. In packed decimal form, the representation of the number −5739 would occupy a total of 2 bytes.

8. In ASCII-8, each numeric character has the same zone bits.

9. A certain EBCDIC character with a parity bit added is coded as 1 1110 0110. The computer is designed to operate with odd parity.

10. All computer words contain 32 bits.

Multiple Choice

11. Which sequence lists the items from the most elementary to the most encompassing?
    a. byte, bit, field, record, file
    b. bit, byte, record, field, file
    c. bit, byte, file, record, field
    d. bit, byte, field, record, file

12. Floating-point numbers are typically represented in:
    a. fixed-length format
    b. binary form
    c. exponential form
    d. all of these

13. Which pairs of terms are synonymous?
    a. byte and character
    b. word and byte
    c. bit and character
    d. floating-point and integer numbers

14. Which of the following statements are *false?*
    a. A word has the same address as the address of its leading byte.
    b. Hexadecimal notation is more compact than binary notation.
    c. All computers use either EBCDIC or ASCII-8.
    d. The sign of a number stored in packed decimal form occupies the last half-byte.

15. Which of the following character codes is represented with odd parity?
    a. 0 1100 0110
    b. 1 1101 1001
    c. 0 1111 0111
    d. 0 1110 0001

16. Integers are represented in:
    a. fixed-length format
    b. variable-length format
    c. either fixed- or variable-length format
    d. EBCDIC code

17. When an integer data value is represented in packed form, the data value:
    a. always packs two integer characters per byte
    b. has a fixed-length format
    c. has a variable-length format
    d. has an exponential representation

18. Which of the following statements are *false?*
    a. Numeric data stored in exponential form are represented in a fixed-length format.
    b. Floating point data may be represented using packed decimal form.
    c. An integer value may be stored using a binary fixed-length format or in packed decimal form.
    d. All of these.

19. In memory, the smallest addressable unit is the:
    a. bit   b. byte   c. word   d. field

Given the data value −129, code the number:

20. in packed decimal form
21. as an integer value in a fixed-length format using a 32-bit word length.

EXCURSION INTO BASIC

SCIENTIFIC NOTATION IN BASIC

Microcomputers will display very small and very large numbers using exponential notation. For example, one popular brand microcomputer will automatically display all numbers less than 0.01 or greater than 999,999,999 in exponential form. These critical values vary from machine to machine. In this form of exponential notation, called *scientific notation*, the mantissa will be between 1 and 10 if the number is positive, or between -10 and -1 if the number is negative. The power of 10 is expressed in *E form*; for example, 10^5 would be represented as $E+05$. (See Table 9-16.)

TABLE 9-16

Number Entered	Scientific Notation	Number Displayed as
1223334444	1.22333444×10^9	$1.22333444E+09$
0.009807	9.807×10^{-3}	$9.807E-03$
-0.0000543	-5.43×10^{-5}	$-5.43E-05$

As another point of interest, in this computer the largest positive number that can be stored is approximately $1.7E+38$. The smallest positive number that can be stored is approximately $2.9E-39$. This particular computer will display nine digits, rounding off in the ninth decimal position. For example, the result of dividing 2 by 3 would be displayed as 0.666666667. This level of performance is typical of today's microcomputers and, coupled with a 64K RAM, represents a great deal of computing power at a very moderate cost.

EXPRESSING POWERS IN BASIC

We have seen, for example, that $2^5 = 32$, where the exponent 5 is written one-half line above the base 2. In BASIC all numbers in a given arithmetic operation must appear on the *same* line. In order to be able to do this, a symbol is needed (just as in addition, subtraction, multiplication, and division) to indicate that a number is to be raised to a power:

Arithmetic	BASIC
2^5	2 ↑ 5 or 2 ∗∗ 5 or 2 ∧ 5

Unfortunately there are several symbols that are used to denote raising to a power: ↑, ∗∗, ∧; the one used depends on the particular machine. Regardless of which symbol is used, the first number represents the base, while the number that follows represents the exponent (the number of times the base will be multiplied together). For example, $2 \uparrow 3 = 8$, since $2 \times 2 \times 2 = 8$.

EXAMPLE

Determine the output of the following program:

```
10   READ B, X
20   IF B = O THEN 70
30   LET P = B ↑ X
40   PRINT B; "RAISED TO THE "; X;
     "POWER ="; P
50   GO TO 10
60   DATA 2, 6, 10, 3, 2, -7, 0, 9
70   END
```

SOLUTION

B	X	P
2	6	64
10	3	1000
2	−7	0.0078125
0	9	

Output
2 raised to the 6 power = 64
10 raised to the 3 power = 1000
2 raised to the −7 power = 7.8125E−03
Program terminates

ORDER OF OPERATIONS

How would the computer evaluate $2 \uparrow 3 + 1$? In the hierarchy of arithmetic operations, exponentiation (raising to a power) is assigned the highest priority. Therefore,

$$2 \uparrow 3 + 1 = 8 + 1 = 9$$

To evaluate arithmetic expressions, the computer follows an established order of operations. Working from left to right, evaluate:

Step 1.   (expressions within parentheses)
Step 2.   ↑ or ** or ∧
Step 3.   * and /
Step 4.   + and −

After each step has been completed, we have to return to the beginning of the line to perform the evaluation indicated in the next step.

EXAMPLES

Evaluate each of the following:
1. $10 \uparrow (1 + 2) + 99$
2. $2 \uparrow 5 / 4$
3. $3 + 100 / 5 \uparrow 2$

SOLUTIONS

1. $10 \uparrow (1 + 2) + 99 = 10 \uparrow 3 + 99 = 1000 + 99 = 1099$
2. $2 \uparrow 5 / 4 = 32 / 4 = 8$
3. $3 + 100 / 5 \uparrow 2 = 3 + 100 / 25 = 3 + 4 = 7$

In writing original programs, it is important to be able to translate formulas into the BASIC language. For example, the area of a square is given by the formula: area $= s^2$. In BASIC it would be expressed as:

line no LET A = S ↑ 2

EXAMPLES

Translate each of the following formulas into BASIC.

1. $V = e^3$
2. $A = P(1 + r)^n$
3. $S = gt - \frac{1}{2}gt^2$

SOLUTIONS

1. LET V = E ↑ 3
2. LET A = P * (1 + R) ↑ N
3. LET S = G * T − $\frac{1}{2}$ * G * T ↑ 2

BASIC EXERCISES

Write a BASIC program to accomplish each of the following.

1. Use a FOR/NEXT loop to generate a table of powers of 2 from 2^0 to 2^8.
2. Input two whole numbers A and B (A less than B). Find the sum of the squares of all whole numbers from A to B, inclusive.
3. Input a base 10 whole number and print its binary equivalent.
4. Input any positive decimal number N and print its value rounded off to the Dth decimal position. For example, if N = 8.163, the value of N rounded off to the nearest hundredth (D = 2) would be 8.17.

TABLE

Summary of Fundamental Program Statements and Commands in BASIC

BASIC Statement/ Command	Type or Purpose of Statement	Sample Statement(s)[a]
1. DIM	The DIMension statement is used in declaring the maximum number of elements in an array.	10　DIM X(25)
2. END	Terminates program execution and indicates the physical end of the program.	90　END
3. FOR/NEXT	Establishes a counting loop or repetition sequence.	10　FOR L = 1 TO 10 ⋮ 80　NEXT L
4. GO TO *line no.*	Unconditionally transfers program control to the indicated line number.	40　GO TO 100
5. GOSUB/RETURN	Creates a program module.	70　GOSUB 500 ⋮ 500　REM***SUBROUTINE*** ⋮　RETURN
6. IF/THEN	Conditionally transfers program control to the line number in the THEN clause when the condition stated in the IF clause is true.	50　IF A = B THEN 90
7. INPUT	Enters data in an interactive mode.	10　INPUT A, B, C

BASIC Statement/ Command	Type or Purpose of Statement	Sample Statement(s)[a]
8. LET	An assignment statement. In the sample statement given, the sum of A and B is found and the result is stored in C, destroying any previous value that may have been stored in memory location C. In most versions of BASIC, the keyboard LET is optional.	30 LET C = A + B
9. LIST	A system command that displays the statements in a stored program. The sample statement commands the computer to list only line 50; if no line number follows the list command, then each statement in the program is listed in ascending line number order.	LIST 50
10. PRINT	An output statement. Expressions enclosed in quotation marks are printed exactly as written.	120 PRINT "SUM="; S
11. READ and DATA	Batch-oriented input of data.	10 READ N, M 90 DATA 5, 19
12. REM	The REMark statement is used to insert nonexecutable comments designed to improve program clarity.	10 REM HARDWARE: IBM PC
13. RUN	System command to initiate program execution.	RUN

14. STOP	Halts program execution.	80 GOSUB 500
		      ⋮
		490 STOP
		500 REM*SORT SUBROUTINE*
		      ⋮

[a]Line numbers have been chosen arbitrarily for illustrative purposes. BASIC program statements are executed in line number sequence rather than in the order in which they may be arranged on a CRT display

ANSWERS TO EXERCISES

CHAPTER 1

1. input; processing; output
2. turnaround
3. storage
4. input
5. processing
6. output
7. calculating
8. summarizing
9. comparing
10. classifying
11. sorting
12. e
13. c
14. a
15. b
16. e
17. a
18. c

Review Exercises

1. turnaround
2. file
3. report
4. alphanumeric
5. input
6. right
7. sorting
8. master
9. source
10. classifying
11. updating
12. batch
13. record
14. left
15. transaction file
16. transaction
17. width
18. comparing
19. master
20. hard copy
21. b
22. b
23. c
24. b
25. b
26. d
27. c
28. c
29. d
30. **a.** 3 **b.** 6

c.	RECORD	NAME FIELD	ACCOUNT NO. FIELD	ACCOUNT BALANCE FIELD
(1)	1	Blue, Carol	1872	$ 75.48
	2	Brown, Susan	9802	1.09
	3	Coral, Mike	4133	295.76
	4	Green, Bob	3298	15.67
	5	Grey, Simon	2426	35.90
	6	Lavender, Louis	0599	66.00
(2)	1	Brown, Susan	9802	$ 1.09
	2	Green, Bob	3298	15.67
	3	Grey, Simon	2426	35.90
	4	Lavender, Louis	0599	66.00
	5	Blue, Carol	1872	75.48
	6	Coral, Mike	4133	295.76
(3)	1	Brown, Susan	9802	$ 1.09
	2	Coral, Mike	4133	295.76
	3	Green, Bob	3298	15.67
	4	Grey, Simon	2426	35.90
	5	Blue, Carol	1872	75.48
	6	Lavender, Louis	0599	66.00

BASIC Exercises

1.

L	W	P
14	6	40

Output is 40.

2.

B	E	M	R
10	4	6	3

Output is 3.

3.

X	Y	Z	A
7	17	6	10

Output is 10.

4.

Line	P
10	13
20	15

Output is 15.

5.

Line	L	B
10	8	
20	24	
30	24	23

Output is 23.

6.

Line	A	M
10	7	
20	7	4
30	7	28

Output is 7 and 28.

7. **a.** 5 **d.** 33
   b. 7 **e.** 13
   c. 3 **f.** 1
8. **a.** `LET W = R / S * T`
   b. `LET W = (R * S) / (R + T)`
   c. `LET W = (T - S) / (T + S)`
   d. `LET W = R * S / T - T`
   e. `LET W = (R + T) * (S + R)`
   f. `LET W = R / S + S / T`

CHAPTER 2

1.

X	S	Output
3	3	3
18	21	21
5	26	26
		?OUT OF DATA IN 20

2.

A	B			Output
7	9	7	9	AVERAGE = 8
4	6	4	6	AVERAGE = 5
13	8	13	8	AVERAGE = 10.5
				?OUT OF DATA IN 10

3.

Line	A	B	Output	
10	9			
20	10			
30	10	100		
40	10	100	10	100

4.

Line	A	B	Output	
10	5	0		
20	5	2		
30	7	2		
40	7	2	7	2
10	13	2		
20	13	4		
30	17	4		
40	17	4	17	4

?OUT OF DATA IN 10

Review Exercises

1. false
2. true
3. false
4. false
5. true
6. false
7. false
8. true
9. true
10. true
11. d
12. c
13. c
14. c
15. a
16. b
17. b
18. d
19. e
20. c
21. d
22. b
23. d
24. a
25. c

BASIC Exercises

1.

X	Y	Z	Output
6	2	3	3
8	1	8	8
2	4	0.5	program terminates

2.

N$	H	OT	Output
Smith	43	3	SMITH 3 HOURS OVERTIME
Jones	35		JONES NO HOURS OVERTIME
Brown	40		BROWN NO HOURS OVERTIME
			?OUT OF DATA IN 10

3.
```
10   READ N$, B
20   IF B < 0 THEN 40
30   GO TO 10
40   PRINT N$, B
50   GO TO 10
60   DATA SMITH, 134.50, JONES, 0.78,
     BROWN, -2.95
70   END
```

or

```
10   READ N$, B
20   IF B > = 0 THEN 10
30   PRINT N$, B
40   GO TO 10
50   DATA SMITH, 134.50, JONES, 0.78,
     BROWN, -2.95
60   END
```

Note Some computers require that alphanumeric data be enclosed within quotation marks in the DATA statement. In this case, line number 50 in the previous program would be rewritten as

```
50   DATA "SMITH", 134.50, "JONES", 0.78,
     "BROWN", -2.95
```

CHAPTER 3

1. **a.** digital **b.** analog
2. Digital computers tend to give more accurate results since numbers are used directly as input. Analog computers must measure physical signals, which makes the accuracy of the input signal dependent upon the sensitivity of the equipment being used.
3. RAM, since user programs, regardless of the application area, are stored in RAM. Specialized operating programs and functions are permanently wired in ROM.

Review Exercises

1.	true	14.	true
2.	false	15.	true
3.	true	16.	b
4.	true	17.	c
5.	false	18.	b
6.	false	19.	d
7.	true	20.	a
8.	true	21.	b
9.	false	22.	b
10.	false	23.	b
11.	true	24.	b
12.	false	25.	d
13.	false	26.	c

CHAPTER 4

Review Exercises

1.	false	18.	true	35.	a
2.	false	19.	true	36.	a
3.	true	20.	true	37.	b
4.	false	21.	true*	38.	b
5.	false	22.	false	39.	d
6.	true	23.	true	40.	a
7.	true	24.	false	41.	d
8.	false	25.	true	42.	c
9.	false	26.	d	43.	b
10.	true	27.	c	44.	c
11.	true	28.	a	45.	c
12.	false	29.	d	46.	a
13.	false	30.	d	47.	d
14.	true	31.	a	48.	c
15.	true	32.	c	49.	c
16.	true	33.	b	50.	a
17.	true	34.	c		

BASIC Exercises

1. Line 30: PRINT *E*. This is an example of an error in logic. The program would execute and print a value of 0, assuming that the variable M has not been defined previously in another program.
2. Line 20: LET P = A ∗ C. This is an example of an error in logic. The program would execute and print that the product has a value of 0, assuming that the variable C has not been defined previously in another program. (The errors illustrated in exercises 1 and 2 are common.)

*A floppy disk drive is necessary to transfer new software from a disk onto a Winchester disk.

3. Line 40 contains two errors: PRINT "QUOTIENT ="; A. Since the value of variable A is required, it must be written outside the quotation marks.
4. The END statement must be assigned a line number. The fact that the output of the program is 1 + 1 = 3 is not necessarily an error; it merely illustrates that the computer only does what it is instructed to do.

Note: The flowchart solutions given are not unique; the reader's may be as good or better.

CHAPTER 5

1. **d.** A flowchart solution is language independent.
2. **a.** The parallelogram-shaped output symbol.
   b. The rectangular process symbol.
   c. The parallelogram-shaped input symbol.
   d. The diamond-shaped decision symbol.
   e. The oval-shaped symbol used to denote the beginning or end of an operation.
3. Definition of variables:

$$A = \text{1st number}$$
$$B = \text{2nd number}$$
$$-9999 = \text{trailer value}$$

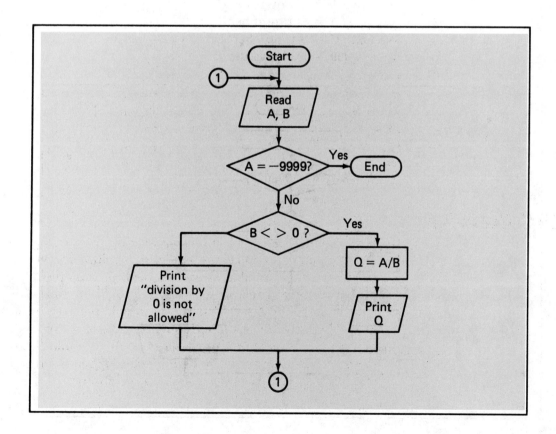

4. Definition of variables:

N = number

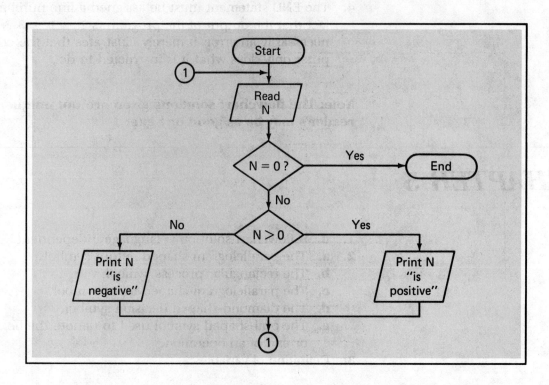

5. Definition of variables:

A = 1st number
B = 2nd number
C = 3rd number
−9999 = trailer value

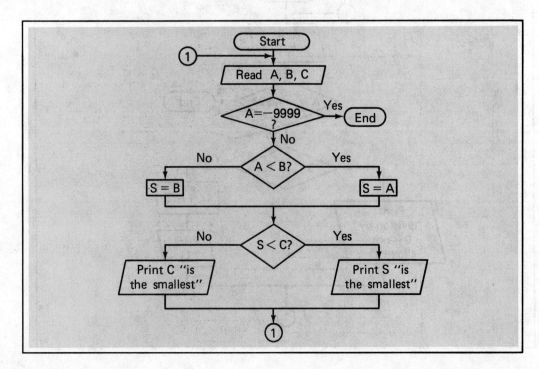

6. Definition of variables:

X1 = 1st test score   X4 = 4th test score
X2 = 2nd test score   AV = Average
X3 = 3rd test score   trailer record = −999, 0, 0, 0

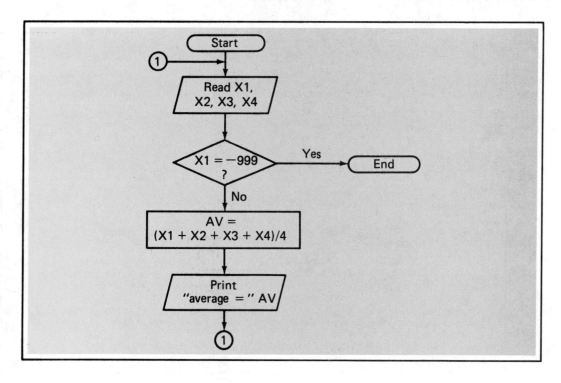

7. Definition of variables:

S\$ = salesperson's name
B = base salary   C = commission
G = gross salary   I   = number of items sold

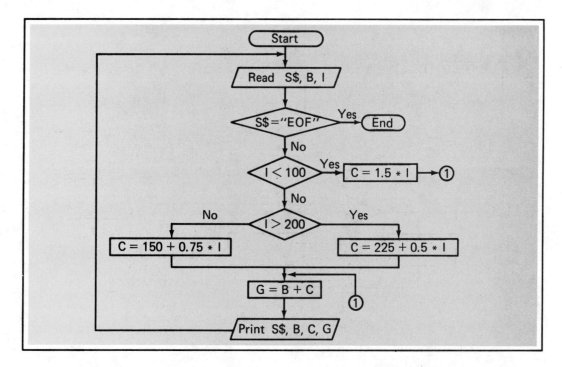

8. Definition of variables:

$$X = \text{data values}$$
$$S = \text{summer}$$
$$N = \text{counter}$$
$$AV = \text{average}$$

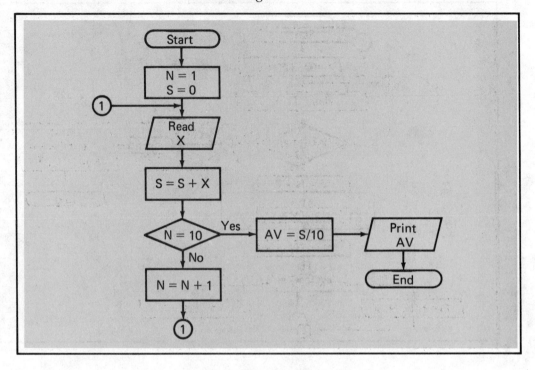

9. Definition of variables:

$$X = \text{data value}$$
$$N = \text{number of negative data values}$$
$$S = \text{sum of positive data values}$$

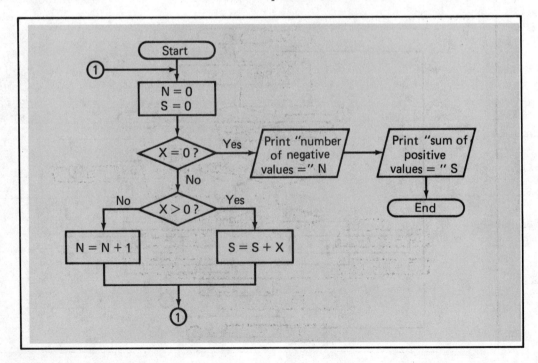

10. Definition of variables:

ID = salesperson's number
N = quantity sold   TV = total value
P = unit price   TN = total number
V = value sold   − 9999 = trailer value

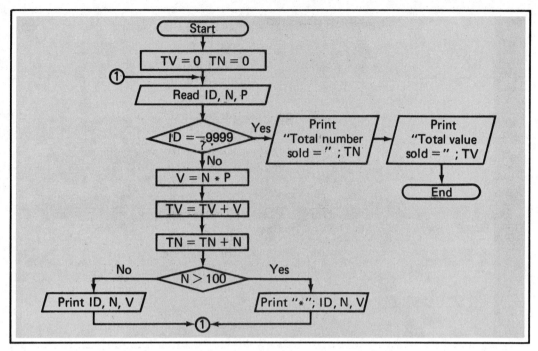

11. Definition of variables:

A = account number
B = balance   S1 = sum of deposits
TA = transaction amount   S2 = sum of debits
TC = transaction code   N = number of records

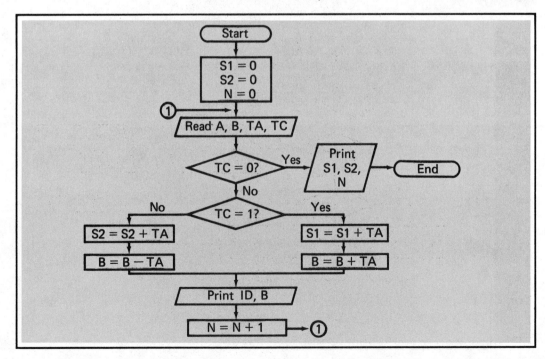

12. A flowchart and a structure chart are fundamentally different. A structure chart focuses on identifying, in hierarchical fashion, *what* tasks are involved in the process. A flowchart, on the other hand, outlines the mechanics of *how* the task is to be accomplished; namely, the sequence of the arithmetic and logical operations that are necessary. For this reason, flowcharts are often used in conjunction with structure charts.

13. Most commercial programs have a long life. It is not unusual for changes in business or government policies and regulations to require that an existing program be modified. For example, a change in the rate of FICA employee withholding taxes would require a modification in an existing payroll program. It is also possible that errors in program logic may not surface until the program is placed into actual use. The process of modifying an existing program is referred to as *program maintenance*, and is not necessarily performed by the person who originally wrote the program. In order to revise an existing program, the programmer must first identify and isolate that part of the program which must be changed. The visibility and the independence of the program modules that are characteristic of a top-down design approach greatly simplify this task.

14. Structure chart for updating employee payroll master record (levels 0 and 1).

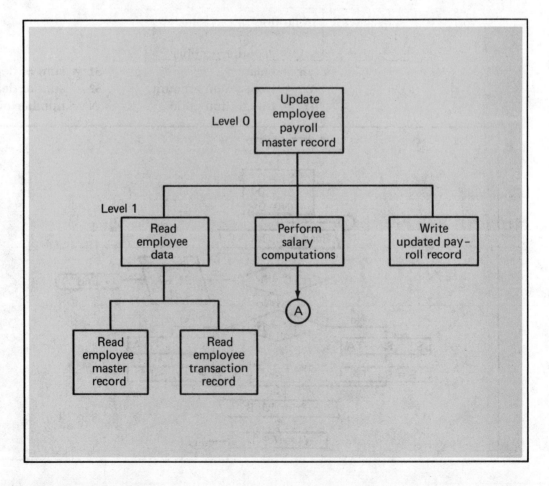

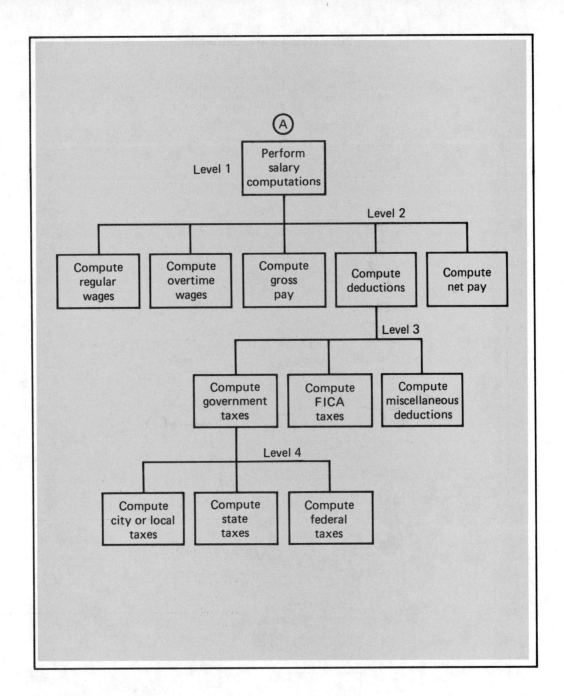

Review Exercises

1.	false	**10.**	true	**19.**	true
2.	true	**11.**	true	**20.**	false
3.	true	**12.**	true	**21.**	b
4.	false	**13.**	false	**22.**	b
5.	true	**14.**	false*	**23.**	d
6.	true	**15.**	false	**24.**	c
7.	false	**16.**	false	**25.**	d**
8.	true	**17.**	true		
9.	false	**18.**	true		

*Program documentation is an *ongoing* process.

**Note: The following flowchart solutions are not unique. The reader's solution
may be as good as or better than the solutions offered.

26. Definition of variables:

X = data value
L = largest data value
S = smallest data value
D = difference

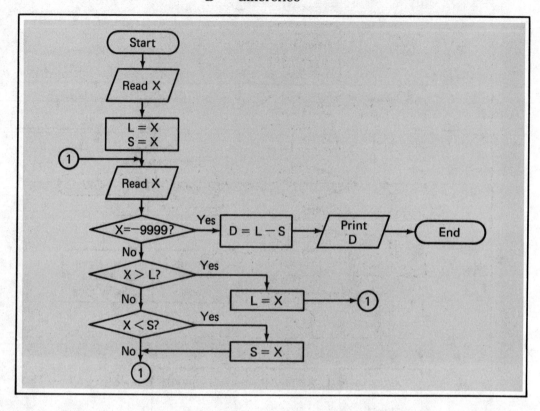

27. Definition of variables:

N = counter
S = summer

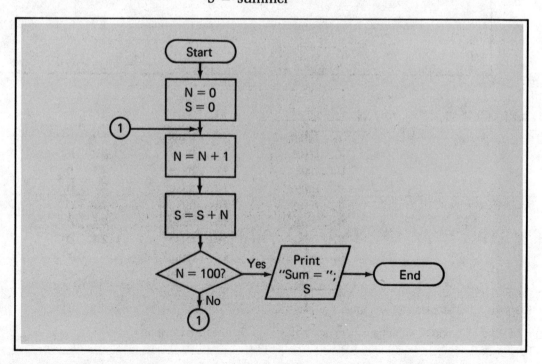

28. Definition of variables:

X = data value
N = number of ones
K = number of zeros

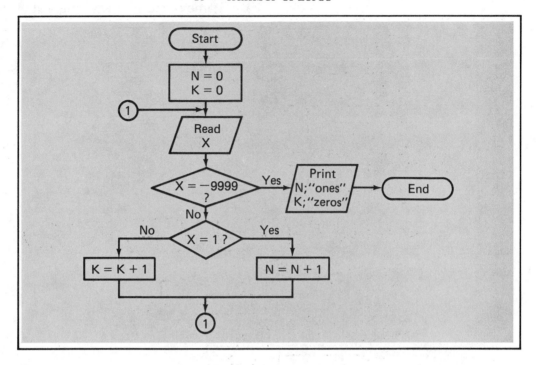

29. See Example 2 in the Excursion Into BASIC.

30. Definition of variables:

X = odd integer
S = sum

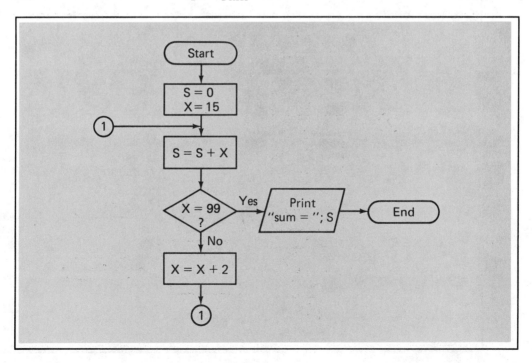

31. Definition of variables:

X1, X2, X3	= test scores	AC	= current average
N$	= name	EOF	= trailer value
AP	= previous average		
L$	= name of student with highest average		

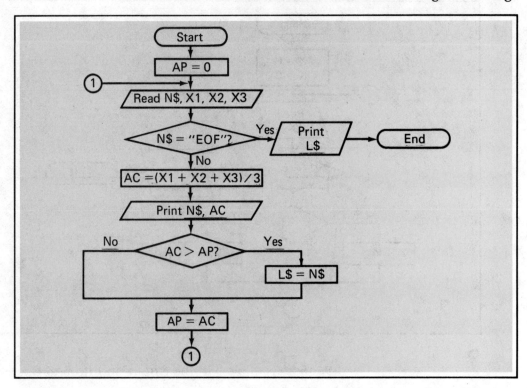

32. Definition of variables:

S = sum of terms

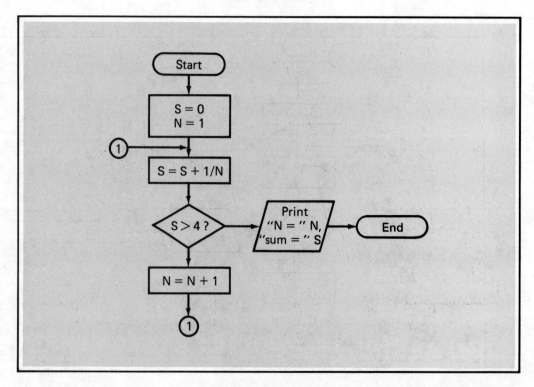

33. Definition of variables:

$N1\$$ = name 1
$N2\$$ = name 2
$N3\$$ = name 3
$F\$$ = first name when arranged in alphabetical order

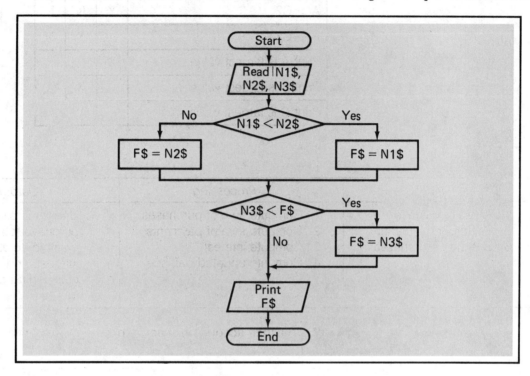

34. Definition of variables:

X1, X2, X3 = data values

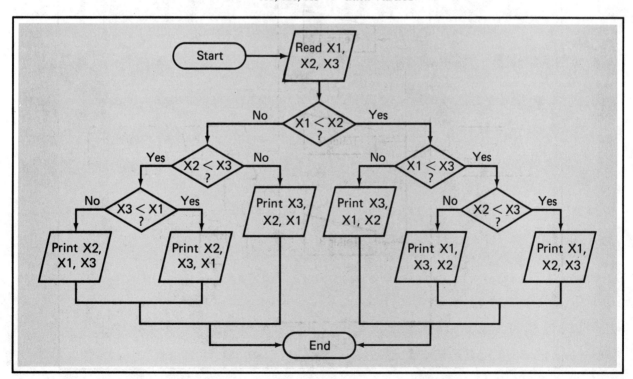

35.

Determine the Largest of Three Data Values	Rules		
	1	2	3
A > B?	Y	N	
A > C?	Y	N	N
B > C?		Y	N
Print A is largest value	X		
Print B is largest value		X	
Print C is largest value			X

36.

Input	Processing	Output
1. Previous balance 2. Customer payments 3. Customer purchases	1. Compute sum of purchases 2. Compute sum of payments 3. Compute interest 4. Compute updated balance	1. Updated values for purchase totals, payment totals, interest, and outstanding account balance.

37. Savings account transaction.

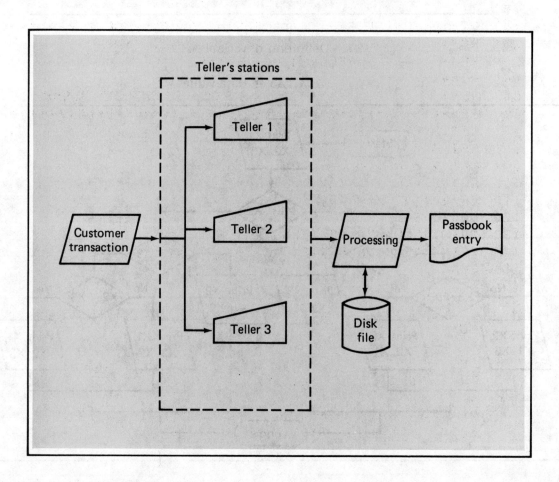

BASIC Exercises

```
1. 10     REM************GENERALIZED AVERAGE PROGRAM ************
   20     REM*                                                     *
   30     REM*              PROGRAM VARIABLES:                     *
   40     REM*                  X = DATA VALUES                    *
   50     REM*                  N = COUNTER                        *
   60     REM*                  S = SUM OF DATA VALUES             *
   70     REM*                 AV = AVERAGE                        *
   80     REM*****************************************************
   90     LET N = 0
   100    LET S = 0
   110    READ X
   120    IF X = -9999 THEN 160
   130    LET N = N + 1
   140    LET S = S + X
   150    GO TO 110
   160    LET AV = S / N
   170    PRINT "AVERAGE ="; AV
   180    DATA 4, 17, 9, -9999
   190    END
```

```
2. 10     REM***SUM OF SERIES EXCEEDING A VALUE OF 4 ************
   20     REM*                                                     *
   30     REM*              PROGRAM VARIABLES:                     *
   40     REM*                  N = COUNTER                        *
   50     REM*                  S = SUM OF SERIES TERMS            *
   60     REM*****************************************************
   70     LET N = 1
   80     LET S = 1
   90     LET N = N + 1
   100    LET S = S + 1 / N
   110    IF S > 4 THEN 130
   120    GO TO 90
   130    PRINT "NUMBER OF TERMS ="; N
   140    PRINT "SUM OF SERIES ="; S
   150    END
```

```
3.  10    REM***TO DETERMINE NUMBER OF ODD AND EVEN NUMBERS *****
    20    REM*                                                  *
    30    REM*      PROGRAM VARIABLES:                          *
    40    REM*          OD = NUMBER OF ODD NUMBERS IN LIST      *
    50    REM*          EV = NUMBER OF EVEN NUMBERS IN LIST     *
    60    REM*           X = DATA VALUE                         *
    70    REM*           T = TOTAL NUMBER OF DATA VALUES IN LIST *
    80    REM*********************************************************
    90    LET OD = 0
    100   LET EV = 0
    110   READ X
    120   IF X = -9999 THEN 180
    130   IF INT(X / 2) = X / 2 THEN 160
    140   OD = OD + 1
    150   GO TO 110
    160   EV = EV + 1
    170   GO TO 110
    180   LET T = OD + EV
    190   PRINT EV; "EVEN NUMBERS"
    200   PRINT OD; "ODD NUMBERS"
    210   PRINT T; "TOTAL DATA VALUES"
    220   DATA 10, 17, 4, -9999
    230   END



4.  10    REM**********CHECKING FOR DIVISIBILITY ****************
    15    REM*                                                  *
    20    REM*      PROGRAM VARIABLES:                          *
    25    REM*          X, Y = PAIR OF DATA VALUES              *
    30    REM*          C = COUNTER                             *
    35    REM*********************************************************
    40    LET C = 1
    50    READ X, Y
    60    IF INT(X / Y) = X / Y THEN 80
    70    PRINT X; "IS NOT DIVISIBLE BY"; Y
    75    GO TO 90
    80    PRINT X; "IS DIVISIBLE BY"; Y
    90    LET C = C + 1
    100   IF C < = 5 THEN 50
    110   DATA 12, 3, 17, 11, 4, 8, 7, 7, 806, 12
    120   END



5.  10    REM******ROUNDING TO THE NEAREST WHOLE NUMBER **********
    20    INPUT "NUMBER (ENTER -999 TO STOP PROGRAM) "; N
    30    IF N = -999 THEN 80
    40    LET R = INT(N + 0.5)
    50    PRINT N, R
    60    PRINT
    70    GO TO 20
    80    END
```

CHAPTER 6

Review Exercises

1.	false		29.	true
2.	true		30.	false
3.	true		31.	b
4.	true		32.	c
5.	true		33.	a
6.	true		34.	d
7.	false		35.	d
8.	true		36.	b
9.	true		37.	b
10.	false		38.	c
11.	false		39.	d
12.	false		40.	c
13.	true		41.	a
14.	false		42.	d
15.	true		43.	c
16.	true		44.	a
17.	true		45.	c
18.	true		46.	d
19.	false		47.	d
20.	true		48.	d
21.	true		49.	b
22.	false		50.	c
23.	true		51.	d
24.	false		52.	b
25.	true		53.	b
26.	true		54.	c
27.	true		55.	c
28.	true			

BASIC Exercises

1.
```
5
4
3
2
1
BOOM!
```

2. 5 FACTORIAL = 120

3.
```
28
10
18
```

4. 5

5.
```
10 LET S = 0
20 FOR K = 1 TO 25 STEP 2
30   LET S = S + K
40 NEXT K
50 PRINT S
60 END
```

6.
```
10 LET S = 0
20 INPUT N
30 FOR K = 1 TO N
40   LET S = S + K
50 NEXT K
60 PRINT S
70 END
```

```
7.  10  LET C = 0
    20  FOR N = 129 TO 497
    30    IF INT(N / 7) = N / 7 THEN 50
    40      GO TO 60
    50      LET C = C + 1
    60  NEXT N
    70  PRINT C; "NUMBERS ARE DIVISIBLE BY 7"
    80  END


8.  10  FOR C = 0 TO 100 STEP 5
    20    LET F = 1.8 * C + 32
    30    PRINT C, F
    40  NEXT C
    50  END


9.  10    LET L = 0
    20    FOR N = 1 TO 10
    30      READ X
    40      IF L < X THEN 60
    50      GO TO 70
    60      LET L = X
    70    NEXT N
    80    PRINT "LARGEST VALUE ="; L
    90    DATA 12, 4, 19, 8, 35, 44, 39, 4, 44, 30
    100   END
```

CHAPTER 7

Review Exercises

1.	true	19.	d
2.	true	20.	b
3.	true	21.	b
4.	false	22.	b
5.	false	23.	b
6.	true	24.	e
7.	false	25.	c
8.	false	26.	a
9.	true	27.	c
10.	true	28.	c
11.	false	29.	b
12.	false	30.	a
13.	true	31.	b
14.	false	32.	b
15.	false	33.	b
16.	d	34.	c
17.	d	35.	b
18.	a		

CHAPTER 8

Review Exercises

1.	true	14.	c
2.	false	15.	c
3.	false	16.	d
4.	false	17.	b
5.	false	18.	d
6.	false	19.	c
7.	true	20.	a
8.	true	21.	d
9.	false	22.	d
10.	false	23.	c
11.	c	24.	c
12.	b	25.	b
13.	a		

BASIC Exercises

1.

9	10
8	18
10	6

2.

10
2
7
1

3. 2 5 10 19 24

4. Change line 70 to:

```
70 IF A(I) < A(I + 1) THEN 90
```

The program solutions that are presented for Exercises 5 to 7 are not unique. It is possible that the reader may devise programs that are as good as or better than the solution programs that are given.

```
5.  5    LET C = 0
    10   DIM Z(10)
    20   FOR K = 1 TO 10
    30     READ Z(K)
    40   NEXT K
    50   INPUT X
    60   FOR K = 1 TO 10
    70     IF X < > Z (K) THEN 90
    80     LET C = C + 1
    90   NEXT K
    100  PRINT X; "APPEARS"; C; "TIMES"
    110  DATA 5, 18, 4, 3, 2, 9, 5, 18, 7, 18
    120  END
```

```
6.  5     LET C = 0
    10    DIM T(12)
    20    FOR K = 1 TO 12
    30      READ T(K)
    40    NEXT K
    50    INPUT L , H
    60    FOR K = 1 TO 12
    70      IF L > = T(K) THEN 110
    80      IF H < = T(K) THEN 110
    90      LET C = C + 1
    100     LET B(C) = T(K)
    110   NEXT K
    120   FOR I = 1 TO C
    130     PRINT B(C);
    140   NEXT I
    150   FOR K = 1 TO 12
    160   PRINT T(K);
    170   NEXT K
    180   DATA . . .
    190   END

7.  10    DIM N$(6)
    20    FOR K = 1 TO 6
    30      READ N$(K)
    40    NEXT K
    50    LET A$ = N$(1)
    60    FOR K = 2 TO 6
    70      IF A$ < = N$(K) THEN 90
    80      LET A$ = N$(K)
    90    NEXT K
    100   FOR K = 1 TO 6
    110     PRINT N$(K);
    120   NEXT K
    130   PRINT "FIRST NAME IN ALPHA ORDER
          IS"; A$
    140   DATA "SMITH", "JONES", "BARNES",
          "LEWIS", "BURNS", "BAER"
    150   END
```

CHAPTER 9

1. **a.** $111111_2 = 63$ **b.** $FFF_{16} = 4095$
2. **a.** 53 **b.** 75 **c.** 531 **d.** 44257
3. **a.** 11101_2 **b.** 111100_2 **c.** 10011101_2
4. **a.** $10F_{16}$ **b.** $7BF_{16}$ **c.** 1718_{16}

5. **a.** $11010100_2 = D4_{16}$

    b. $0110101110_2 = 01\ 1010\ 1110_2 = 0001\ 1010\ 1110_2 = 1AE_{16}$

    c. $1001111_2 = 100\ 1111_2 = 0100\ 1111_2 = 4F_{16}$

    d. $1110110101001_2 = 1\ 1101\ 1010\ 1001_2 = 0001\ 1101\ 1010\ 1001_2 = 1DA9_{16}$

6. **a.** $C7_{16} = 1100\ 0111_2 = 11000111_2$

    b. $BAD_{16} = 1011\ 1010\ 1101_2 = 101110101101_2$

    c. $9F04_{16} = 1001\ 1111\ 0000\ 0100_2 = 1001111100000100_2$

7, 8.

Hexadecimal (EBCDIC)	Character	Hexadecimal (ASCII-8)
F0	0	50
F1	1	51
F2	2	52
F3	3	53
F4	4	54
F5	5	55
F6	6	56
F7	7	57
F8	8	58
F9	9	59
C1	A	A1
C2	B	A2
C3	C	A3
C4	D	A4
C5	E	A5
C6	F	A6
C7	G	A7
C8	H	A8
C9	I	A9
D1	J	AA
D2	K	AB
D3	L	AC
D4	M	AD
D5	N	AE
D6	O	AF
D7	P	B0
D8	Q	B1
D9	R	B2
E2	S	B3
E3	T	B4
E4	U	B5
E5	V	B6
E6	W	B7
E7	X	B8
E8	Y	B9
E9	Z	BA

9.

	Character	EBCDIC Code	With Even Parity	With Odd Parity
a.	P	1101 0111	0 1101 0111	1 1101 0111
b.	D	1100 0100	1 1100 0100	0 1100 0100
c.	1	1111 0001	1 1111 0001	0 1111 0001
d.	9	1111 1001	0 1111 1001	1 1111 1001

10.

	Character	ASCII-8 code	With Even Parity	With Odd Parity
a.	P	1011 0000	1 1011 0001	0 1011 0000
b.	D	1010 0100	1 1010 0100	0 1010 0100
c.	1	0101 0001	1 0101 0001	0 0101 0001
d.	9	0101 1001	0 0101 1001	1 0101 1001

11.

	Character	BCD Code	With Even Parity	With Odd Parity
a.	P	10 0111	0 10 0111	1 10 0111
b.	D	11 0100	1 11 0100	0 11 0100
c.	1	00 0001	1 00 0001	0 00 0001
d.	9	00 1001	0 00 1001	1 00 1001

12.

a.   9   1   8

1001	0001	1000	1111

b.   9   1   8   +

1001	0001	1000	1100

c.   9   1   8   −

1001	0001	1000	1101

13.

a.   0   1   4   6   3

0000	0001	0100	0110	0011	1111

b.   0   1   4   6   3   +

0000	0001	0100	0110	0011	1100

c.   0   1   4   6   3   −

0000	0001	0100	0110	0011	1101

14. a. $219 = 11011011_2$

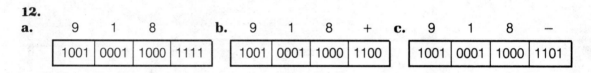

31	30	29	28	. . .	8	7	6	5	4	3	2	1	0
0	0	0	0	. . .	0	1	1	0	1	1	0	1	1

b. $-111 = -1101111_2$

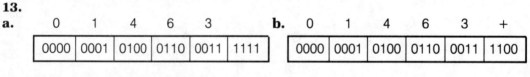

31	30	29	28	. . .	8	7	6	5	4	3	2	1	0
1	0	0	0	. . .	0	1	1	0	1	1	1	1	1

15. a. 0.10251464
  b. 3; 67; 0.81509321; 0.81509321
  c. −3; 0.123987; 61; 0.123987; 0.123987
  d. 2; −0.1290913756; 66; −0.12909137; −0.12909138
  e. 5; 0.115190005; 69; 0.11519000; 0.11519001
  f. 1; 0.133333333; 65; 0.13333333; 0.13333333

Review Exercises

1.	true	**11.**	d
2.	false	**12.**	d
3.	true	**13.**	a
4.	true	**14.**	c
5.	false	**15.**	c
6.	false	**16.**	c
7.	false	**17.**	c
8.	true	**18.**	b
9.	false	**19.**	b
10.	false		

20.

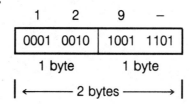

21. $129 = 10000001_2$

1	000 . . .	10000001

— mantissa is right-
justified in its field

BASIC Exercises

1.
```
10  FOR N = 0 TO 8
20    LET X = 2 ↑ N
30    PRINT X
40  NEXT N
50  END
```

2.
```
 5  LET S = 0
10  INPUT A, B
20  FOR N = A TO B
30    LET S = S + N ↑ 2
40  NEXT N
50  PRINT "SUM ="; S
60  END
```

3.
```
 5   REM ** CONVERTING A DECIMAL NUMBER INTO BINARY FORM **
10   INPUT "NUMBER: "; N
20   FOR I = 1 TO 100
30     LET R(I) = N - 2 * INT(N / 2)
40     LET N = N / 2
50     IF N = 0 THEN 70
60   NEXT I
70   FOR K = I TO 1 STEP -1
80     PRINT R(K);
90   NEXT K
100  END
```

```
4.  5   REM *** ROUNDING OFF ANY POSITIVE DECIMAL NUMBER ***
   10   INPUT "NUMBER: "; N
   20   INPUT "DECIMAL POSITION ACCURACY (D = 1, 2, ETC.) "; D
   25   PRINT:PRINT
   30   LET R = INT(N * 10↑D + 0.5) / 10↑D
   40   PRINT N, R
   50   END
```

INDEX